# Faithful Dissent

## Charles E. Curran

Sheed & Ward

With deep gratitude and affection for
the many people who have sustained and supported me
in the midst of this controversy

Sheed & Ward™ is a service of National Catholic Reporter Publishing,
Inc.

Library of Congress Catalog Card Number: 86-62884

ISBN: 1-55612-045-1

Published by: Sheed & Ward
115 E. Armour Blvd. P.O. Box 414292
Kansas City, MO 64141-4292

To order, call: (800) 821-7926

# CONTENTS

# Introduction

This book attempts to give both the historical record and my interpretation of my controversy with the Congregation for the Doctrine of the Faith over the legitimacy of theological and practical dissent from noninfallible hierarchical teaching on a number of issues primarily in sexual ethics. The book is divided into two parts.

The first part of the book involves my commentary on the dispute. One possibility was to make some commentary or notes in the midst of the correspondence between the congregation and myself. However, it seemed better to keep the documentary section as objective as possible and to reserve my commentary for a separate section. This commentary evolves through three chapters — my personal record of the historical developments, a theological analysis, and my evaluation of all that is involved. In the historical section I have tried to develop the historical parameters so that the reader can understand the dispute better. The theological perspectives attempt to give a systematic summary of the issues involved in and connected with the controversy without repeating the materials contained in the correspondence. The final chapter develops personal reflections on the dispute and my own work as a Catholic moral theologian.

In this part I have tried to be fair, and to explain my own position as honestly as I can. I am aware of the fact that I am bound to see the entire affair through a limited and even biased perspective. However, since so many others have been commenting on this dispute, I thought it important for me to explain my interpretation and understanding of what is involved.

The second part is documentary. All the correspondence exchanged between the congregation and myself is contained here. In a final section, a few other appropriate documents are added. On the basis of this documentation, readers will be able to make their own judgments and draw their own conclusions about the controversy.

This is also the appropriate place to publicly express gratitude to all who have been of assistance to me. It is impossible to thank adequately all those who have supported and assisted me. The book is dedicated to the many people who have supported and sustained me in this dispute. Some of these people are mentioned in the text, but there are many others who will always have a place in my mind and heart. However, a special word of thanks goes to Donnalee Kulhawy and Bonnie Gould, who have been both gracious and efficient in typing this manuscript and a great volume of correspondence in the last year. I am grateful to James Coriden, George Higgins, and Johann Klodzen for critically reading the manuscript. An earlier version of the second chapter was delivered as an address to the 1986 convention of the College Theology Society and appears in the Proceedings of that meeting.

# Part One
# The Story

# Chapter One
# The Historical:
# A Personal Record

On August 2, 1979, I was informed that my theological positions were being investigated by the Vatican Congregation for the Doctrine of the Faith. On that date, Cardinal Baum, the Chancellor of the Catholic University of America and the Archbishop of Washington, called me to the Chancery Office of the Archdiocese and handed me a letter from the congregation, dated July 13, and sixteen pages of "Observations." Baum was gracious throughout the meeting and asked if I was surprised by the investigation. I responded in the negative and handed him a paper I had in my coat pocket. His face showed both surprise and embarrassment at what he read.

When I was called on the telephone to make the appointment to see Cardinal Baum, I knew immediately that it was bad news coming from Rome. There were many indications pointing in this direction, and the most telling sign was a letter dated April 29, 1979, from Archbishop Jerome Hamer, the Secretary of the Congregation for the Doctrine of the Faith, to Bishop Joseph V. Sullivan of Baton Rouge, Louisiana. Hamer congratulated Sullivan for refusing to allow "the use of diocesan facilities for a talk by Rev. Charles Curran at the University of Louisiana in Baton Rouge" and "for providing public clarification of some of the ambiguous and erroneous teachings of Fr. Curran." Reports first appeared in the extremely conservative wing of the Catholic press about the existence of the letter from Hamer to Sullivan, to prove that Sullivan was in good standing with Rome. Someone sent me a copy of the letter itself. This was the letter I handed to Baum on August 2.

Only a few hours later, I realized that the protocol number on the Hamer letter to Sullivan was the protocol number they assigned to me — 48/66. According to Vatican custom, 66 refers to the year that the file began. My dossier had apparently been growing for some time. I later learned that Edward Schillebeeckx, the Dutch theologian, had the protocol number 46/66.[1] The first section of this chapter will describe the circumstances leading up to my being informed about the Vatican investigation.

## I. Before 1979

My interest and work in moral theology was not something I planned. In the 1950s, I was studying for priestly ministry and was a typical product of United States Roman Catholicism of the pre-Vatican II times. In 1947 I entered high school in a day seminary of the Diocese of Rochester, New York. After completing high school at St. Andrew's Seminary, I finished my college work at the major seminary of St. Bernard's in Rochester. I was then assigned to study theology at the North American College in Rome. At that time, my superiors as well as my peers probably looked upon me as a bright, docile, dedicated, and rather passive young man.

While in residence at the North American College in Rome for four years, I studied theology at the Pontifical Gregorian University and learned the standard pre-Vatican II theology. My professors in the first year of theology (Timothy Zapalena, S.J., for ecclesiology and Sebastian Tromp, S.J., for revelation) had been teaching at the Gregorian University since before the Second World War. However, some of the professors were even then beginning to break away from the theology manuals. Again I was for the most part the intelligent, dutiful, and unquestioning seminarian. I was named the student liaison between the North American College and the Gregorian University. In 1959, after completing my licentiate (S.T.L.) at the Gregorian, I was awarded the Papal Bene Merenti medal. Each year the one winner of the medal was chosen from among the many students who did well in their grades. As a matter of fact, the ultimate choice was not always by lot, for in my time the liaison from the American College (with the biggest number of students at the Gregorian) often won the medal!

I was ordained to the priesthood at the end of my third year of theology in 1958 and informed during my fourth and last year of seminary theology that the Diocese of Rochester wanted me to return to Rome to study for a doctorate in moral theology so that I could teach in the diocesan seminary of St. Bernard's. This was how I came to the discipline of moral theology — I received a letter from my bishop telling me to get a degree. Such was the way the pre-Vatican II church operated. To add to the irony, I had originally decided to become a diocesan priest because I did not want to be a teacher but to be involved in pastoral work. For all practical purposes, I have done nothing but teach for almost thirty years. I have found great satisfaction in teaching and researching in moral theology — thanks to the order I received from my bishop in 1958.

After finishing my licentiate in theology (S.T.L.) in 1959 I began the two-year program for the doctorate. I chose to continue my studies at the Gregorian University. I had appreciated the classical pre-Vatican II theology I received there. In addition people like Bernard Lonergan in dogmatic theology and Joseph Fuchs in moral theology had been preparing and developing somewhat new approaches in their disciplines, although at first I did not really understand what they were trying to do.

One of the professors at the Gregorian was Father Francis Hürth, a German who was described once in class by the American moralist Edwin Healy as often writing under the penname of Pope Pius XII. It was a well known fact that Hürth wrote most of the moral addresses of Pope Pius XII and was a very influential consultor of the Holy Office. This most powerful Vatican Congregation was originally called the Congregation of the Inquisition. It became the Congregation for the Doctrine of the Faith in 1965. On a number of occasions I had long talks with Hürth in Latin about various moral problems. Once an American Jesuit was fearful that the Holy Office was going to condemn the Doyle cervical spoon — a device inserted into the vagina to protect the male semen immediately after insemination from being harmed by the acids of the vagina, thereby improving the possibility of fertility. He asked me to sound out Hürth to see if the Holy Office was going to condemn this device. We talked about it for an hour. Hürth explained why he thought the Doyle cervical spoon was morally wrong, and I tried to argue the other side. I think he really understood what was happening, because near the end of the conversation he smiled and said in his precise Latin that this was an American problem and he was not going to become involved in it. I had my answer — the Holy Office would not condemn the Doyle cervical spoon!

In keeping with the spirit of the times and my own inclinations, I wrote and defended in 1961 a doctoral dissertation at the Gregorian University, under Father Francis Furlong, on the prevention of conception after rape. It was a typical problem of casuistry which required some acquaintance with biological and medical knowledge.

While debating where to do my doctoral studies for moral theology, I had come across the existence of the Academia Alfonsiana — an institute in moral theology run by the Redemptorist Fathers, whose founder Alphonsus Liguori (d. 1787) was the patron saint of moral theologians. At that time (1959), the Alfonsiana was not yet empowered to give the doctoral degree but provided a two-year program of classes and seminars leading to a diploma, with the purpose of acquainting future teachers with the many different areas of moral theology — biblical, historical, theological, sacramental, philosophical, psychological, sociological, etc.[2] In 1959 I enrolled there to take some of these courses, because they would help to prepare me to teach moral theology.

It was at the Alfonsiana in 1959 that I first came into contact with Father Bernard Häring. The year before, I had read the Italian translation of Häring's groundbreaking three-volume work entitled the *The Law of Christ,* which proposed a new approach to moral theology and broke away from the format and approach of the traditional manuals of moral theology. Joseph Fuchs had first introduced me to a newer approach to moral theology, and I found Häring's classes intellectually stimulating and spiritually inspiring. The older manuals of theology were based primarily on natural law and had the limited aim of training confessors as judges in the sacrament of penance, so they could decide what is a sinful act and the difference between mortal and venial sin. Häring's approach was life-centered, biblically based, holistic, and stressed the universal call of all disciples of Jesus to holiness. At the Alfonsiana I was not personally close to Häring, but I was greatly impressed by his work, his writing, and his person. I encouraged others living with me in the American graduate priest students' residence in Rome to come to his classes.

There can be no doubt that Bernard Häring has been the greatest influence in my intellectual development, a magnificent example of one who lives what he teaches, and one who has been an unfailing source of support for me throughout the last thirty years. Häring has consistently argued against legalism and hypocrisy and has courageously written and acted in defense of the freedom of the children of God — a freedom that is both faithful and life-giving. My gratitude to Häring knows no bounds. Little did I realize in 1959 that twenty-seven years later Häring would volunteer to be my counselor and advocate as I met face to face with the Prefect of the Congregation for the Doctrine of the Faith, who was accusing me of not being a Catholic theologian. As I climbed the stairs of the Holy Office behind the resolute steps of Bernard Häring on my way to meet Cardinal Ratzinger on March 8, 1986, the memories of my first encounters with him at the Alfonsiana flooded my mind.

Häring was not the only professor at the Alfonsiana. The faculty of about twenty specialized in different areas of moral theology. In keeping with the Roman custom, the classes were based mostly on the lecture system, but I enjoyed them because they opened up to me many different aspects of moral theology. The lecture system certainly has many weaknesses, and I would never use it for doctoral seminars myself.

After I took the regular complement of classes during the 1959-60 school year at the Alfonsiana, one of the professors, Domenico Capone, urged me to work for a doctorate there. Beginning in the summer of 1960, the Alfonsiana was accredited to offer the degree of doctorate in theology with a specialization in moral theology. I mentioned that I had spent most of the summer working on my dissertation for the Gregorian and just wanted to spend the 1960-61 school year preparing myself to teach. In addition, why did I need another doctorate? However, Capone insisted that it would be good for me and the Academia. He proposed a dissertation topic on invincible ignorance in St. Alphonsus and promised to allow me to take out of the library all the books I needed — this was against the usual Roman library custom. I am still proud of the fact that I was the first person to be officially awarded the doctorate at the Alfonsiana.

Before returning from Rome in the summer of 1961 I went to lunch and spent a long afternoon with Francis X. Murphy, an American Redemptorist who had been teaching Patristic Moral Theology at the Alfonsiana. That day Murphy filled me in on some of the Roman gossip. (That conversation, plus the fact that I knew his mother's maiden name was Rynne, helped me solve the puzzle of the author of the famous "Letter from Vatican City" which first appeared in the *New Yorker* at the beginning of the Second Vatican Council in 1962.)

Murphy also gave me some important advice that day. He felt that my new approach to moral theology might not go over that well at St. Bernard's Seminary in Rochester, which was nicknamed "the Rock" because of its reputation as a very conservative Catholic seminary. In that environment, it was too easy to get off on the wrong foot and not last too long. The wise and politically astute Murphy suggested that I start teaching my classes in Latin. I knew Latin well and could use it in class with no trouble. There had been a tradition in the past of using Latin in classes at St. Bernard's Seminary. After a while, I could switch into English. By then the first and the most enduring experience of the new kid on the block would be that he taught his classes all in Latin.

## Teaching at St. Bernard's Seminary — 1961-65

I thus arrived at St. Bernard's Seminary in August of 1961 with my degree, my newer approach to moral theology, and my advice from F. X. Murphy. I was still wet behind the ears with little or no pastoral experience, at best a couple of years older than my students, and with the august title of Professor of Moral Theology and of Canon Law at "the Rock." The Canon Law part of the work and the title was by far the funnier, or the more tragic, depending on your viewpoint. In the pre-Vatican II church, moral theology was heavily intertwined with canon law. Often the same person taught both disciplines. United States seminaries, with their somewhat practical and legalistic bent, required even more canon law of their students than did the Roman universities. In fact, some of my students had studied more canon law than I.

Those of us who teach know that teaching is the best way to learn. The first time through a course is always the hardest but also the most rewarding. Often in those years I was typing out notes for the students at 5:30 a.m. in preparation for an 8:00 a.m. class. Some days I even fell behind the proverbial "one page ahead of the students." Moral theology was taught in a three-year cycle so that for three years I taught a new course. My experience was all the more exhilarating because for all practical purposes I was the only one teaching this newer approach to theology which was simultaneously influencing the Second Vatican Council, which had begun in the fall of 1962.

I began by following Murphy's advice of lecturing in Latin but then "relented" and switched into English. But the word about Curran was out. I was known as the one who tried to restore the use of Latin. I decided to keep the manual or textbook which had been used previously, but I became famous for my long introductions. One school year I finished the introduction in March! I explained that moral theology should deal with the fullness of the Christian life and the call to holiness, and not just with the sinfulness of particular acts. Conversion and the law of the spirit were primary considerations in my introduction.

One of the three-year cycles dealt with the sacraments. The

textbook treated the subject in the usual manner of discussing the obligations involved in administering and receiving the sacraments. I developed a much broader treatment of the sacraments as the saving encounter of the individual with God in and through Jesus, the Spirit, and the community of the Christian church. I relied heavily on Schillebeeckx's *Christ the Sacrament of the Encounter with God,* which was then available only in French. One of the liveliest discussions that year was on the fruits of the mass or the problem of the one and the many masses. Are two, three, or four masses better than one? The accepted spirituality and theology strongly maintained that the more masses, the more grace. Following Karl Rahner, I disagreed and pointed out that the Eucharist was the celebration of the community gathered together. It would be better for an ordained priest not to say a private mass but to share in the community eucharist. In the early 1960s, this was bound to cause a great uproar. These first years of teaching were both tiring and exhilarating at the same time.

The faculty at the seminary were considerably older than I, and most of them were formed in the typical neo-scholastic theology of the pre-Vatican II period. A good number of them had been my own teachers. Many were very helpful and solicitous for my well-being, and I have continued to remain on a friendly basis with a number of them to this day.

Some of my professors in Rome and one or two faculty colleagues at St. Bernard's urged me to do some writing in the field of moral theology. In this way I could develop in the United States a greater interest in the new approach to moral theology. I was first asked in the fall of 1961 by Father Godfrey Diekmann, the editor of *Worship,* to contribute a short piece to counteract a negative review of Häring's *The Law of Christ,* which had just appeared in his review.[3] I was then asked, in the spring of 1962, to contribute a twenty-five page pamphlet on "Morality and the Love of God" as part of a new Paulist Press Doctrinal Pamphlet series. This pamphlet gave me the opportunity to discuss the general approach to a more positive and life-centered moral theology. A few years ago in the introductory course in moral theology I gave this pamphlet to my students to criticize as part of their final exam. To their credit, they were quite negative in what they said!

I was invited to give one of the major papers at the groundbreaking Roman Catholic-Protestant Colloquium sponsored by Harvard

University in March 1963. Cardinal Augustin Bea gave three addresses on this occasion. I was reluctant to accept, in the light of
my comparative youth as a scholar, but the organizers insisted
that I was the right person to give the address on conscience.[4] It
was obvious that the conference organizers wanted someone with
a new approach to moral theology, and there was no one else available. I found it to be a great learning experience, and appreciated
the concern and the consideration of my Protestant respondent
Professor Paul Lehmann, with whom I have remained in touch
ever since.

There were many invitations to speak to various groups within
the diocese on this new approach to moral theology. In addition I
was asked with increasing frequency to speak outside the diocese.
From February to May 1964, I gave a series of eight talks on moral
theology to the priests of the Archdiocese of Boston under the auspices of an official clergy continuing education program. I spoke at
the annual conventions of the National Conference of Catholic Men
in 1963, the Canon Law Society in 1964, and the Catholic College
Teachers of Sacred Doctrine (now called the College Theology Society) in the spring of 1965.

From 1961 to 1965, the primary question in moral theology was
responsible parenthood and artificial contraception. Looking back,
it is hard to believe that there were no theological writings
disagreeing with the official Catholic teaching until the very end of
1963. The most widely discussed article that appeared questioning
the official teaching was written by Canon Louis Janssens of Louvain and published in the December 1963 issue of *Ephemerides
Theologicae Lovanienses.*[5] In retrospect, it is interesting to note
that Janssens argued only for the moral legitimacy of the pill.
Other early contributions in favor of change in the official teaching
were made by Bishop Josef Maria Reuss in Germany, William van
der Marck in Holland, and Louis Dupré in the United States.[6] I
wrote an article for the August 1964 issue of *Jubilee,* which in a
popular way addressed the question of family planning.[7] Despite
expressing problems with the traditional position and sympathy
for the need to question it, I was unwilling to say that artificial contraception is morally good and the teaching of the church should be
changed. However, within a few months I was convinced and expressed the need for the church to change its teaching in a review
in the December 4, 1964 issue of *Commonweal.* That same month I

gave a talk to the Catholic Club of Harvard giving my reasons why I thought the church should change its teaching on artificial contraception for married couples.[8]

The bishop and officials of the Rochester diocese called me in on a few occasions to warn me about what I had said and where I had said it. In early 1965, they expressed concern over what I was saying about artificial contraception and asked me to restrict what I was writing and saying in a more popular and public vein. Most of my dealings were with Auxiliary Bishop Lawrence Casey, who was really running the diocese at that time.

I also experienced two other phenomena which were to occur again in later years. On February 19, 1965, Hugo Maria Kellner, a Catholic layman who had come over to the United States at the time of the Second World War, wrote a letter to the rector of the seminary, pointing out what I was saying in sermons at his church (St. Columba's in Caledonia, a suburb of Rochester) and in my published writings. I was, like Bishop G. Emmett Carter of Canada, "a representative of extreme kerygma"; my theology was "no longer based on orthodox Catholic dogma and morality"; I "spread heretical and moral subverting ideas." On March 30, Kellner sent copies of the six-page mimeographed letter to all the rectors of seminaries in the United States and to most of the religious provincials. Kellner had started sending out these mimeographed articles on different subjects a few years before, when he addressed all the cardinals in the world and the United States bishops. He decried the opening address of Pope John XXIII to the Second Vatican Council, the proposed schema on religious liberty, the Directory on Ecumenism of the Archdiocese of St. Louis, and many other contemporary developments. I was in good company.

A second incident at this time involved a cancelled talk. I had agreed to give a talk in the fall of 1964 and another one in the following spring for an updating program for religion teachers, sponsored by the Archdiocese of New York at Fordham University. I enjoyed the fall session and was well received by the audience and especially by those who arranged the program. In the winter, I received a call from the Monsignor who was organizing the program to say that they were going to have to cancel things for the spring. He was most apologetic and said he wanted to come up to Rochester sometime to visit me. My naiveté was shattered when I received a letter later in the spring from a woman religious which said she was sorry that I could not make the spring date because they really missed not hearing me!

During these years I received offers to teach elsewhere. In June of 1962 Walter Schmitz, S.S., the Dean of the School of Theology at the Catholic University of America, first contacted me about coming to teach at Catholic University. Albert Schlitzer, C.S.C., Chair at Notre Dame, invited me to teach in the graduate theology program there and come for just one semester if I were not able to come full-time. There were also some other feelers. I sent these invitations to Bishop Casey, thinking it would not hurt my reputation in the diocese. The bishop responded that I could not be released by the diocese at that time to accept any of these offers. Gerard Sloyan invited me to teach full-time and also in the summer program in the Department of Religious Education at Catholic University. I enjoyed a very pleasant summer there in 1964 (despite the heat) and was invited back to teach a three-week session in the summer of 1965.

Upon returning to Rochester in late July 1965 from my teaching in Washington, I was informed by Bishop Casey that I could no longer teach at St. Bernard's. The shoe had finally dropped! In addition to dissatisfaction within the diocese of Rochester there also had been problems expressed by Bishop Forey of Syracuse, who sent all his students to St. Bernard's Seminary. The final straw was apparently an article in the Niagara Falls, Canada paper about a talk I gave to the Carmelites in Niagara Falls in June, in which I urged a change in the church's teaching on artificial contraception. I expressed some interest in perhaps staying as an associate pastor in the diocese, but Casey strenuously urged me to accept the invitation to Catholic University. He wrote a letter to the rector of Catholic University in the name of Bishop Kearney to say that I was now released from the diocese of Rochester to accept a position that fall in theology at Catholic University. Thus I came to Washington.

## Early Years at The Catholic University

I started teaching in the graduate school of theology at Catholic University in September 1965. My past followed me. On September 7, Hugo Maria Kellner sent his original six-page letter to the rector of St. Bernard's Seminary, together with a two-page cover letter, to all the priest faculty of The Catholic University of America. My new faculty colleagues frankly seemed to pay no attention to this diatribe, but the university administration was nervous. The vice-rector called me in and advised me to be very careful and prudent.

I quickly settled into my new environment and found myself quite at home. Fides Publishers of Notre Dame agreed in the fall to publish a book of my essays in moral theology, and I prepared the essays for publication together with a new introduction. *Christian Morality Today* was published in 1966. At the June 1966 meeting of the Catholic Theological Society of America, I gave a paper on the morality of masturbation.[9] This paper argued against the official position that masturbation is always objectively gravely wrong. As in the case of contraception, I appealed to the experience of Christian people, a better understanding of sin, and a less biological and more personal understanding of both the natural law and the reality of masturbation.

In those days it became increasingly evident to me that the two major issues of a practical nature facing moral theology were the teaching authority of the church in moral matters and the existence of absolute universal norms, especially in those areas where the forbidden behavior was described in terms of the physical or biological structure of the act — e.g. contraception, masturbation, sterilization, or direct killing. I still recognized and insisted that moral theology should involve more than actions and norms, but those two specific issues needed great attention. It was also important for people to realize that there were an ever increasing number of Catholic moral theologians in the United States who were thinking along these newer lines. In late 1966 and early 1967, with the help of my colleague and friend Daniel Maguire, I planned a book of essays to be written by different Catholic moral theologians on various aspects of this question. A contract was signed in the early months of 1967 and *Absolutes in Moral Theology?* was published in the spring of 1968.[10]

It is difficult now to remember the exact state of Catholic moral theology in 1966. Two vignettes from the 1966 meeting of the Catholic Theological Society of America will help to recall the atmosphere of the time. A number of U.S. Catholic moral theologians in January 1964 attended a meeting of the Society of Christian Ethics and became members of this society, which heretofore had been totally Protestant. The ecumenical movement had arrived in Catholic moral theology. In 1966, the Board of Directors decided to invite a Protestant theologian as an observer to the annual meeting of the Catholic Theological Society of America. They invited Paul Ramsey, who was known to some of the board members (especially Warren Reich) through membership in the Society of Christian Ethics. But there was some hostility on the part of a good number of the members to the presence of Ramsey. Ramsey was treated cordially, if a bit coolly at first, and invited to the presidential suite, after the sessions of the first night, to have a drink and join in the conversation. By the end of the evening Ramsey had charmed everyone. At one point he exclaimed, "What would my fundamentalist, preacher father say to see me now with a scotch in one hand, a pipe in the other hand, and a guest of the Catholic Theological Society of America!" More to the point, Ramsey's positions were quite conservative and nonthreatening. Those who were most cool to the idea of inviting him spent the night reverently asking him his opinion about every issue under the sun. Thus ecumenism came to the Catholic Theological Society in 1966.

A woman also came to the Catholic Theological Society in 1966. This society was male, clerical, and composed almost totally of seminary professors. One breakthrough had been the admittance of religious brothers who had obtained pontifical doctoral degrees in theology. At the cocktail hour before the banquet at the 1966 meeting, a woman appeared at the entrance to the hall. One of the officers said she could not come in. I overheard the conversation, called the president on the phone, requested that he come down, and insisted that the woman be allowed to come in. That night I ate with Elizabeth Farians, who was the first woman to attend the banquet of the Catholic Theological Society. There is still much to be done about the role of women in Catholic theology, but we have come a long way since 1966.

In my first year at Catholic University I was busy with teaching, researching, writing, and lecturing throughout the country. In the 1966-67 school year, I was unanimously approved by my colleagues from the school of theology and by the academic senate of the university for promotion to the rank of associate professor. However, there had been some meetings with the administration and the rector of the university. The rector was troubled by an article about me in the *National Catholic Reporter* and by my being a member of the Board of Directors of the Institute for Freedom in the Church, an organization which had recently been founded to promote and defend the legitimate rights of Catholics. In October of 1966, my theology faculty colleagues unanimously expressed confidence in my teaching and orthodoxy and objected to the harassment and unspecified charges that were being made against me. I had no inkling of what was really going on at the time.

On April 17, 1967, I was summoned by Bishop William McDonald, the rector, and told that the Board of Trustees at their meeting in Chicago on April 10 had voted not to renew my contract. No reasons were given. Later press reports indicated that in accord with the statutes of the university a three-member committee composed of Cardinal Krol of Philadelphia, Archbishop Hannan of New Orleans, and Rector McDonald had studied my writings and reported to the full board, who voted with one exception to terminate my contract. An article in *The Washingtonian,* a few years later, reported that Archbishop Egidio Vagnozzi, the apostolic delegate at the time, claimed he was responsible for my firing. Rome wanted to make an example of a liberal American priest, and I was chosen.

That afternoon I confided in a few friends. Ideas and plans rapidly developed. A public rally was held Tuesday night, April 18, at which my colleagues Robert Hunt, Daniel Maguire, and Sean Quinlan explained the nature of the controversy and voiced their strong support for me. A steering committee of students from all parts of the university was formed to help coordinate and execute the different strategies and activities. On Wednesday, at noon, the theology faculty met and unanimously concluded, "We cannot and will not function unless and until Father Curran is reinstated. We invite our colleagues in other schools of the university to join with us in our protest."

At a public meeting and press conference at 2:00 that Wednesday afternoon, Dean Schmitz, Father Eugene Burke, and I spoke to explain what was happening. The strike was on. Students from the various schools and their respective faculties joined almost unanimously in the strike. The university was effectively closed down on Thursday morning. The full faculty of the university met on Thursday at noon, while a student rally was planned for 1:00 outside the building in which the faculty was meeting. The faculty voted 400 to 18 to support the strike. The campus was full of demonstrators, pickets, and placards. The papers and the public media gave the story extensive coverage. Some cracks began to appear when Cardinals Lawrence Sheehan and Richard Cushing publicly criticized the action that had been taken against me. Some negotiations began, with Dean Schmitz staunchly standing up for his faculty. After a long and tough negotiation session with Cardinal Patrick O'Boyle, the chancellor of the university, Bishop William McDonald, and the theology faculty, it was publicly announced on Monday, April 21, that the action of the Board of Trustees was rescinded, and I would be given a new contract, with promotion to the rank of Associate Professor, as of September 1, 1967.

One campus historian proclaimed that this was the first successful university strike since the middle ages. There had been many problems smoldering within the university and there was much built-up resentment against the administration. Although the real reason was obviously my ethical position on issues such as contraception and masturbation, no reasons were ever explicitly given by the administration for the termination. The only issue thus involved in the controversy was the fact that the trustees had directly gone against the unanimous faculty recommendation for my promotion and continued employment. This made it very easy to obtain strong faculty support. The role of Dean Schmitz in this strike was very significant. He was a well-known and respected figure in Catholic circles, and he and a few others gave great respectability to the case. In a sense Walter Schmitz risked more than most others and I shall always be grateful to him. Schmitz had taken over as dean of the School of Theology in the early 1960s and was successfully attempting to change the image of a faculty which had been heavily identified with the conservative positions of Joseph Clifford Fenton and Francis Connell.

Little did I realize at that time that the strike of 1967 was setting the stage for another significant event. As a result of the strike, I came to be publicly identified as a leading proponent for the Catholic Church to change its teaching on artificial contraception. I had thought change would come in the official hierarchical teaching. The majority of Pope Paul VI's famous birth control commission had come out in favor of a change in the official teaching. But as 1968 began there were signs that perhaps the pope would not change. I kept in contact throughout the spring of that year with many theological friends and colleagues on this issue. I was spending the summer of 1968 at St. Bonaventure University in Olean, New York, trying to study German and giving just three lectures during the course of the summer. On Sunday evening, July 28, the radio and television reported that an encyclical would be issued the following day, reaffirming the condemnation of artificial contraception.

The encyclical was released on Monday morning, July 29, 1968. A number of us had concluded that in this event it would be important to point out to Roman Catholics that it was not necessary for married couples to choose between using artificial contraception and being Roman Catholic. A loyal Catholic could dissent from such noninfallible teaching. I flew back to Washington at noon and met, through prearrangement, with a group of ten theologians to study the document and decide what we would do. Later on, a good number of people charged that we had never read the document. This accusation was entirely false, which should have been evident even on the basis of the intrinsic reasoning we produced in our statement. However, the fact that many bishops in the United States had not yet received a copy of the encyclical gave some credence to the charge that we had not seen the document. We concluded that a statement signed by theologians would be very appropriate and then agreed on the wording of such a statement, which I finally typed out.

Our statement was respectful, pointed out positive aspects of the encyclical, but also pointed out the flaws we saw in the document from the perspective of moral theology and ecclesiology. The statement recognized the possibility of dissent from such noninfallible teaching and concluded: "Therefore, as Roman Catholic theologians, conscious of our duty and our limitations, we conclude that spouses may responsibly decide according to their conscience that artificial contraception in some circumstances is permissible and indeed necessary to preserve and foster the values and sacredness of marriage."[11] That Monday evening, this small group called colleagues throughout the country to join our statement. I acted as the spokesperson for the original group of 87 signers at a press conference on Tuesday morning, July 30. Letters were subsequently sent to about 1200 Catholic theologians asking for public support for the statement. Eventually over 600 persons qualified in the sacred sciences publicly signed this statement.

There can be no doubt that this dissent was public, organized, and put together in a comparatively short period of time. However, in my judgment the statement was responsible, and it has held up very well over the years. We were concerned that some Catholics would be upset by our statement, but we thought that the good of many others and the good of the church called for us to do what we did, so that Catholics would know that they did not have to choose between practicing artificial contraception and being loyal Roman Catholics. The debate about such dissent obviously continues to exist within the Catholic Church.

This theological statement was quickly identified by the press as the "Washington Statement" or the "Catholic University Statement" because its original signers were from the Washington area, and primarily from The Catholic University of America. Eventually, twenty professors from Catholic University signed the statement. There were other statements made by individuals and groups at this time, but this statement remained the primary one in the United States.

There was further public discussion about the whole matter of the encyclical. Cardinal O'Boyle, Archbishop of Washington and Chancellor of The Catholic University, publicly supported the encyclical on July 29 and later took a firm stand against any possible dissent. On July 31, Archbishop John Dearden, the President of the National Conference of Catholic Bishops, issued a mild and general statement calling for all to receive the encyclical with sincerity, to study it carefully, and to form their consciences in its light. We organized a press conference on August 1, at which the lay members of the papal commission on artificial contraception from the United States spoke and defended the position of dissent. On that occasion, in response to reporters' questions, I replied that I did not think that our statement was irreconcilable with the statement that had been made by Archbishop Dearden. However, on August 2, Bishop Joseph Bernardin, the General Secretary of the National Conference of Catholic Bishops, emphasized that the previous general statement in no way implied that there was any difference between the United States bishops and the pope.

Catholic University was then being administered by Father John Whalen, as acting rector or president. Whalen suggested and organized a small meeting between bishops and theologians which took place in New York City on August 18 and 19. I worked with him to represent the dissenting theologians and set the parameters for the meeting, which would involve an equal number of those who dissented and those who were opposed to such dissent. The meeting was truly cordial, but it did not resolve the problem. On August 20, Archbishop O'Boyle, as Chancellor, convoked a meeting with the faculties of theology and religious education at Catholic University, but the meeting achieved no tangible results.

A special meeting of the Board of Trustees of Catholic University was called for September 5. Cardinal James Francis McIntyre of Los Angeles began the meeting by introducing a resolution stating that the utterances of Father Curran and his associates on *Humanae vitae* constituted a breach of their contract with the university, which thereby justified their termination. Such a resolution did not prevail, probably because many on the board were conscious of the problems raised by my attempted firing the year before. The Board of Trustees ultimately called for an inquiry, in accord with academic norms and due process, to determine if the Catholic University theologians had violated their manifold responsibilities as professors of theology at this institution.

The 1968-69 academic year was spent in this inquiry. Our defense was a collaborative effort of all the colleagues involved, but Robert Hunt and I organized and directed the effort. Thanks to the generosity of the law firm of Cravath, Swaine, and Moore of New York, John F. Hunt and his associate Terrence R. Connelly presented our case with great professional skill and deep personal care. In April the faculty hearing committee vindicated the declarations and actions of the professors. The Board of Trustees received the report but never really accepted the spirit of the report. Our written submissions to the faculty inquiry board were published in a slightly modified form in two volumes by Sheed and Ward.

After the successful outcome of the inquiry, our group was quite elated. It seemed that we had established the principle of university autonomy and academic freedom at Catholic University and for all Catholic higher education in the United States. The role of the theologian, with its interpretive function which sometimes might conclude by dissenting from noninfallible teaching, was also accepted. Recall that during this very academic year the United States bishops issued their pastoral letter, "Human Life in Our Day," in which they accepted the legitimacy of public theological dissent under three conditions: if the reasons are serious and well-founded, if the manner of dissent does not impugn the teaching authority of the church, and is such as not to give scandal.[12] The whole experience was trying and tiring, but at the end it all seemed worthwhile. In our judgment, the possibility of public theological dissent and the need for academic freedom were good, not merely for theology, but for the church itself. However, time and history have reminded all of us that the battle was not won in 1968-1969.

The realization that the administration of Catholic Univerity and the trustees had not really accepted the results of the inquiry was not long in coming. Roland Murphy, a distinguished Old Testament scholar, was the faculty choice to replace the retiring Walter Schmitz as the dean of the School of Theology in the fall of 1969. However, the new President, Clarence Walton, said he could not appoint Murphy as dean because Murphy had signed the *Humanae vitae* statement. Murphy maintained that if he could not be dean he could not stay on the faculty either. So in September 1970, Murphy went to Duke University. This event was a good indication that the troubles at Catholic University were not all behind us.

After the successful outcome of the faculty inquiry in the 1968-69 academic year, I determined to stay at Catholic University and continue my work of teaching, researching, writing, and lecturing. It was obvious that the conditions calling for a change in the church's teaching on artificial contraception would also logically call into question some other official teachings. I had already questioned the official position that masturbation is always an objectively grave evil. In the next few years, I dealt with the topics of homosexuality, divorce, sterilization, and abortion. In addition to addressing the specific problems, it was necessary to address the methodological approach behind these questions. Thus I gave attention to a critical analysis of the natural law question, the existence of absolute norms, and the need for greater pluralism in the life of the church on specific complex moral questions which are somewhat remote from the core of faith.

Although these specific issues are important, in my writing and in my teaching I tried to make the point that moral theology involves much more than just the morality of individual actions and the existence of universal norms. I investigated the significant methodological questions of the role of the Scriptures in moral theology, the distinctiveness and uniqueness of Christian ethics and Christian morality, the fundamental stance or perspective of moral theology, the different levels of moral discourse, and the role of the sciences and empirical data in moral decision making. Articles and essays on these subjects were originally published in journals or books and collected in a series of my books, published originally by Fides Publishers and then later by the University of Notre Dame Press.

Throughout the 1970s I continued writing in the area of medical ethics, but I made a conscious decision in 1974 to move more into the area of social ethics. I really developed no new positions in sexual ethics after 1974, although occasionally I wrote in this area. I also continued to address methodological issues and to insist that moral theology involves more than questions about norms and specific actions. One new controversial issue emerged in the 1970s — abortion laws. I proposed a theory of the function of law in relationship to morality and concluded that at the present time one should not work for a constitutional amendment to overturn the Supreme Court's ruling supporting very liberal abortion laws.

In these years at Catholic University I found that I really enjoyed teaching. I have consistently taught the introductory course in moral theology to about 40 students each year. My courses have been very well received by students who, according to course evaluations, have appreciated my enthusiasm, clarity, and respect for students and their positions. The negative aspects in these evaluations centered on my attempt to cover too much material and my assignment of too much work. In doctoral level seminars, I have tried to make my students think critically and have developed a seminar style which stresses a well-organized, student-run discussion. In the process I have always had a good rapport with students. They have even appreciated, although somewhat grudgingly at times, that I have made them work hard. I also directed many doctoral dissertations and have been pleased that a number of these students have gone on and written in the field of moral theology.

I have received many invitations to give lectures, institutes, and retreats throughout the country and abroad. This has been an enjoyable experience and brought me into contact with a good number of people. I have also used these opportunities as a way to discover what is happening in the church in different parts of the country and the world. Although there were often some pickets and opponents, my talks were generally very well received.

In academic circles I was well received and supported by my peers. I was promoted to the rank of Ordinary Professor in 1971, after serving the minimum of four years in the rank of Associate Professor. For a long time I represented my faculty to the Academic Senate of the University. I served as President of the Catholic Theological Society of America in 1969-70, and was the first Roman Catholic elected President of the Society of Christian Ethics (1971-72). In the 1970s there were many feelers about moving to other universities, but I rejected them all. Despite the normal problems of daily existence , as well as some other tensions which will be described shortly, I enjoyed what I was doing.

However, there is another aspect of this history that needs to be mentioned. My various involvements, especially the strike in 1967 and the *Humanae vitae* controversy in 1968, together with my continuing questioning and dissent on a few moral issues, attracted opposition and protest from a number of different sources. I was never asked in the 1970s to serve on any official groups or committees sponsored by the United States bishops, such as the various ecumenical dialogues with other churches. One incident illustrated the tension between theologians and bishops. The Catholic Theological Society every year chooses a theologian to be recognized for outstanding accomplishment in theology. From the beginning of the society, Cardinal Francis Spellman of New York offered to give a small monetary prize to the individual selected by the society and the award was named in his honor. When Cardinal Terence Cooke succeeded Cardinal Spellman as Archbishop of New York, he willingly agreed to continue funding the Spellman Award. In 1972 my colleagues elected me the winner of the award. However, the sponsor of the award had difficulties with the selection. The Board of Directors of the Catholic Theological Society of America then decided to change the name of the award to the John Courtney Murray Award and made me the first recipient. I shall always be grateful for their action and for the moving citation written for the occasion by my colleague and friend Richard McCormick.[13]

As previously noted, I have been invited to give many retreats, lectures, and institutes throughout this country and abroad. In the process I have spoken to many different kinds of groups in all parts of the country and beyond. However, there were and are a number of dioceses where I am not welcome to speak. Occasionally I have had engagements cancelled because of episcopal displeasure — and not only in this country. In 1969 I accepted an invitation to speak to English-speaking priests in a foreign country, but the local hierarchy forbade me to come. A similar situation occurred again in 1982 in a different country. In these and similar controversies, I try to go out of my way not to cause any unnecessary problems for people who might have invited me. On a number of occasions when there were protests against my coming to speak, I called the sponsoring people and volunteered not to come if it was going to cause them a problem. Almost invariably they were grateful for my concern, but they insisted that I come.

There are also other instances of disinvitations. In March 1978, I was informed by the editor of the *Linacre Quarterly* that at the suggestion of the Board of the National Federation of Catholic Physicians' Guilds, the *Linacre* was going to change some members of the Editorial Advisory Board, including myself, in order to bring in new blood. I sensed this was not the real reason. The editor finally admitted that he had been told to get me off the advisory board. I offered a face-saving compromise that they would rescind their action, keep me on the advisory board for a very short time, and then I would resign. They were unwilling to accept such an arrangement. (Richard McCormick, who had intervened on my behalf, resigned in protest from the advisory board at that time.)

There have been some amusing situations. I gave a workshop at an exempt religious community, but the local bishop forbade any publicity in the diocesan paper. After the institute, I travelled by car with two priests of the diocese to go to another speaking engagement. While we were eating lunch in a restaurant the bishop himself came in and, upon seeing the two priests, pulled up a chair and joined us for lunch. He and I had a very friendly conversation about the cooperatives in Nova Scotia.

At one institute there was a mystery man in the back who refused to identify himself but only said that his tuition had been paid for by a Father Sullivan. By Thursday of the week, with help from a phone call from the apostolic delegate's office in Washington, the organizer of the institute realized that the mystery man was an Archbishop who was Papal Nuncio in a different part of the world!

The more conservative and right-wing Catholic press has frequently attacked me, and in some cases, especially in the *Wanderer*, these attacks have in my judgment been irresponsible. In the 1970s, editorials in the *National Catholic Register, Our Sunday Visitor*, and *Twin Circle* occasionally disagreed with me, questioned my orthodoxy, and raised questions about my continued teaching at Catholic University. Various columnists in these journals sometimes raised the same questions. The late Archbishop Robert Dwyer strongly urged my removal from Catholic University.[14]Editorials and articles in *The Homiletic and Pastoral Review* occasionally took the same tone.

I was a frequent target in the *Wanderer*. Many different articles and columns attacked me and urged my dismissal from Catholic University. On a number of occasions, the *Wanderer* encouraged its readers to participate in a campaign of letter writing to remove me from Catholic University. I once urged a *Wanderer* columnist to at least let his readers know that I tried to be responsible in what I was doing. In a later column he acknowledged my request and said, "Alas, Curran fully appreciates that he is a thorough-going relativist and subjectivist."[15]

One consequence of all this was frequent opposition and protest to my speaking in a good number of different places. Often there would be a protest before and pickets would appear at the talk itself. One incident in particular deserves special mention. A former student of mine, Daniel Drinan, was the pastor of the campus ministry team at Louisiana State University and first asked me in the spring of 1977 to give a talk there. I begged off because of other pressing concerns but finally agreed that I would be willing to give a talk while on sabbatical leave in 1979. We finally agreed on the date of Monday, February 19, and the topic, "American Catholic Social Ethics in the Twentieth Century." However, as the time approached there were indications of trouble. I was asked to speak under the auspices of The Uniting Campus Ministry and not that of the Catholic Campus Ministry. I had no problem with that arrangement when Drinan suggested it to me. But further trouble lay ahead. Before the talk, Bishop Sullivan of Baton Rouge announced he could not allow me the use of the facilities of the Catholic Center, even though rent was being paid to the Center by The Uniting Campus Ministry. At the same time Bishop Sullivan issued a statement and held a press conference comparing my positions with those of the church on a number of issues — abortion, fornication, sterilization, divorce, *Humanae vitae*.[16] The quotations from my books on four of these five issues were taken exactly from the quotations given in an earlier series of articles which appeared in the *Wanderer*.[17]

When informed about these developments, I told Drinan that I was very willing not to come if that would be better for all concerned, but he insisted that I come. As fate would have it, I was fortunate to make the engagement because I avoided one of the worst snowstorms in Washington history. The headline in the campus paper the morning after my talk speaks for itself: "Curran Doesn't Live Up To Radical Expectations."[18] This incident was quite well publicized throughout the Catholic press and served as the occasion for a number of very negative articles in the more conservative and right-wing press.

Soon there were other signs that this Louisiana incident would not simply go away and die. I accepted an invitation to speak at a workshop on sexuality sponsored by the Office of Religious Education of the Archdiocese of Milwaukee in the middle of June 1979. On May 12, a group called the St. Thomas More Educational Foundation, Ltd. took out quarter-page ads in the two Milwaukee daily papers to protest my appearance as well as that of another priest. They quoted from Bishop Sullivan's statement contrasting my positions with those of the official teaching of the church. On June 2, this same group published an even larger ad in the secular paper which reprinted the May 17, 1979, editorial from the *Wanderer,* urging their readers to write to a number of different people, including the Chair of the Board of Trustees of The Catholic University of America, the Vatican Secretary of State, and the Prefect of the Vatican Congregation for the Doctrine of the Faith, to urge that Curran be silenced and removed from Catholic University. Again, I offered not to come, but the organizers wanted me to be there. There was heavy security (at least by campus standards) for the talk which was given on the Marquette University campus, and no one was admitted who had not signed up for the entire workshop.

Father Matthew Lamb of the Marquette theological faculty wrote a very ironic article for the Op- Ed page of the *Milwaukee Journal.* Lamb wanted to bring to the attention of the St. Thomas

More Education Foundation the writings of a Catholic author which were readily available in practically every library. This author advocated communism, euthanasia, and toyed with the idea of women priests and priests being elected by the community. Lamb wrote that he could almost hear this author — Thomas More — having a good and hearty laugh at the pretensions of the Foundation. Maybe in four hundred years a group of like-minded Catholics might start a Father Charles Curran Educational Foundation, Ltd.![19]

There is no doubt that the contretemps in Baton Rouge had mobilized some of the extreme conservative Catholic groups in the country. There were more frequent public protests when I was invited to speak in various places throughout the country. For example, a full-page ad appeared in the St. Louis *Globe-Democrat* of April 10, 1980, protesting my coming to lecture that summer at St. Louis University and citing the statement of Bishop Sullivan about me. I was scheduled to give a lecture in a summer course which eventually had an enrollment of about fifteen students. My contribution was one evening in a three-week course.

I have recounted this history to give some background and also to explain why I was not surprised to discover on August 2, 1979, that I was under investigation by the Vatican Congregation for the Doctrine of the Faith. From what I have been able to piece together, I do not think that the incident with Bishop Sullivan was the spark that set off the entire investigation. In accord with its own procedures, the Congregation for the Doctrine of the Faith admitted to me in its letter of July 13, 1979, that my investigation began long before the incident in Baton Rouge. In addition, Cardinal Ratzinger himself admitted recently that the Curran investigation has been going on for more than ten years.[20]

## II. Under Investigation

Upon receiving the letter and "Observations" from Cardinal Franjo Seper, the then Prefect of the Congregation for the Doctrine of the Faith in August 1979, I consulted with a number of friends and colleagues. While preparing my response, I contacted Catholic moral theologians I knew in Belgium, England, France, Germany, and Italy to see if there were other moral theologians under investigation at the time. My inquiries turned up some communications between the congregation and moral theologians, but the bottom line was that there were no other moral theologians under investigation at that time through the formal process of the Congregation for the Doctrine of the Faith. Since my positions in moral theology were basically shared by many others, I thought there might be others involved. The fact that I was the only one raised interesting questions in my own mind.

I had determined it was better not to give any publicity to this investigation. However, word of it leaked out. I thought that perhaps some of the people I contacted might have given out this information, but one archbishop was convinced that someone in Rome had leaked it. *Le Monde* had an article which among other things mentioned that Schillebeeckx and I had been called to Rome.[21] Similar information appeared in England in *The Economist,* the London *Times,* and the *Tablet.*[22] In response to press inquiries generated by these reports, I said in late November of 1979 that I was in correspondence with the Congregation for the Doctrine of the Faith, but I had not been called to Rome. This was the standard phrase I used whenever questions were raised on this matter. I also indicated that there was some correspondence between Rome and other theologians. At the same time I communicated with my faculty colleagues in theology about the investigation. (Throughout the subsequent years, I kept these colleagues informed by inviting them to come to update sessions with the proviso that they would be willing to keep confidentiality.)

At the end of October, I responded to the "Observations," concentrating on the question of magisterium and dissent which the congregation had called my fundamental flaw. I raised five questions to ascertain exactly what was the position of the congregation on dissent. The long, subsequent correspondence indicates that I never received an answer to those basic questions. The letters back and forth also reveal my frustration when the congregation never replied to my response of October 1979 until February 1981. But in reality, the February 1981 letter to me was no response but rather a request for me to address the other aspects mentioned in the first set of "Observations" from July 1979. That letter could have been written in November 1979. I was greatly disappointed by the lack of any true dialogue and by this unnecessary delay and decided that in the future I would follow the same time schedule as that used by the congregation. I would take as long to respond to them as they took to answer me. Following this time schedule, I submitted my response to the particular moral questions under dispute in June 1982. By then Cardinal Ratzinger was Prefect of the Congregation for the Doctrine of the Faith. I interpreted the letter and "Observations" from Ratzinger, under date of May 10, 1983, as strong and ominous. I was asked if I wanted to "revise those positions in clear public dissent from the magisterium." I was being given a final chance to change my positions. Again,I tried unsuccessfully to determine when and under what conditions the congregation would allow public dissent, but they refused to say. I finally completed my last response to them on August 24, 1984. At that time I was convinced that they were now seriously holding their position and that they apparently wanted to make it very clear that they would not allow any public theological dissent on these issues.

Other events also made me feel that a hard-line approach on their part was inevitable. In general, there seemed to be a number of signs in the United States of a more conservative swing in Catholic Church matters — the Vatican investigations of United States seminaries, United States religious (especially women), and even of two bishops; the removal of imprimaturs from some books, including Philip Keane's *Sexual Morality.* Earlier the congregation had pointed out the errors in the book, *Human Sexuality.*[23] The principal author of the book left his teaching post and could no longer teach sexual or medical ethics. Also there was no doubt that Rome was appointing conservative new bishops and passing over more moderate candidates. Richard McCormick, in recounting these and other events, described the situation as "the big chill."[24]

In addition to the content and tone of the correspondence, as well as the general atmosphere, there was a very specific indication of problems ahead for me. At his regular Wednesday audience on July 11, 1984, Pope John Paul II began a series of talks on *Humanae vitae* in which he reaffirmed the official teaching that the conjugal act in marriage must always be open to procreation. After this first talk in the projected series, the Vatican press office took the very unusual step of having a press briefing for reporters given by Msgr. Carlo Caffarra, President of the Pontifical Institute for Studies in Marriage and the Family, which was established by Pope John Paul in 1982, and also a consultant for the Congregation for the Doctrine of the Faith. Caffarra named four theologians —

Hans Küng, Franz Böckle (both of Germany), Marc Oraison of France, and myself — who bear a very grave responsibility because from the beginning they have contested *Humanae vitae,* have caused confusion and doubt in the minds of the faithful, and have helped prevent the encyclical from having its effect.[25] In response to inquiries from the press, I expressed amazement that the Vatican would believe that the lack of reception of *Humanae vitae* by the vast majority of Catholic faithful came about because of the dissent of four theologians, one of whom was now dead.[26] The message from this press briefing was very clear. There was only one question in my mind — did Msgr. Caffarra speak on his own or was he saying these things in the name of higher authority? Some friends in Rome told me they thought he was speaking on his own, but the message was still quite ominous.

The position taken by the congregation in its correspondence with me was not only opposed to the thinking of the vast majority of Catholic theologians writing at the time, but also was contrary to the Catholic tradition itself. I still hoped there might be some way of avoiding what I thought would cause great harm to the church. I was also concerned about myself, but I knew that I would never have difficulty finding a teaching job in theological ethics because over the years I have been offered many such opportunities at other institutions. I tried to take some initiatives.

Was there any type of compromise I could offer at this time which might prevent the impending impasse? After discussing the matter with some friends, I offered a possible compromise. I would be willing to move from the Department of Theology at Catholic University, which is an ecclesiastical faculty which gives pontifical degrees, is subject to special Vatican regulations, and is the place where seminarians are taught, to the Department of Religion and Religious Education which is not an ecclesiastical faculty, does not give church-accredited degrees, and does not teach seminarians. A canon lawyer carefully drew up a six-page document indicating how this could be done in accord with the statutes of our university. I signed a two-page declaration of intent, with copies to Fr. William Byron, S.J., the President of the University, and to John F. Hunt, my legal counsel. I would be willing to make this move quietly within the university, if the Vatican dropped its investigation. I gave this declaration to an intermediary who had connections to get the message to some concerned bishops. I urged President

Byron to do what he could to see if this compromise would float. Apparently this offer was brought to the attention of some concerned bishops, but no action was taken on my offer. At the end of December, I wrote President Byron, saying that from what I knew my offer was not accepted although it was not necessarily rejected.

On August 10, 1984, I sent a confidential memo to inform any and all faculty colleagues in theology willing to accept the confidentiality. I concluded that things looked bleak. A group of colleagues met during the Fall to discuss the problem. On November 30, thirteen faculty colleagues sent a joint letter to Cardinal Ratzinger expressing strong support for me as a theologian and as a person of faith.

I had also been in contact with a number of colleagues who were past presidents of the Catholic Theological Society of America, and we agreed that a private letter to Ratzinger signed by some past presidents of this society might be both helpful and appropriate. Richard McBrien, Richard McCormick, and David Tracy took the initiative in this endeavor. The letter signed by them and many other past presidents strongly defended my orthodoxy as a Roman Catholic theologian. In late August 1984, a group of about twenty concerned graduate students in theology met and ultimately formed a group called FACT — Friends of American Catholic Theology. They studied the whole issue of dissent, sponsored a forum of three public talks at the university focussing on problems confronting American Catholic theology in this area, and discussed ways and means to support me if any action was taken against me. The FACT group put much time and energy into their efforts and continued to meet throughout the 1984-85 school year.

Later in the fall of 1984, there was another strong indication that the congregation was going to take action against me and deny the legitimacy of public theological dissent. The November issue of *Jesus* printed parts of the interview that Cardinal Ratzinger had given in August to the Italian journalist Vittorio Messori. In part of the interview Ratzinger pointed out the problems confronting the church in different parts of the world. The following is the entirety of what he said about the United States:

> Looking at North America, we see a world where riches are the measure and where the values and style of life proposed by Catholicism appear more than ever as a

scandal. The moral teaching of the church is seen as a remote and extraneous body which contrasts not only with the concrete practices of life but also with the basic way of thinking. It becomes difficult if not impossible to present the authentic Catholic ethics as reasonable since it is so far distant from what is considered normal and obvious. Consequently many moralists (it is above all the field of ethics in which North Americans are involved, whereas in the fields of theology and exegesis they are dependent on Europe) believe that they are forced to choose between dissent from the society or dissent from the magisterium. Many choose this latter dissent, adapting themselves to compromises with a secular ethic which ends up by denying men and women the most profound aspect of their nature, leading them to a new slavery while claiming to free them.[7]

After reading this passage I had little doubt about where Cardinal Ratzinger stood. However, I was saddened that such a gross oversimplification came from a person who should know better.

In October 1984, Cardinal Ratzinger acknowledged receipt of my August response, but I heard no more. My faculty colleagues and the past presidents of the Catholic Theological Society of America told me that they never even received an acknowledgement of the letters they sent to the congregation.

In February of 1985, Theological College, the diocesan seminarians' house of formation at Catholic University, and the Department of Theology were visited by a committee investigating United States seminaries under the general direction of Bishop John Marshall of Burlington, Vermont . Marshall himself was the chair of this particular visiting committee and met with me on February 21. After a few pleasantries, he zeroed in on the question of the magisterium and dissent. I explained that this constituted less than one class hour of all the classes I taught during a semester. I summarized my position as recognizing that the presumption of truth lies with the teaching of the noninfallible, hierarchical magisterium; but that this teaching has been wrong in the past, and the presumption must always cede to the truth in the present.

Marshall explained that Rome would obviously expect his committee to say something about me, and he thought it might be appropriate for them to write an appendix about me. Would I be willing to read such an appendix? I responded negatively and forcefully. It would be gravely unjust to single me out when they had not read my writings or the writings of my colleagues, a good number of whom held the same position on the legitimacy of dissent. They had no right to make any judgments on me without a full hearing such as was held at Catholic University in the 1968-69 school year.

Marshall then asked my reaction to a second possible approach. What if the committee recommended that the seminarians from Theological College be forbidden to take my classes? Again I pointed out the total unfairness of the suggestion. After that session, I had a scheduled meeting with another member of the visiting committee and recounted to him my earlier discussion with Marshall. After some discussion involving others, I was told that an effort would be made to make sure that nothing was said about me or dissent in the final report of the committee. When the committee made its oral exit report the next day, there was no mention of either myself or dissent. I was pleased by the change of heart on the part of the committee.

The 1984-85 school year saw me involved with my usual pursuits, and there was no reaction from Rome. However, I was convinced that the congregation would not accept my defense of legitimate public theological dissent, even though I was willing to accept the same position as that proposed by the United States bishops in 1968.

In June I met privately and on the spur of the moment with an American archbishop to discuss the matter. The archbishop was somewhat sympathetic to the need to clarify the underlying issue of dissent but said he was not really involved in the case. However, when I mentioned that some people thought Rome might still back off my case, he indicated very strongly that in the light of all that was happening he judged that Rome would in no way back off.

I mentioned to the archbishop that I had never talked to my own bishop about the matter but would do so immediately. I did not want to discuss my issue with other bishops without first discussing the matter with him. It was my understanding that Bishop

Matthew Clark of Rochester as my diocesan bishop had received copies of the correspondence from Rome but was not directly involved in the case. I saw him in Rochester at the end of June. I was heartened by the support he expressed for me and my work at that time. I also mentioned to him that I often wondered in the last few years if Rome would try to solve the problem by having my bishop call me back to Rochester.

After a busy summer of studying, writing, and lecturing, with two weeks vacation in August, I returned to teaching in the 1985 fall term. On Saturday afternoon October 8, Archbishop James A. Hickey telephoned me to say that he had received a letter from Cardinal Ratzinger and wanted to set up a meeting with himself, Cardinal Bernardin, and me for October 10 so that he could, in accord with his instructions, hand over this letter to me. I agreed but thought the meeting would be more profitable if I had a chance to read the letter beforehand. I was willing to go out then and pick it up at his residence. He agreed, but with the understanding that the letter would not be officially handed over to me until the meeting on October 10.

Thus I received the September 17 letter from Cardinal Ratzinger asking me to retract and reconsider my positions on contraception and sterilization; abortion and euthanasia; masturbation, premarital sexuality, and homosexuality; the indissolubility of marriage. If I did not retract, I could not be called a Catholic theologian and could not teach in the name of the church.

What to do? I could not in my own conscience and with integrity change my positions. After consulting some others, I worked out a strategy to try to convince Hickey and Bernardin to accept some type of compromise which they would then urge Rome to accept. I met with the two of them on four different occasions — October 10, November 9, December 4, and January 16. To avoid any misunderstandings, I sent the two of them detailed minutes of our meetings and asked them to correct any inaccuracies. At first, Archbishop Hickey tried to get me to change my positions but I told him that I had taken these positions after study and prayer and in all integrity I could not change. However, I realized it would also be impossible for the congregation to change its positions. As a result any substantive compromise would not work.

I proposed the need for some type of "procedural compromise."

Finally I suggested three points that would serve as the basis for a compromise with each side able to interpret things in one's own way. I had not been teaching the course in sexual ethics for about fifteen years, so I would be willing to accept an arrangement whereby Rome forbade me to teach this course. Second, Rome could issue a document pointing out the "errors" of my theology, provided the bottom line was that I was still a Catholic theologian able to teach in the name of the church. Third, I would be on a sabbatical for the calendar year 1986 and would not be teaching anyway. Obviously Hickey and Bernardin would have wanted more, but they realized this was as far as I could go.

To convince them of the need to accept and propose such a compromise to the Vatican, I tried to point out the disastrous consequences that would follow for the church if the actions threatened in the letter were carried out. In addition, I again consulted with others, especially those who had written to Ratzinger on my behalf in the fall of 1984. I shared with them in strict confidentiality the letter I received from Cardinal Ratzinger. The former presidents of the CTSA, McBrien, McCormick, and Tracy, all wrote forceful letters to Hickey and Bernardin pointing out the negative effects on theology and the church if Rome acted in accord with the Ratzinger letter. Francis Schüssler Fiorenza, the current President of the Catholic Theological Society of America, and William Shea, the current President of the College Theology Society, wrote personal letters indicating the grave damage to theology and Catholic higher education if the proposed action were taken. In the fall of 1984, within my own theology faculty there emerged a core group of five who organized and led the faculty in their 1984 discussions and subsequent letter to Ratzinger. I shared the new information with them and they wrote a magisterial eight-page letter to Hickey dealing with all the aspects of the case but stressing its disastrous impact on theology at Catholic University.

A number of very convincing reasons were proposed in both conversation and writing to move Hickey and Bernardin to work for the acceptance of the compromise. The Ratzinger letter confused the assent of faith and the religious submission of intellect and will which is owed to noninfallible teaching. The congregation apparently denied any public theological dissent from noninfallible teaching and thereby went against not only the vast majority of Catholic theologians but even against the teachings proposed by the United States bishops in 1968. Action against Curran would be unfair because many other theologians hold similar and even more radical positions. The contemplated action would have disastrous effects on Catholic University and all of Catholic higher education in the United States perhaps even leading to civil suits about the constitutionality of state funding for Catholic higher education. The proposed action would be a blow to ecumenism and would inevitably be self-defeating by driving more Catholic theologians out of Catholic institutions.

In the light of all this, Hickey and Bernardin agreed to take the compromise to Rome and to see if the congregation was willing to accept it. It was evident to me that Archbishop Hickey would have preferred greater willingness on my part to change my positions. I recognized why he would have preferred such an approach but again told him that I could not change. Bernardin agreed to take some soundings while he was in Rome in November for a meeting of all the cardinals. We also agreed that I would write to Archbishop Hickey a preliminary response to the Ratzinger letter, indicating that my positions on all these issues were quite nuanced and there was not as much disagreement between myself and the congregation as appeared by merely reading the September 17 letter.

Archbishop Hickey was scheduled to go to Rome on December 10, but he was ill and unable to go. The trip was rescheduled for early January. Hickey's secretary called me at 11:00 p.m. on January 15, asking if I could come to a meeting with Hickey and Bernardin on the next morning at 9:30. In light of the circumstances of this call, I did not need to be told what had happened in Rome.

Archbishop Hickey met with both the Pope and Cardinal Ratzinger. His message to me was that Rome cannot continue to allow me to teach in the name of the church while holding my positions on the questions under discussion. Apparently they are not questioning me as a Catholic, as a priest, or even as a theologian of ability. I was given two options. The congregation would receive me for an informal meeting to discuss the issues but I had to ask for the meeting, agree to a joint press release afterward, and recognize that this meeting was not part of their official procedure. The official procedure called for a colloquy only if the congregation deemed it necessary, but in my case my positions were clear and there was no need for a colloquy. Their process was finished.

If I did not ask for the colloquy, I was to give the congregation in writing by February 15 my final response to their request to reconsider and retract my positions. Frankly I held out little hope, but thought that I should leave no stone unturned. To go to Rome could do no harm. After some further dialogue, the meeting was set for March 8 in Rome.

In the meantime, I had to think about strategy. James Coriden, a close friend and confidant who had advised me on every aspect of the correspondence throughout the years, raised the pointed question. What did I expect and want to happen? I recognized that I would probably lose in the short term, so in the long term I wanted to make this a teaching moment for the good of theology and the good of the church. The Catholic Church ultimately has to recognize the legitimacy of public theological dissent from some noninfallible teaching and the possibility of such dissent in practice by members of the church. I am a teacher and I wanted this to be a teaching moment. The whole episode would become public after my trip to Rome, so I wanted to make sure that the public understood that I was neither a rebel nor a guerilla but a loyal Catholic theologian working for what I and many others thought to be the truth and therefore the good of the church. I have always maintained that such dissent is ultimately necessary to enhance the credibility of the hierarchical teaching office. I wanted to avoid any anger, name-calling and arrogance, and any unfair attributions of motives to anyone involved. The tone and manner of my words and actions had to be respectful.

The goal was clear, but what about the strategy? The student group FACT had been meeting regularly and studying the issues and the case since September 1984. The group now comprised 32 members. I never met with the group but from the beginning FACT asked my colleague David Power to meet with them and be somewhat of a faculty liaison with the FACT group. (David Power wore more hats and spent more time on my behalf than any other colleague at Catholic University during these tense times.) However, after receiving the Ratzinger letter in October, I began meeting regularly with the coodinators of FACT — Johann Klodzen, Mary Zelinski Hellwig, and Sally Ann McReynolds, N.D. FACT, on the basis of their study and discussion, had decided that the best strategy to aid me would be a campaign to obtain signatures for a statement of support and to encourage individuals to write letters to the relevant church authorities. They also had formed an alumni committee and agreed on a basic wording of a letter to send to the alumni as well as a general letter to be sent to others. FACT had taken steps to legally incorporate themselves as a nonprofit organization so they could receive tax exempt status to finance their plans. All of these basic strategies were developed without my input. However, beginning in October of 1985, I met regularly with the coordinators and made them an important part of my group of advisors. In addition, we agreed that FACT as a group would execute the tactics that we agreed upon. FACT had already written their statement of support for me, with their various cover letters, and now went to work on preparing mailings. McBrien, McCormick, and Tracy agreed to compose a statement on my behalf and to obtain additional signatures from representative past presidents of both the Catholic Theological Society of America and the College Theology Society, with the purpose of sending this statement to all the members of both societies for their public endorsement. FACT agreed to take care of mailing and tabulation.

After some dialogue back and forth with Rome, the date of Saturday March 8 was set for my informal meeting in Rome with the congregation. From the very beginning Msgr. George Higgins, who retired after almost forty years at the United States bishops' conference specializing in the area of social action and labor, said that he was going to go to Rome with me to show his solidarity in a visible way. I tried to discourage him, but he insisted. In the end I was most grateful for his presence. It would have been a much more difficult experience without George Higgins' companionship and counsel. Throughout this whole time I have appreciated his support and his realistic assessments. William Cenkner, the Dean of the School of Religious Studies, also asked to accompany me to express the solidarity of the faculty and his own personal support. The three of us flew out of Washington on Wednesday night and returned on Saturday night March 9.

Bishop Clark had told me when I first talked to him in June 1985 that he wanted me to feel free to ask him to do whatever I thought might be helpful. He might not be able to do what I asked, but he wanted me to ask. I told him I did not want to ask him to come to Rome with me. I pointed out that he had different responsibilities from mine and had to think of his role as a bishop, leader, and center of unity of the Church of Rochester. However, I suggested that he might write a personal letter to Ratzinger before my meeting and also that he should be prepared for questions once the matter became public. From the very beginning of this process, I had hoped that, if there were to be a meeting with the congregation, Bernard Häring would be willing to accompany me as my advocate. He had graciously agreed to that request long ago. This magnanimous gesture of support just added more to the many gifts I have received from Bernard Häring.

Cenkner and Higgins accompanied Häring and myself to the meeting in the Holy Office on Saturday March 8. We were given a copy of Bishop Clark's letter to Cardinal Ratzinger and read it just before entering the building. It was a magnificent letter and buoyed up our spirits. Häring resolutely led the way up the stairs and around the corners of the Holy Office building without having to ask for any directions. At his request he had a private meeting earlier that week with Cardinal Ratzinger in order to discuss my case. The cardinal greeted us in the anteroom and ushered Häring and myself into the meeting. There were six people at the meeting — Cardinal Ratzinger and Archbishop Alberto Bovone, the Secretary of the Congregation. In addition, Fr. Thomas Herron, an American member of the congregation's staff, was there to take notes and was assisted by Fr. Edouard Hamel, a Jesuit who teaches moral theology at the Gregorian University. The meeting lasted from 11:00 a.m. to 1:00 p.m. The cardinal was unfailingly civil and polite and had a half smile etched on his face throughout most of the meeting.

There had been no agenda for the meeting so Häring asked the permission of all to begin. Häring had prepared and passed out a two-page paper with the title, "The Frequent and Long-Lasting Dissent of the Inquisition/Holy Office/CDF From and Against the *Opinio (Sententia, Convictio) Communior* as a Major Ecclesiological, Ecumenical and Human Problem." What a way to start the meeting! It was vintage Häring. He pointed out errors on the part of the Holy Office in the past — the power of the church in the temporal sphere, the torture and burning of witches, interest taking, slavery, some Biblical teachings, the *nouvelle theologie,* religious liberty. Maybe in this case of Curran the Holy Office is again the real dissenter.

Such an opening was not necessarily conducive to good dialogue! In addition, we all seemed a bit nervous and ill at ease. However, in the course of the two hours we did manage to cover the main issues involved in the case even though the conversation was quite scattered and did not have a logical order or progress. Cardinal Ratzinger and Archbishop Bovone spoke in Italian; I used English with a little bit of Latin and Italian; while Häring used both English and Italian. Although all the important issues were discussed, both sides merely reiterated the positions they had already taken. I noticed one change on Ratzinger's part. He was backing away somewhat from the charge that I was not a Catholic theologian. I think he agreed that I was in no way denying matters of faith. However, he did not back away from the position that I could not teach in the name of the church nor from his position that dissent on these matters was unacceptable.

One testy moment occurred when I was making the point that many other Catholic theologians in all different parts of the world held positions similar to my own. Ratzinger asked me to name some of the individuals. I did. Then he responded by saying that if I wished to accuse any of these people, the congregation would be glad to begin an investigation. I strongly insisted that I was there to accuse no one. I was talking to a well-known and well-read Catholic theologian, Joseph Ratzinger, who had to know that many other Catholic moral theologians held similar positions.

Midway through the meeting, the cardinal offered coffee, but I suggested we not adjourn but have it at the table so that the conversation could continue. Once or twice, in the midst of other points, Bernard Häring mentioned the compromise I had proposed, but Ratzinger did not pick up on it. When this happened again, I asked Ratzinger if he was familiar with the compromise. He acted surprised and hesitated. Archbishop Bovone then interrupted and said something about the "different hypotheses" that had been mentioned. I then read to them the notes from my meeting with Hickey and Bernardin (which the two of them had seen and declared to be accurate), in which the compromise was spelled out. Häring eloquently urged Ratzinger to accept such a compromise. There should be no winners or losers; such an approach would be best for the church and for all concerned. Ratzinger reminded us that no decision could be made at this meeting and that the final decision rested not with himself or the officials of the congregation but with the cardinal members. However, he promised to give attention to the compromise. At the end we talked about a joint press release and ultimately agreed on a bland statement that was to be released that afternoon. I told Ratzinger that I had agreed to avoid any publicity whatsoever before the meeting but now it would be impossible. I had to defend my position, but I intended to do so in a responsible manner. He indicated that it was up to me to do what I had to do in this matter. I suggested that we pray together at the end of the meeting and the cardinal led us in prayer.

There was really no change in positions at the meeting, but Häring was somewhat optimistic that the compromise would be accepted. On Sunday morning before leaving Rome, Cenkner, Higgins, and I agreed to go to Häring's residence at St. Alphonsus Church for a liturgy. Two people from Rochester who were in Rome for a meeting of the vicars for religious and who had hand delivered Bishop Clark's letter to the congregation on Friday joined us for the liturgy, together with another good friend of mine who was at their meeting. It was a very moving liturgy, with Häring presiding. In the light of the reading of the parable of the prodigal son, his homily developed the themes of God's great graciousness, hope, forgiveness for all, and the need to avoid a "winners and losers mentality."

We arrived back in Washington late Sunday night March 9. The *New York Times* ran a long story on Monday. On Tuesday March 11, I held a press conference and explained my positions in the case. I insisted that I considered myself to be a loyal Roman Catholic who upheld the need for papal and episcopal leadership in the church while still holding on to the need at times for responsible, public theological dissent from some noninfallible teachings such as the ones under consideration.

On Wednesday noon, March 12, FACT held a "call for action." The coordinators — Klodzen, Hellwig, and McReynolds — announced that they were sending mailings throughout the country seeking signatures for their statement attesting to the educational work and Christian witness of Fr. Curran and deploring any action that might be taken against him. FACT also announced that a statement signed by nine past presidents of the CTS and the CTSA was being sent to all members of the two societies seeking public support. The Theologian's Statement disagreed with the assumption in the congregation's position that any dissent from noninfallible teaching places one outside the body of Catholic theologians.

The statement pointed out the injustice in singling me out, the negative effect on Catholic University and Catholic instutitions of higher learning by any action against me, and pointed out that Curran was one of the most respected and admired Catholic theologians in the country. At the same session two graduate students — Kevin Mullen and John Lombardi — spoke of the substantial contributions Curran makes to theology in general and to the theology department at Catholic University in particular.

On Friday March 14, a "FACT Forum: A Teaching Moment" was held in order to explain to the university community what were the issued involved. At that forum, Patricia Hackett, a graduate student in theology and three faculty colleagues — John Tracy Ellis, Alexander DiLella, and John Ford — addressed various aspects of the issues. Thus, thanks to the efforts of FACT, the teaching moment became a reality. In the matter of a few days the issues involved in my case were explained in a responsible way, without in any way denigrating or impugning the teaching authority of the church.

One other group should be mentioned. I am a priest of the Diocese of Rochester, New York, and still have many friends there. A group of people, ultimately calling themselves "Friends for Charles Curran," met in the fall of 1985 and agreed to study the issues involved and discuss possible strategies. The group ultimately sent out letters seeking signatures for the FACT statement and sponsored three informational forums in different parts of the diocese, with special emphasis on informing pastoral staffs about what was taking place. The "Friends for Charles Curran" letter was signed by Rev. Daniel P. Tormey, Rebecca J. Gifford, Rev. James Lawlor, Joan Sobala, S.S.J., and Rev. Raymond H. Fleming. Many priests and pastoral workers discussed the issues in their bulletins, in conjunction with their Sunday eucharist, or in special sessions. The teaching moment became a very living reality in Rochester. Fr. John Philipps, a local pastor, wrote a very supportive and lucid statment in his parish bulletin which was later reprinted by many other parishes. My mother had died in Rochester in the summer of 1985 and had been very active to the end of her 85 years. In thumbing through the signatures on the FACT statement before they were sent to Rome, I came across the pages from her home parish and recognized on one page the group which daily celebrated the 7:00 a.m. Eucharist. I was touched to see that one of her friends

had signed my mother's name and put the address down as
"heaven."

Reactions to the whole affair came quickly. I was both grateful
and humbled by the statement released by my own bishop. Bishop
Clark described me as a priest whose personal life could well be
called exemplary and as a moral theologian of notable competence
who in no way is an extremist. According to an N.C. news story,
Cardinal Bernardin "supported a compromise that would allow Fr.
Curran to retain his tenured professorship on the theology faculty
in exchange for an agreement not to teach a course in sexual
ethics." Bernardin said that he had "spoken informally" to Ratzinger, but it would be "inappropriate" to publicly discuss the content of the conversation.[28] However, there was little or no public
support from other bishops.

Within Catholic University there was much discussion of the issues. After returning from Rome with me, Dean Cenkner of the
School of Religious Studies explained to our faculty that he had accompanied me to Rome to show support for one "who is recognized
at this university and beyond for his theological acumen, pastoral
concern, and ecclesial loyalty." Within the university, the faculties
of the Departments of Psychology and of Education passed statements of support for me and urged that I be allowed to continue to
teach at Catholic University. Twenty members of the theology faculty expressed solidarity with the sentiments expressed by Bishop
Clark and urged that the congregation accept the compromise I
proposed as being in the best interest of all concerned. This same
statement was then passed by the departmental theology faculty
(13 yes, 4 no, and 3 abstentions) and sent to the faculty of the
School of Religious Studies. At its meeting, the School of Religious
Studies changed some of the wording of the statement but en-
dorsed the same conclusion of strongly supporting the compromise
by a vote of 25 yes, 3 no, 1 abstention. The School of Religious
Studies sent this resolution to the Academic Senate of the University. The Academic Senate at its May 8 meeting returned the resolution to the School of Religious Studies for clarification and
adopted its own milder resolution (25-5-1) expressing concern for
the effect of the proceedings of the congregation on Professor Curran.

President Byron had maintained in interviews and newspapers
that the university was neutral in this case and not involved. At a

special meeting at the Catholic Theological Society of America convention in Chicago in June 1986, the Catholic University faculty person and the FACT coordinator on the panel expressed disappointment about their respective conversations with the president. I personally had only one conversation with President Byron after I was informed that Rome had turned down the compromise. It took place by chance at National Airport on Friday morning, January 17, 1986, the day after both of us had been informed by Hickey and Bernardin that the compromise was turned down. Byron said he was sorry things had not worked out, but he pledged to do everything possible to keep me at the university and thought it would be practical to work out a position for me at the law school. There I could continue researching some of the issues I had recently been interested in. I thanked Byron and pointed out that in the light of the Marshall report which had just been circulated to the faculty, I could only call his proposed offer completely cynical. I could not accept it. Byron strenuously objected to my characterization.

I explained. The Marshall Committee report had been given to the faculty just the day before, but it had gone through a number of drafts since late summer with all the appropriate university officials, including the president, being asked for comments on the different drafts. The president admitted to me he had purposely not made any comments. I had earlier discussed with him what happened when the Marshall Committee visited in February 1985. Word had circulated in our faculty that Rome had refused to accept the Marshall report without some mention of dissent. So the committee began to revise its report. According to the final report, the committee judged that dissent at the university could do harm to seminary formation and may be in opposition with the governing Roman documents. The report said that "only one of the signers of the original statement of dissent remains a member of the theology faculty today." The committee also made the judgment that dissent is still found "in one or another" of the faculty at the present time.

I was outraged at the report. They had made these judgments on the basis of outside pressure without having read the works of those concerned and without any real investigation or opportunity for people to defend themselves. Also the description of the teaching on dissent at Catholic University was not true. The legitimacy of theological dissent from noninfallible teaching was accepted by a good number of my faculty colleagues, as was later made apparent. In my conversation with Byron I pointed out that both truth and justice demanded that he set the record straight. It was now too easy to move me to another faculty and then to claim that the one remaining original signer was no longer on the theology faculty. I accused Byron of putting institutional survival ahead of truth and justice. Unless I saw a copy of his letter disagreeing with the Marshall report, I could draw no other conclusions. I have never seen such a memo or letter from him.

The response from the theological community was overwhelmingly favorable. Over 750 members of the College Theology Society (CTS) and the Catholic Theological Society of America (CTSA) signed the theologians' statement on my behalf. One small but vocal objection came from the Fellowship of Catholic Scholars which had been created about ten years ago by a group committed to uphold the teachings of the magesterium. Even the few who disagreed with my position had to admit the fact that the theological community is overwhelmingly in agreement with the legitimacy of my positions. The presidents of the CTS and the CTSA in their 1986 presidential addresses to their respective meetings pointed out the urgency of the problem and their perceived need to strongly support the legitimacy of my positions. I gave a principal address to the CTS and received a standing ovation before the talk began. The CTSA put on an informational panel about my case and in the business meeting on June 13 adopted by a 171-14 vote a resolution which strongly urged that no action be taken against Charles Curran that would prohibit him from teaching on the theological faculty at the Catholic University of America. However, my Catholic University colleague William May then sent out a statement asking for my removal from the university which was signed by thirty-three scholars, almost all of whom are members of the Fellowship of Catholic Scholars.[29] At the suggestion made in an earlier joint letter from the presidents of the CTS and the CTSA, a number of forums were held on many campuses and some individual faculties signed collective statements.

The ecumenical dimensions of the issue were pointed out in statements of support from past presidents of the Society of Christian Ethics, the annual meeting of the American Theological Society, Wesley Theological Seminary Faculty, the Faculty of the General Theological Seminary in New York and others. Often these statements recognized the rights of the Catholic Church leaders to deal with their own doctrinal and disciplinary questions, but they pointed out their respect for me, my standing in the theological community, the harmful effects on ecumenism of any action against me, and the need for universities, if they wish to be true universities, to protect academic freedom.

Within the general Catholic public, FACT and Friends for Charles Curran did admirable work. The thoroughness of FACT preparation and execution was proved by their reaching their goal of more than 20,000 signatures on their statement which was sent to Ratzinger and Hickey. In addition their mailings encouraged many people to write to the church authorities involved. I have no way of knowing what kind of mail was received by others. Many sent me copies of what they wrote to church officials. I received about a thousand pieces of mail with 15% negative. Some national groups such as the National Federation of Priests' Councils and the National Conference of Diocesan Directors of Religious Education passed resolutions in my favor. I received copies of resolutions on my behalf from a number of different priests' councils and groups throughout the country. There was also one notable organized attempt to work for action against me. The April 17, 1986 issue of *The Wanderer* supplied a post card addressed to Cardinal Ratzinger so that the readers could inform Ratzinger of their position in support of his action against Curran. *The Wanderer* also urged that action be taken against Curran as a priest and that the Holy See apply appropriate sanctions against anyone who dissents or allows people under one's authority to dissent. The Catholic press often editorialized about the issue, but I have no accurate way of correlating all the different editorials. Letters to the editor in secular and Catholic magazines and papers represented both sides of the issue. The freedom of some Catholic diocesan newspapers is well illustrated by the fact that the Rochester *Courier Journal* carried some very negative (and in my judgment, irresponsible) letters against the local bishop.

A summary of the response might go something like this. Very little public support for me from bishops, but not much public opposition either. However, it seems many influential bishops are opposed to me. The vast majority of Catholic theologians expressed agreement, but the Fellowship of Catholic Scholars supported the congregation. Most people probably could have predicted how the different Catholic publications would editorialize on the issue. In the general Catholic populace there was support for me from some liberal and moderate Catholics, but strong opposition from some conservative quarters. However, the vast majority of Catholics were not even touched by this case or issue. They probably know nothing about it and just continue to live their daily lives.

On March 10, Ratzinger wrote Hickey, asking for my definitive response to the September 17 letter. I responded on April 1 saying that in conscience I could not change my positions, but I once again urged acceptance of the compromise.

From the very beginning I was pessimistic about the acceptance of the compromise. As the spring of 1986 turned into summer, I was even more convinced that the congregation would take action against me to deprive me of my status as a Catholic theologian and my ability to teach in the name of the church. All the indications were negative. There was no real visible support for me by American bishops. In fact, I knew that most of the bishops in major sees were opposed to me. Cardinal Ratzinger's continued public comments were unyielding. Friends from Rome wrote about very negative rumors, and even Bernard Häring counselled me to prepare for a negative judgment. At Catholic University, the bishops on the Board of Trustees on a first ballot turned down the tenure application of James Provost, a well-known moderate canonist who was also the executive secretary of the Canon Law Society of America. However, in August Provost was granted tenure. There also continued to be much talk about a conservative swing in the United States hierarchy, and a general chill or pall seemed to be settling in over the church in the United States. I prepared myself for a negative decision. In fact, these pages are first being written precisely at this time of waiting, in June of 1986.

The negative decision reached me on August 18. During my vacation in early August, I was contacted by Archbishop Hickey. I agreed to come to a meeting at his office on Monday, August 18, at 4:00 pm. At that meeting Hickey gave me the July 25 letter from Cardinal Ratzinger informing me that I will "no longer be considered suitable nor eligible to exercise the function of a Professor of Catholic Theology." The congregation's decision had been approved by the Pope on July 10. Hickey also handed me his press release and said that the Ratzinger letter to me as well as his press release were already in the hands of the public media. This story was carried on the national TV news that night and was front page news the next morning.

On Tuesday Archbishop Hickey held a press conference at which he and William J. Byron, S.J., the President of Catholic University, gave prepared remarks and then fielded questions. In response to a question, Hickey said that "there is no right to public dissent." I held a news conference on Wednesday, August 20, and responded to the Ratzinger letter. At that conference I pointed out the enormous consequences of Hickey's statement. No Catholic theological journal could ever publish any position dissenting from any noninfallible church teaching. I also promised to continue my own theological work including my efforts to support the need at times for theoretical and practical dissent from some noninfallible teachings and the importance of academic freedom for Catholic theology and for Catholic institutions of higher learning.

One other aspect of the case must be mentioned. In a letter to me under date of August 18, 1986, Archbishop Hickey informed me that as Chancellor of Catholic University he was initiating "the withdrawal of the canonical mission which permits you to teach theology at this University." Hickey reminded me of my right to request the hearing procedures spelled out in the Canonical Statutes, but unilaterally imposed a September 1 deadline for my action. On August 29, I informed Hickey that I was requesting such a process without prejudice to, and without waiving, my fully documented academic and legal rights.

Thus my case with the Congregation for the Doctrine of the Faith came to a close. In their judgment I am neither "suitable nor eligible to exercise the function of a Professor of Catholic Theology." The larger issues of the role of Catholic theologians and the possibility and legitimacy of dissent will continue to be burning issues within the Catholic Church. The process under way at Catholic University will ultimately decide my fate within Catholic University as well as Catholic University's understanding of academic freedom.

Notes

[1]Ted Schoof, ed., *The Schillebeeckx Case* (New York: Paulist Press, 1980), p. 15.

[2]For a history of this institution, see *Academia Alfonsiana, 1957-1982* (Rome: Academia Alfonsiana, 1982).

[3]Charles E. Curran, "Communication," *Worship* 36, n. 1 (December 1961), 58-61.

[4]Charles E. Curran, "The Problem of Conscience and the Twentieth Century Christian," in Samuel H. Miller and G. Ernest Wright, eds., *Ecumenical Dialogue at Harvard: The Roman Catholic-Protestant Colloquium* (Cambridge: Belknap Press of Harvard University Press, 1964), pp. 262-273.

[5]Louis Janssens, "Morale conjugale et progestogenes," *Ephemerides Theologicae Lovanienses* 39 (1963), 787-826.

[6]Josef Maria Reuss, "Eheliche Hingabe und Zeugung," *Tübinger Theologische Quartalschrift* 143 (1963), 454-476; William van der Marck, "Vruchtbaarheidsregeling," *Tijdschrift voor Theologie* 3 (1963), 386-413; Louis K. Dupré, "Toward a Re-examination of the Catholic Position on Birth Control," *Cross Currents* 14 (Winter 1964), 63-85.

[7]Charles E. Curran, "Christian Marriage and Family Planning," *Jubilee* 12 (August 1964), 3-7.

[8]Charles E. Curran, "Birth Control," *The Current* 5 (Spring 1965), 5-12.

[9]Charles E. Curran, "Masturbation and Objectively Grave Matter: An Exploratory Discussion," *Proceedings of the Catholic Theological Society of America* 21 (1966), 95-112.

[10]Charles E. Curran, ed., *Absolutes in Moral Theology?* (Washington: Corpus Books, 1968).

[11]Charles E. Curran, Robert E. Hunt, *et al, Dissent In and For the Church: Theologians and Humanae Vitae* (New York: Sheed and Ward, 1969), p. 26. This book and its companion volume, John F. Hunt, Terrence R. Connelly, *et al., The Responsibility of Dissent: The Church and Academic Freedom* (New York: Sheed and Ward, 1969), propose the case made by the Catholic University theologians in defense of their declarations and actions concerning *Humanae vitae.* These volumes also describe the historical situation outlined in the next few pages of this text.

[12]*Human Life in Our Day: A Collective Pastoral Letter of the American Hierarchy* (Washington: United States Catholic Conference, 1968), p. 18.

[13]*Proceedings of the Catholic Theological Society of America* 27 (1972), 175, 176.

[14]Archbishop Robert J. Dwyer, "Catholic University: Who's in Charge?" *Twin Circle,* April 13, 1975, pp. 2, 15, and 16. Dwyer again singled me out

in an undelivered letter he twice tried to give to the pope at a private audience in Rome. "Undelivered Letter of the Late Archbishop Robert J. Dwyer to the Holy Father Pope Paul VI," available as a reprint from *Orthodoxy of the Catholic Doctrine Periodical Review* 6, n. 1.

[15]Frank Morris, "CU's Fr. Curran," *Catholic Standard,* October 31, 1974, p. 8.

[16]Bishop Joseph V. Sullivan, "An Open letter to the Academic Community of Louisiana State University," *Catholic Commentator,* February 21, 1979, p. 1.

[17]Charles R. Pulver, "In Curran's Own Words. . .," *The Wanderer,* December 8, 1977; December 28, 1977; January 12, 1978.

[18]*The Daily Reveille,* February 20, 1979, p. 1.

[19]Father Matthew L. Lamb, "In My Opinion," *The Milwaukee Journal,* June 13, 1979, p. 21.

[20]*National Catholic Register,* May 11, 1968, p. 5; *Trenta Giorni,* maggio 1986, p. 15.

[21]*Le Monde,* Jeudi, 25 octobre, 1979, p. 17.

[22]*The Ecnonomist,* November 10, 1979, p. 66; *Tablet* 233 (November 3, 1979), 1081; London *Times*, December 3, 1979.

[23]"Doctrinal Congregation Criticizes 'Human Sexuality' Book," *Origins* 9 (August 30, 1979), 167-169.

[24]Richard A. McCormick, "The Chill Factor: Recent Roman Interventions," *America* 150 (June 30, 1984), 475-481.

[25]*NC News Service,* July 12, 1984, pp. 3, 4.

[26]*National Catholic Reporter,* July 20, 1984, pp. 1, 22.

[27]*Trenta Giorni,* Novembre 1984, p. 77.

[28]*NC News Service,* March 12, 1986, p. 10.

[29]*Catholic Standard,* July 10, 1986, p. 7.

# Chapter Two
# The Theological:
# An Analysis

The purpose of this chapter is not to repeat what has been developed in the course of my correspondence with the Congregation for the Doctrine of the Faith.[1] This chapter will summarize in a systematic way what I believe to be the primary theological issues involved in my dispute with the congregation. At the same time some of the more recent comments on these primary issues of disgreement will be discussed.

## Context and Presuppositions

The general context for this chapter and for the entire case is that of the Roman Catholic Church and Catholic theology. I have made it very clear that I am a believing Catholic and intend to do Catholic theology. Despite my intentions, I still might be wrong; but I maintain that my positions are totally acceptable for a Catholic theologian and a believing Roman Catholic.

The mission of the entire church is to be faithful to the word and work of Jesus. God's revelation has been handed over and entrusted to the church, which faithfully hands this down from generation to generation through the assistance of the Holy Spirit. Roman Catholicism recognizes that revelation was closed at the end of apostolic times, but revelation itself develops and is understood in the light of the different historical and cultural circumstances of the hearers and doers of the word.

Roman Catholic faith and theology have strongly disagreed with emphasis on the Scripture alone. The Scripture must always be understood in light of the thought patterns of our own time. The Catholic insistence on the Scripture and tradition recognized the need to develop and understand God's revelation in Jesus Christ

in the light of contemporary circumstances. The early Councils of the fourth, fifth, and subsequent centuries illustrate how in matters touching the very heart of faith — the understanding of God and of Jesus Christ — the living church felt the need to go beyond the words of the Scripture, to understand better and more adequately the revelation of God. Thus, the Christian Church taught there are three persons in God and two natures in Jesus. Fidelity to the tradition does not mean merely repeating the very words of the Scripture or of older church teaching. The Christian tradition is a living tradition, and fidelity involves a creative fidelity which seeks to preserve in its own time and place the incarnational principle. Creative fidelity is the task of the church in bearing witness to the word and work of Jesus.

In carrying out its call to creative fidelity to the word and work of Jesus, the church is helped by the papal and episcopal roles in the church. The existence of this pastoral teaching function of pope and bishops in the church must be recognized by all. However, there has been much development in the understanding of the exact nature of that teaching office, how it is exercised, and its relationship to the other functions connected with the offices of pope and bishops in the church. Much of the following discussion will center on what is often called today the ordinary magisterium of the papal office. This term ordinary magisterium, understood in this present sense, has only been in use since the nineteenth century.[2] A Catholic must recognize the pastoral office of teaching given to pope and bishops, but also should realize that this teaching function has been exercised in different ways over the years.[3]

These aspects, briefly mentioned in this opening section, are very important and could be developed at much greater length and depth. However, in this chapter they are being recalled as the necessary context and presuppositions for the discussion of the issues raised by the case involving the Congregation for the Doctrine of the Faith and myself. I understand myself to be a Catholic theologian and a Catholic believer, who recognizes the call of the church to be faithful in a creative way to the word and work of Jesus and who gratefully and loyally accepts the papal and episcopal functions in the church.

This chapter will now focus on what in my judgment are the primary issues involved in my case. In the process I will state briefly my own position on these issues. Five issues will be considered: the role of the theologian, the possibility of public theological dissent from some noninfallible, hierarachical church teachings, the possibility and right of dissent by the Christian faithful, the justice and fairness of the process, and academic freedom for theology and Catholic institutions of higher learning. The September 17 letter from Cardinal Ratzinger calls upon me to retract my positions in the following specific areas: contraception and sterilization; abortion and euthanasia; masturbation, premarital intercourse, and homosexual acts; the indissoluability of marriage. However, as Richard McCormick perceptively points out, these issues and agreement with my positions on these issues do not constitute the major points of contention in the dispute between the congregation and myself.[4] These are important topics, but they are primarily illustrative of the more fundamental issues involved. I have developed and defended my positions on these issues in my responses to the congregation.

## The Role of the Theologian

There has been much written on the role of the theologian and the relationship between the function of bishops and theologians in the church. It is impossible to add to this discussion in this short space, but rather my purpose is to raise the underlying issues involved in the present controversy. Many, and probably the majority of, Catholic theologians writing today see the role of the Catholic theologian as somewhat independent and cooperative in relationship to the hierarchical office, and not delegated or derivative from the role of pope and bishops. The theologian is a scholar who studies critically, thematically, and systematically Christian faith and action. Such a scholar must theologize within the Catholic faith context and must give due importance to all the *loci theologici,* including the teaching of the hierarchical magisterium. The Catholic theologian to be such must give the required assent to official church teaching, but the theologian does not derive his or her theological office from delegation by the hierarchical office holders. The pastoral teaching function of pope and bishops is connected with their offices in the church and differs from the teaching role of theologians. Note that I have described this understanding of the Catholic theologian as somewhat independent and cooperative with regard to the hierarchical role in the church. That independence is modified by the call of the theologian and all believers to give due assent to the pastoral teaching role of bishops and pope.

However, there is a very different understanding of the role of the theologian found in more recent church legislation. The new Code of Canon Law, which came into effect in the fall of 1983, and the Apostolic Constitution for ecclesiastical faculties and universities, *Sapientia Christiana,* understand the role of the theologian as primarily derived from the hierarchical teaching office and functioning by reason of delegation given by the hierarchical teaching office. A good illustration of this understanding of the theologian as delegate and representative of the hierarchical teaching office is found in canon 812 of the new Code of Canon Law: "Those who teach theological subjects in any institute of higher studies must have a mandate from the competent ecclesiastical authority." According to the Code, this mandate is required for all those who teach theology in any Catholic institution of higher learning. Earlier versions of the Code spoke of a "canonical mission" instead of a mandate. *Sapientia Christiana,* the Apostolic Constitution governing ecclesiastical faculties, requires a canonical mission from the chancellor for those teaching disciplines concerning faith or morals.[5] The final version of the Code uses the word mandate, and not canonical mission, because canonical mission appears to imply the assignment of a person to an ecclesiastical office.[6] The implication of this new canon and of other recent legislation is that the Catholic theologian in a Catholic institution officially exercises the function of teaching in that school through a delegation from the bishop. The role of the Catholic theologian is thus derived from the hierarchical teaching function and juridically depends upon it.

It seems there has been an interesting, even contradictory, development in Catholic documents within the last few years. The more theoretical documents seem to recognize a somewhat independent and cooperative role for theologians, whereas the legislative documents understand the theological role as derivative and delegated from the hierarchical teaching office. There is no doubt that from the nineteenth century until recent times, the role of the theologian was seen as subordinate to and derivative from the hierarchical teaching office. However, Vatican Council II, in its general ecclesiology and in its understanding of theologians, can be interpreted to adopt a more cooperative and somewhat independent understanding of the role of theologians vis-à-vis the hierarchical magisterium.[7] The cooperative model does not deny the official role of the hierarchical office in protecting and proclaiming the faith, but theology is a scholarly discipline distinct from but related to the proclamation of the faith by the hierarchical teaching office. However, canonists recognize that recent canonical legislation, including the new Code of Canon Law, understands the theological function as derivative from the hierarchical teaching function. In the older Code of Canon Law, there was no requirement for theologians in Catholic institutions to have a canonical mandate or mission to each theology. The older Code saw the role of the ordinary or diocesan bishop in terms of negative vigilance with regard to individual teachers of theology and not one of positive deputation.[8]

There can be no doubt that present church legislation tends to see the theological function as derivative from the hierarchical teaching function. However, very many Catholic theologians today appeal to more recent developments in Catholic understanding to substantiate a somewhat cooperative and independent understanding of the theological role vis-à-vis the hierarchical role. The correspondence between the Congregation for the Doctrine of the Faith and myself never explicitly goes into this question as such, but the congregation is operating out of a derivative understanding of the role of the theologian, while I adopt the somewhat independent and cooperative understanding.

In my understanding the teaching function is committed to the whole church. In addition, there is a special pastoral teaching office given to pope and bishops in the church. As important as this hierarchical teaching function is, it is not identical with the total teaching function of the entire church. There are many teaching roles in the church. The teaching role of theologians does not depend on an office in the church but finds its authority in the faithful expertise of the scholar. This understanding of teaching authority in the Catholic Church which is proposed by many contemporary Catholic theologians has been called a pluralistic approach as distinguished from the hierocratic approach which reduces the teaching authority in the church to the teaching offices of pope and bishops.[9]

# Public Theological Dissent from Some Noninfallible Hierarchical Church Teachings

The correspondence from the congregation indicates that the problem is public dissent from some hierarchical noninfallible teaching and not just private dissent. However, the meaning of "public" is never developed. The entire investigation centers on my theological writings so the only logical conclusion is that public here refers to theological writings. Private dissent apparently means something that is not written and is not spoken publicly.

From the very beginning the position of the congregation surprised me, because the congregation was denying the legitimate possibility of public theological dissent from the noninfallible teachings under discussion. My surprise was rooted in the fact that some Catholic bishops and very many theologians have recognized the possibility of such public theological dissent.

In 1979, after receiving the first set of "Observations" from the congregation, I had the feeling that the investigation would soon focus clearly on the manner and mode of public dissent. Past experience was the basis for this judgment. Recall that in 1968 I acted as the spokesperson for a group ultimately numbering over 600 theologians and issued a public statement at a press conference, which concluded that Catholic spouses may responsibly decide according to their conscience that artificial contraception in some circumstances is permissible and even necessary to preserve and foster the values and sacredness of marriage. In response to this statement, the trustees of the Catholic University of America, on September 5, 1969, mandated an inquiry in accord with academic due process to determine if the Catholic University professors involved in this dissent had violated by their declarations and actions their responsibilities to the university.[10]

A few months later, the object of the inquiry had definitely changed. "Hence the focus of the present inquiry is on the style and method whereby some faculty members expressed personal dissent from papal teaching, and apparently helped organize additional public dissent to such teaching."[11] The Board of Trustees did not question the right of a scholar to dissent from noninfallible church teaching. In the context of the inquiry, it became clear that public and organized dissent referred primarily to holding a press conference and to actively soliciting other theologians to sign the original statement. The primary question of public dissent thus was not regular theological publication but the use of the more popular media. In response to this new focus, the professors subject to the inquiry at Catholic University, through their counsel, pointed out the changed focus but went on to show that such public and organized dissent in the popular media was a responsible action by Catholic theologians. The shift in the focus of the inquiry seemed to come from the fact that the trustees, including the bishops on the Board of Trustees, were willing to recognize the possibility of even public dissent in theological journals as being legitimate, but objected to the use of the popular media. As mentioned in the last chapter, the faculty inquiry committee fully agreed with the thrust of the argument proposed by the professors, and the professors were exonerated in this hearing.

However, to my surprise, the investigation from the congregation never moved explicitly in the direction of the manner and mode of dissent and even at times the use of popular media. The conclusion logically follows from the position taken by the congregation, that the only acceptable form of dissent on these issues is that which is neither written nor spoken publicly.

The controversy explicitly deals with dissent on the specific questions under dispute. However, the correspondence seems to imply that the theologian cannot legitimately dissent from any noninfallible hierarchical teaching. I have always pointed out in the correspondence that I have been dealing with the noninfallible hierarchical teaching office. This position was explicitly accepted by the congregation in all of the correspondence prior to the September 17, 1985 letter to me from Cardinal Ratzinger. A very few Catholic theologians have maintained that the teaching on artificial contraception, is infallible from the ordinary teaching of pope and bishops throughout the world.[12] However, this position is not held by the vast majority of theologians and has not been proposed or defended by the congregation. One could also maintain that the Catholic teaching on divorce is infallible, by reason of the teaching of the Council of Trent. However, the phrasing of the canons with regard to the indissolubility of marriage, the attempt not to condemn the practice of *"economia"* of the Greek Church, and the somewhat broad understanding of *"anathema sit"* at the time of Trent, argue against the infallible nature of the Catholic Church's teaching on the indissolubility of marriage. Accepted standard textbooks, such as that of Pierre Adnès, recognize that the teaching on absolute intrinsic indissolubility is not infallible.[13] Thus, my position all along has been that I have never denied an infallible teaching of the church.

However, in the September 17 letter, Cardinal Ratzinger seems to claim that the assent of faith is somehow involved in my case. I have strenuously maintained that the assent of faith is not involved. We are dealing with the *obsequium religiosum* (this term's translation will be dealt with below) which is due in cases of noninfallible teaching. I hope as a result of my meeting with Cardinal Ratzinger in Rome on March 8 that we agree that the assent of faith is not involved. However, it is very clear that the congregation definitely maintains that the *obsequium religiosum* due to noninfallible teaching does not allow the theologian to dissent publicly in these cases.

Cardinal Ratzinger himself has called the distinction between infallible and noninfallible teaching "legalistic." Only in this century have theologians made this distinction in such a sharp way. "When one affirms that noninfallible doctrines, even though they make up part of the teaching of the church, can be legitimately contested, one ends up by destroying the practice of the Christian life and reduces the faith to a collection of doctrines." Abortion, divorce, and homosexuality, even with a thousand distinctions that can be made, are acts that go against Christian faith.[14] Ratzinger deemphasizes the distinction between infallible and noninfallible teaching, to help support his position that a theologian cannot dissent publicly from these noninfallible church teachings. What is to be said about Ratzinger's understanding?

It is true that the sharp distinction between infallible and noninfallible teaching is recent, for it became prevalent only at the time of the first Vatican Council (1870) which defined the infallibility of the pope. After that time, theologians quite rightly distinguished the two levels of teaching and the two different assents which are due to such teachings. All the faithful owe the assent of faith to infallible teaching and the *obsequium religiosum* of intellect and will to authoritative or authentic, noninfallible teaching. The distinction became well entrenched in the theology manuals of the twentieth century before Vatican II.[15] Such a distinction helped to explain that official teaching on some issues had been wrong and had subsequently been corrected (e.g. the condemnation of interest taking, the need for the intention of procreation to justify conjugal relations). At the time of Vatican Council I and later it was also pointed out that Popes Liberius (d. 366), Vigilius, (d. 555) and Honorius (d. 638) all proposed erroneous teachings, which were subsequently rejected through theological dissent. Vatican Council II changed many earlier teachings, such as those on religious freedom and the relationship of the Roman Catholic Church to other Christian churches and to the true church of Jesus Christ. Scripture scholars, for the last generation or so, have publicly disagreed with the teachings that were proposed by the Biblical Commission in the first two decades of this century. The theologians thus recognized the distinction between infallible and noninfallible teaching, and used it among other purposes to explain why certain earlier errors in church teaching did not refute the Vatican I teaching on papal infallibility. These theologians likewise recognized the possibility of dissent from such noninfallible teaching at times, but did not explicitly justify public dissent.[16]

The theologians are not the only ones to use this distinction. *Lumen Gentium,* the Constitution on the Church of the Second Vatican Council, recognizes this distinction between infallible and noninfallible teaching and the two different types of assent which are due (par. 25). The new Code of Canon Law clearly distinguishes between the assent of faith and the *obsequium religiosum* of intellect and will which is due to the authoritative teaching of the pope and college of bishops even when they do not intend to proclaim that doctrine by a definitive act (canon 752). This distinction is thus accepted not only by theologians but also by official documents and by the new Code of Canon Law.

Some theological manuals and many contemporary theologians understand the *obsequium religiosum* owed to authoritative, noninfallible teaching to allow at times the possibility of theological dissent, and at the present time even public dissent. Some bishops' conferences explicitly recognized the legitimacy of dissent from the papal encyclical *Humanae vitae* issued in 1968. Also documents from bishops' conferences have acknowledged the possibility of public theological dissent from some noninfallible church teaching. The United States bishops in their 1968 pastoral letter "Human Life in Our Day" recognize that in noninfallible teaching there is always a presumption in favor of the magisterium. However, the pastoral letter also acknowledges the legitimacy of public theological dissent from such teaching if the reasons are serious and well-founded, if the manner of the dissent does not question or impugn the teaching authority of the church, and if the dissent is such as not to give scandal.[17] Since I have developed at great length in my correspondence with the congregation both the arguments justifying the possibility of public dissent and the many theologians and others in the church who recognize such a possibility, there is no need to repeat this here.

One significant aspect of the question deserves mention here because of some recent developments — the understanding and translation of *obsequium religiosum. Obsequium* has often been translated as submission or obedience. Bishop Christopher Butler was, to my knowledge, the first to translate the word *obsequium* as "due respect."[18] Francis Sullivan, a Jesuit professor and former dean at the Pontifical Gregorian University in Rome, in his book on the magisterium rejects the translation of "due respect" but still allows the possibility of legitimate, public theological dissent from noninfallible church teaching.[19] (Sullivan in a recent interview strongly defends the distinction between infallible and noninfallible church teaching.[20] Sullivan sees the position taken by the Vatican congregation in its correspondence with me as threatening the critical function of the theologian with regard to the nondefinitive teaching of the magisterium. "The idea that Catholic theologians, at any level of education, can only teach the official church position, and present only those positions in their writings, is new and disturbing." Sullivan, who considers his approach "rather moderate" and "standard," has been teaching the possibility of public theological dissent from some noninfallible teaching at the Pontifical Gregorian University in Rome. Sullivan adds that "no one has ever questioned what I teach.") Sullivan claims that "submission" and not "due respect" is the proper translation of *obsequium,* but the Gregorian University professor still recognizes the possibility and legitimacy of public theological dissent from authoritative, noninfallible teaching.

The English text of the Code of Canon Law, found in the commentary commissioned by the Canon Law Society of America and authorized by the executive committee of the National Conference of Catholic Bishops in the United States, translates *obsequium* as "respect."[21] Ladislas Orsy, in a recent commentary on canon 752, recognizes difficulties in translating *obsequium* but opts for "respect." Orsy also accepts the possibility of legitimate public dissent from some authoritative, noninfallible teaching.[22] The discussion over the proper understanding and translation of *obsequium* has been an occasion for many to recognize the possibility of legitimate public dissent from some noninfallible church teaching.

There can be no doubt that church documents, the Code of Canon Law, theologians in general, and canonists in general have accepted the importance of the distinction between infallible and noninfallible hierarchical teaching. Although I believe the distinction between infallible and noninfallible teaching is very important and necessary, there is a need to say more in dealing with the possibility of public dissent. I disagree with Cardinal Ratzinger's attempt to smooth over somewhat the clear distinction between infallible and noninfallible teaching. What about the danger of reducing the Christian faith in practice to a small, abstract core? Are abortion, divorce, and homosexuality, even with nuanced distinctions, acts which go against Christian faith?

In my own comments about this case in the popular media, I have been careful not only to use the distinction between infallible and noninfallible teaching but also to talk about what is core and central to the faith as distinguished from those things that are more removed and peripheral. Also I have consistently spoken about the right to dissent publicly from *some* noninfallible church teaching. The distinction between infallible and noninfallible church teaching is absolutely necessary, but not sufficient. The older theology tried to deal with questions of the relationship of church teaching to the core of faith through the use of "theological notes." These notes, and their opposites in terms of censures, recognized the complexity by categorizing many different types of noninfallible teaching.[23] In a true sense, there is a need today to redevelop the concept of theological notes in the light of the realities of the present time.

As important as the concept of infallible teaching is, there are some very significant limitations involved in it. Infallible teaching, especially of the extraordinary type by pope or council, has usually come in response to an attack on or a denial of something central to the faith. However, some points which have never been denied by believers, such as the existence of God, have never been defined by the extraordinary hierarchical teaching office. Something can be infallible by reason of the ordinary teachings of the pope and all the bishops, but the conditions required for such infallibility are often difficult to verify. On the other hand, the limits and imperfections of any infallible teaching have been rightly recognized. Infallible teaching itself is always open to development, better understanding, and even purification. Thus, one must be careful when speaking about infallible teaching both because some things might pertain to the core of faith which have at least not been infallibly taught by the extraordinary teaching function of the pope and bishops and because even infallible teaching itself is open to development and further interpretation. However, in the present discussion the distinction between infallible and noninfallible is very important. It allows me to deal with a limited area — the area of noninfallible teaching.

Within this large area of what is noninfallible, it is necessary to recognize various degrees and levels of relationship to faith. Here an updating of the older theological notes would be very useful. It is true that I have not attempted to develop all the distinctions involved in noninfallible teaching, but in light of the purposes of the present discussion I have tried to show that the particular issues under discussion are remote from the central realities of Christian faith.

The Catholic tradition in moral theology has insisted that its moral teaching is based primarily on natural law and not primarily on faith or the Scripture. The natural law is understood to be human reason reflecting on human nature. Even those teachings which have some basis in Scripture (e.g.,the indissolubility of marriage, homosexuality) were also said to be based on natural law. This insistence on the rational nature of Catholic moral teaching recognizes that such teaching can and should be shared by all human beings of all faiths and of no faith. Such teachings are thus somewhat removed from the core of Catholic faith as such. The distance of these teachings from the core of faith and the central realities of faith grounds the possibility of legitimate dissent.

In addition, the issues under discussion are specific, concrete, universal moral norms existing in the midst of complex reality. Logic demands that the more specific and complex the reality, the less is the possiblity of certitude. Moral norms in my judgment are not the primary, or the only, or the most important concern of moral teaching and of moral theology. Moral teaching deals with general perspectives, values, attitudes, and dispositions, as well as norms. Values, attitudes, and dispositions are much more important and far-reaching for the moral life than are specific norms. These values and dispositions, by their very nature, are somewhat more general and can be more universally accepted as necessary for Christian and human life. Within the church, all can and should agree that the disciples of Jesus are called to be loving, faithful, hopeful, caring people who strive to live out the reality of the paschal mystery. Disrespect for persons, cheating, slavery, dishonesty, and injustice are always wrong. However, the universal binding force of specific, concrete material norms cannot enjoy the same degree or level of certitude. Norms exist to protect and promote values, but in practice conflicts often arise, in the midst of the complexity and specificity involved.

Thus the issues under consideration in this case are quite far removed from the core of faith and exist at such a level of complexity and specificity that one has to recognize some possibility of dissent. It is also important to recognize the necessary distinction between the possibility of dissent and the legitimacy of dissent on particular questions. Reasons must be given which are convincing in order to justify the dissent in practice. The central issue involved in the controversy between the Congregation for the Doctrine of the Faith and myself is the possibility of public theological dissent from some noninfallible teaching which is quite remote from the core of faith, heavily dependent on support from human reason, and involved in such complexity and specificity that logically one cannot claim absolute certitude.

There is a further question which has not received much discussion from the Catholic theological community but which should at least be raised. We have generally talked about the responsibilities and rights of Catholic theologians in general. Are there any distinctions that must be made concerning theologians? Are the rights and responsibilities of Catholic theologians and the particular right to dissent in these areas the same for all Catholic theologians? Is there a difference between the theologian as teacher and as researcher and writer? Is there a difference if the theologian teaches in a seminary, a college, or a university? In the particular cases under discussion, I would develop the thesis that these differences do not affect the possibility and legitimacy of public theological dissent. All of us can agree on the need to explore this question in much greater depth. In addition, more attention must be given to the limits of legitimate dissent.

## The Christian Faithful and Dissent

There is a third aspect or issue which has not received the attention it needs — the possibility and legitimacy of dissent on the part
of the members of the church. In a very true sense, my present controversy involves more than just the role of theologians in the
church.

There can be no doubt that much of the friction between theologians and the hierarchical magisterium has occurred on more
practical questions, including moral issues touching on sexuality.
The issues are not just abstract questions about which people
speculate, but they involve concrete decisions about specific actions which are to be performed. Problems arise in these areas precisely because they involve more than speculation. Here the position proposed by theologians might have some practical bearing on
how people live. All must recognize that the distinction between
the roles of bishops and theologians would be much clearer if the
role of theologians were restricted to the realm of speculation, with
no effect on what people do in practice. However, life is not so easily
compartmentalized.

Elsewhere I have defended the thesis that on some issues a loyal
Catholic may disagree in theory and in practice with the church's
noninfallible teaching and still consider oneself a loyal and good
Roman Catholic.[24] In a sense, under certain conditions, one can
speak of a right of the Catholic faithful to dissent from certain
noninfallible teachings. In the aftermath of *Humanae vitae* in
1968, some bishops' conferences recognized that dissent in practice
from the encyclical's teaching condemning artificial contraception
could be legitimate and did not cut one off from the body of the
faithful. The congregation in its correspondence with me has not
gone explicitly into this issue. Those who deny the legitimacy of
such dissent in practice would seem to face a difficult ecclesiological problem when confronted with the fact that the vast majority of
fertile Catholic spouses use artificial contraception. What is the relationship of these spouses to the Roman Catholic Church?

The possibility of legitimate dissent by the faithful stands on its
own and is not directly dependent on theological dissent. In the
next chapter, I point out how I have learned from the experience of
Christian people. However, the importance of recognizing this possibility and even right on the part of the faithful greatly affects how
the theologian functions. If there is such a possibility of dissent,
then the individual members of the Catholic Church have a right

to know about it. I hasten to add that the individual members also have a right to know what is the official teaching of the church and should be conscious of the dangers of finitude and sin that can skew any human decision. Public dissent by a Catholic theologian would then be called for, not only because theologians must discuss with one another in the attempt to understand better God's word and to arrive at truth, but also because the people of God need this information to make their own moral decisions. Thus, for example, in the light of the situation present at the time of the issuance of the encyclical *Humanae vitae* in 1968, it was important for Roman Catholic spouses to know that they did not have to make a choice between using artificial contraception under some conditions and ceasing to be members of the Roman Catholic Church. The Catholic theologian, among others, had an obligation to tell this to Catholic spouses.

The possibility of legitimate dissent in practice by the faithful also affects the matter of scandal. The United States bishops in their 1968 letter proposed three conditions under which public theological dissent is in order. One of these conditions is that the dissent be such as not to give scandal. In my correspondence with the congregation, I repeatedly asked them for criteria which should govern public theological dissent in the church. No developed criteria were ever forthcoming. However, in the April 1983 "Observations" from the congregation, it was mentioned briefly that to dissent publicly and to encourage dissent in others runs the risk of causing scandal.[25]

Scandal in the strict sense is an action or omission which provides another the occasion of sinning. In the broad sense, scandal is the wonderment and confusion which are caused by a certain action or omission. The existence of sin and of scandal understood in the strict sense is logically dependent on whether the dissent itself is legitimate.[26] What about scandal as the wonderment and confusion caused among the faithful by public theological dissent? There can be no doubt that in the past there has been a strong tendency on the part of the hierarchical leaders of the church to look upon the faithful as poor and ignorant sheep who had to be protected and helped. This same vision and understanding of the ordinary common people also lay behind an older Catholic justification of monarchy and government from above. Catholic social teaching itself has changed in the twentieth century and accepted the need for, and importance of, democratic political institutions. No longer are the citizens the poor sheep or the "ignorant multitude," to use the phrase employed by Pope Leo XIII. So, too, the members of the church can no longer be considered as poor sheep. Greater importance must be given to their increased education and rights in all areas, including religion.[27]

Perhaps at times theologians, who often associate with people who are well educated, will fail to give enough importance to the danger of disturbing some of the faithful with their teachings. However, in this day and age it seems many more Catholic lay people would be scandalized if theologians were forbidden to discuss publicly important topics of the day, such as contraception, divorce, abortion, and homosexuality. These issues are being discussed at great length in all places today, and theologians must be able to enter into the discussion, even to the point of dissenting from some official Catholic teaching. In addition, if the faithful can at times dissent in practice and remain loyal Roman Catholics, then they have the right to know what theologians are discussing.

In this entire discussion, it would ultimately be erroneous to confine the question just to the possibility and right of theologians to dissent publicly from some noninfallible teachings. There is need for further development and nuancing, but on all the moral issues under consideration, I have carefully tried to indicate in my writings what the legitimate possibilities are for the faithful in practice. The right of the faithful in this matter definitely colors one's approach to public theological dissent and to the dangers of scandal brought about by such dissent or the lack of it.

## Justice and Fairness of the Process

Catholic theology has always emphasized the incarnational principle, with its emphasis on visible human structures. Catholic ecclesiology well illustrates this approach by insisting on the church as a visible human community — the people of God with a hierarchical structure. The visible church strives to be a sacrament or sign of the presence of God in the world in and through this visible community. Within the community there are bound to be tensions involving the role of bishops and the role of theologians. Both strive to work for the good of the church, but there will always be tensions. To claim there is no tension would be illusory and ultimately would deny that the church is a living, pilgrim community. The church is always striving to know and live better the word and work of Jesus in the particular historical and cultural circumstances of time and place. The role of the theologian, by definition, will often be that of probing, exploring, and tentatively pushing the boundaries forward. The hierarchical teaching office must promote such creative and faithful theological activity, while at the same time it must rightly wait until these newer developments emerge more clearly. The church in justice must find ways to deal with this tension in the relationship between theologians and the hierarchical teaching office. The good of the church, the credibility of its teaching office, and the need to protect the rights of all concerned call for just ways of dealing with these inevitable tensions.

The present case raises questions of justice and of the credibility of the teaching office in the church. It is recognized by all that there are many Catholic theologians who publicly dissent from some noninfallible teachings. Likewise there are many Catholic theologians who hold similar positions, and even more radical positions, on the moral issues involved in the present case. However, the issues of justice and credibility go much deeper.

First, it is necessary for the congregation to state its position on public theological dissent from noninfallible teaching. Is such dissent ever allowed? If so, under what conditions or criteria? From the correspondence it would seem that the congregation is claiming that all theological dissent is wrong, or at least public dissent on these particular issues is wrong. Does the congregation truly hold such a position? As mentioned earlier, the United States bishops in 1968 in the light of the controversy engendered by *Humanae vitae* proposed three conditions for justifying public dissent from noninfallible teaching. I have consistently maintained that my dissent has been in accord with these norms. The congregation was unwiling to accept these norms. Does the congregation disagree with the United States bishops and with the vast majority of Catholic theologians?

Archbishop John Quinn, then of Oklahoma City, at the Synod of Bishops in 1974 pointed out the real need to arrive at some consensus and understanding about dissent, and urged discussions between representatives of the Holy See and representatives of theologians to arrive at acceptable guidelines governing theological dissent in the church.[28] Archbishop Quinn brought up the same problem again at the Synod of Bishops in 1980.[29] For the good of the church, there continues to be a "real need" to arrive at some guidelines in this area.

In addition there is need for juridical structures which better safeguard justice and the rights of all concerned. Some of the problems with the present procedures of the congregation have already been pointed out in the correspondence. The congregation, in a letter to me, has defended its procedures because the *"Ratio Agendi"* is not a trial but rather a procedure designed to generate a careful and accurate examination of the contents of published writings by the author. However, since the process can result in severe punishment for the person involved, it seems that such a process should incorporate the contemporary standards of justice found in other juridical proceedings.

One set of problems stems from the fact that the congregation is the prosecutor, the judge, and jury. Some people have objected strongly to the fact that the cardinal prefect has commented publicly on the present case and disagreed in the public media with my position while the case has been in progress. Problems have also been raised against the existing procedures from the viewpoints of the secrecy of the first part of the process, the failure to allow the one being investigated to have counsel, the failure to disclose the accusers and the total record to the accused, and the lack of any substantive appeal process.[30] There have been many suggestions made for improvements in the procedures. The German Bishops have adopted procedures for use in Germany.[31] Cardinal Ratzinger in 1984 admitted that the plenary session of the congregation had decided to revise the current procedures of the congregation. The proposals made by the German Conference of Bishops have been accepted in principle. However, because of the workload and time constraints, the decree has not been put into effect.[32]

In 1980 a joint committee of the Catholic Theological Society of America and the Canon Law Society of America was formed to address the question of cooperation between theologians and the hierarchical magisterium in the United States, with a view toward developing norms that could be used in settling disputes. The committee prepared a detailed set of procedures in 1983, but they are still under study by the United States bishops.[33] In the meantime there has been one case involving the investigation of a theologian's writings by the doctrinal committee of the United States bishops. Little is known about the process itself, but the final statement from the committee indicates that the dialogue was fruitful and that the theologian in question, Richard McBrien, had the right to call other theologians to defend and explain his positions.[34] Perhaps the process used in this case might prove helpful in similar cases.

A detailed discussion of proposed guidelines lies beyond the scope of this present chapter. The major points made here are that justice and the credibility of the church's teaching office call for a recognition of the norms or criteria governing public dissent in the church, the equitable application of these norms, and the review of existing procedures to incorporate the safeguards of contemporary justice in the process of examining theologians. The call for these changes has been repeatedly made in the past. The need is even more urgent today.

## Academic Freedom, Theology, And Catholic Institutions of Higher Learning

Catholic higher education in the United States well illustrates the tension between being Catholic and being American which has challenged Catholic life and institutions in our country. In this particular case the pertinent question was often phrased in the following terms: Is a Catholic university a contradiction in terms? Colleges and universities in the United States have stressed the importance of institutional autonomy and academic freedom as two essential characteristics of what constitutes a college or university.

Until 1960, most Catholic institutions of higher learning emphasized their uniqueness and either implicitly or explicitly denied the need for academic freedom and institutional autonomy. However, as the '60s progressed, there was a growing acceptance of the need for these characteristics. By the end of the 1960s the major Catholic institutions of the United States had expressed a strong commitment to a true autonomy and academic freedom in the face of authority of whatever kind, lay or clerical, external to the academic community itself.[35]

Many reasons help explain this change — a greater Catholic interest in higher education at that time; the influx of people from secular universities into Catholic academe; the growing recognition of the greater compatibility between Catholicism and American institutions; the realization of the meager Catholic contribution to intellectual life in this country; a theoretical and practical appreciation of the role of the laity in higher education; a greater acceptance of professionalization in all aspects and departments of Catholic institutions of higher learning, including theology and religion departments.

Today the leaders of Catholic higher education in the United States strongly insist on the need for academic freedom and institutional autonomy.[36] The crux of the problem is to reconcile the existence of academic freedom and institutional autonomy with the truth claims made by the Catholic Church and its hierarchical teaching office. More specifically, the question is: can and should Catholic theology be responsibly taught and researched in the context of academic freedom and institutional autonomy? From the viewpoint of the American academy, there is a greater awareness today of the bankruptcy of an older insistence on being value-free or value-neutral. Values should be very important in all the human disciplines. Thus there is in general a greater openess in American academe today to accept the academic respectability of disciplines like theology. However, the question is, can Catholic theology accept the American concept of academic freedom? There has not been as much discussion in this area as there should be.

I will briefly describe how I think academic freedom and Catholic theology are compatible.[37] Academic freedom and institutional autonomy mean that any decisions affecting promotion, hiring, or dismissal of faculty members must be made by peers in the academy and not by outside persons or forces of any kind. Academic freedom respects the freedom of the scholar to pursue truth, with no limits placed on scholarship other than truth, honesty, and competency. The accepted principles of academic freedom recognize that even tenured faculty members can be terminated if they are incompetent and the judgment of incompetency is made by academic peers. Competency for the Catholic theologian demands that one theologize within the pale of Roman Catholic faith. The Catholic theologian must teach Catholic theology as such; otherwise one is incompetent as a Catholic theologian. Peers, in judging the competency of a Catholic theologian, must give due weight to the teaching of the hierarchical magisterium. However, the ultimate decision with juridical effects must be made by peers in the academy. The hierarchical magisterium is always free, if it deems it necessary, to point out the errors and ambiguities in the work of a theologian, but it cannot make decisions having direct juridical effect in the academy.

There is no doubt that academic freedom gives some added protection to the rights of the Catholic theological scholar. However, in my judgment, such protection is totally compatible with the understanding of the role of the Catholic theologian as somewhat cooperative with and somewhat independent of the role of the hierarchical teaching office. Such protection is not only good for the discipline of Catholic theology but also is good for the total church as it strives for creative fidelity to the word and work of Jesus. In this way, I maintain, one can do justice both to the demands of the academy and to the demands of Catholic theology and the good of the Catholic Church.

The academic freedom of Catholic institutions and of Catholic theology is an important theoretical question with many practical consequences. I think that the issue has to be settled on grounds of good theory, but one cannot ignore the practical consequences. Perhaps the most significant practical consequence at the present time concerns the financial threat to the very existence of Catholic higher education in the United States. Catholic colleges and universities receive a large amount of financial help, in different forms, from the public monies of the state. In the past the Supreme Court has ruled such public funding is acceptable for Catholic higher education but not for Catholic elementary and high schools. The difference between higher and lower education is that in higher education there is no indoctrination and the principles of academic freedom are observed. Thus, if there were no academic freedom and institutional autonomy for Catholic higher education, it might very well be that the Court would rule that public funding for Catholic institutions of higher learning is unconstitutional.[38] There are many complex and intricate questions that need to be discussed, but the general outline of this possible outcome is clear. The leaders of Catholic higher education are quite aware of and worried by these implications.

If the Vatican congregation or any ecclesiastical authority can declare someone no longer a Catholic theologian and unable to teach in the name of the church and thereby prevent that professor from continuing to teach Catholic theology in a Catholic institution, this seems to be a violation of academic freedom. However, in the present context, some maintain that this is the case only for the very few ecclesiastical faculties or universities such as the Catholic University of America, but it does not apply to the vast majority of American Catholic colleges and universities which are not canonically accredited by the Vatican.[39]

Yes, there is some difference between Vatican-accredited ecclesiastical faculties or institutions and the vast majority of Catholic colleges and universities in the United States. However, in the light of the new Code of Canon Law with its canon 812, the same problems about academic freedom exist for all Catholic institutions of higher learning. According to canon 812, teachers of theological disciplines need a mandate from a competent ecclesiastical authority. Thus the decisions of ecclesiastical authority can have a direct effect in the hiring, promotion, and dismissal of faculty members. The proposed Schema for Catholic colleges and universities, now being circulated by the Congregation for Catholic Education, enshrines and develops the same basic structural understanding. Catholic leaders of higher education in the United States have strongly disagreed with the new canon 812 and with the proposed new Schema for Catholic higher education. Such legislation and proposed legislation are seen as threats to the academic freedom and institutional autonomy of Catholic higher education in the United States.[40] I insist that the question of the academic freedom and institutional autonomy respecting Catholic higher education and Catholic theology should not ultimately be decided because of practical consequences for Catholic higher education; but, on the other hand, one cannot ignore these possible consequences.

In conclusion, this chapter has examined what I think are the five most significant issues involved in my dispute with the Congregation for the Doctrine of the Faith — the role of the Catholic theologian, the possibility of public theological dissent from some noninfallible hierarchical teaching, the possiblity of dissent by the faithful in such cases, the fairness of the process, and academic freedom. In discussing all these issues, I have also indicated my approach to the questions under discussion.

## Notes

[1]Some of the pertinent documentation in my case has been published in *Origins* 15 (March 27, 1986), 665-680.

[2]John P. Boyle, "The Ordinary Magisterium: Toward a History of the Concept," *The Heythrop Journal* 20 (1979), 380-398; 21 (1980), 14-29.

[3]For a discussion of all sides in the contemporary debate about morality and the hierarchical teaching office, see Charles E. Curran and Richard A. McCormick, eds., *Readings in Moral Theology No. 3: The Magisterium and Morality* (New York: Paulist Press, 1982).

[4]Richard A. McCormick, "L'Affaire Curran," *America* 154 (April 5, 1986), 261-267.

[5]*Sapientia Christiana,* art. 27, in *Origins* 9 (June 7, 1979), 34-45.

[6]John A. Alesandro, "The Rights and Responsibilities of Theologians: A Canonical Perspective," in Leo O'Donovan, ed., *Cooperation Between Theologians and the Ecclesiastical Magisterium: A Report of the Joint Committee of the Canon Law Society of America and the Catholic Theological Society of America* (Washington: Canon Law Society of America, 1982), pp. 106-109.

[7]Jon Nilson, "The Rights and Responsibilities of Theologians: A Theological Perspective," in O'Donovan, pp. 53-75. Many contemporary theologians hold a similar position. This understanding of the role of the theologian also appears in some papers prepared for a discussion of the magisterium sponsored by the United States Bishops' Committee on Doctrine. See U.S. Bishops' Committee on Doctrine, "Report: An Ongoing Discussion of Magisterium," *Origins* 9 (1980), 541-551.

[8]Alesandro in O'Donovan, pp. 107-109.

[9]Avery Dulles, *The Resilient Church* (Garden City, New York: Doubleday, 1977), pp. 99ff.

[10]John F. Hunt, Terrence R. Connelly, *et al., The Responsibility of Dissent: The Church and Academic Freedom* (New York: Sheed and Ward, 1970), pp. 23ff. This volume treats the academic and legal aspects of the defense made by myself and my colleagues at Catholic University. For the theological aspects, see Charles E. Curran, Robert E. Hunt, *et al., Dissent In and For the Church* (New York: Sheed and Ward, 1970).

[11]Hunt and Connelly, p. 39.

[12]John C. Ford and Germain Grisez, "Contraception and the Infallibility of the Ordinary Magisterium," *Theological Studies* 39 (1978), 258-312.

[13]Pierre Adnès, *Le Mariage* (Tournai, Belgium: Desclée, 1963), pp. 159ff.

[14]Lucio Brunelli, "Interview with Cardinal Ratzinger," *National Catholic Register*, May 11,1986, p. 5. The original interview appeared in *Trenta Giorni*, Maggio 1986, pp. 10, 11.

[15]Francis A. Sullivan, *Magisterium: Teaching Authority in the Catholic Church* (New York: Paulist Press, 1983).

[16]Curran and Hunt, pp. 66ff.

[17]National Conference of Catholic Bishops, *Human Life in Our Day* (Washington: United States Catholic Conference, 1968), pp. 18, 19.

[18]B. C. Butler, "Authority and the Christian Conscience," *Clergy Review* 60 (1975), 16.

[19]Sullivan, pp. 159ff. Sullivan refers only to a later article by B. C. Butler, "Infallible: *Authenticum: Assensus: Obsequium.* Christian Teaching Authority and the Christian's Response," *Doctrine and Life* 31 (1981), 77-89.

[20]John Thavis, "Interpretation of Dissent Could Threaten Theologians, Says Former Dean," *NC News Service,* Tuesday, May 6, 1986, pp. 19, 20.

[21]James A. Coriden, Thomas J. Green, and Donald E. Heintschel, eds., *The Code of Canon Law: A Text and Commentary* (New York: Paulist Press, 1985), canon 752, p. 548.

[22]Ladislas Orsy, "Reflections on the Text of a Canon," *America* 154 (May 17, 1986), 396-399.

[23]Sixtus Cartechini, *De Valore Notarum Theologicarum* (Rome: Gregorian University Press, 1951).

[24]E.g., Charles E. Curran, *Ongoing Revision: Studies in Moral Theology* (Notre Dame, IN: Fides Publishers, 1975), pp. 37-65; *Transition and Tradition in Moral Theology* (Notre Dame, IN: University of Notre Dame Press, 1978), pp. 43-55; *Critical Concerns in Moral Theology* (Notre Dame, IN: University of Notre Dame Press, 1984), pp. 233-256.

[25]*Origins* 15 (March 27, 1986), 670.

[26]McCormick, *America* 154 (April 5, 1986), 266, 267.

[27]Cardinal Ratzinger emphasizes the faith of the simple faithful and the duties of the shepherds and teachers in the church to these simple faithful. See Cardinal Ratzinger, "The Church and the Theologians," *Origins* 15 (May 8, 1986), 761-770.

[28]Archbishop John R. Quinn, "Norms for Church Dissent," *Origins* 4 (1974-5), 319, 320.

[29]Archbishop John R. Quinn, "New Context for Contraception Teaching," *Origins* 10 (1980), 263-267.

[30]Patrick Granfield, "Theological Evaluation of Current Procedures," in O'Donovan, pp. 125-132.

[31]"Beschluss der Deutschen Bischofskonferenz vom 21 September 1972 zur Regelung eines Lehrbeanstandsungsverfahrens,"*Archiv für katholischen Kirchenrecht* 141 (1972), 524-530.

[32]*National Catholic Register,* August 12, 1984, p. 6.

[33]Joint Committee of the Canon Law Society of America and the Catholic Theological Society of America, "Doctrinal Responsibilities: Procedures for Promoting Cooperation and Resolving Disputes between Bishops and Theologians," *Proceedings of the Catholic Theological Society of America* 39 (1984), 209-234.

[34]U.S. Bishops' Committee on Doctrine, "Father Richard McBrien's *Catholicism," Origins* 15 (1985), 129-132.

[35]For the historical development of the attitude of Catholic higher education to academic freedom see the various writings of Philip Gleason including the following: "Academic Freedom and the Crisis in Catholic Universities," in Edward Manier and John W. Houck, eds., *American Freedom and the Catholic University* (Notre Dame, IN: University of Notre Dame Press, 1967), pp. 33-56; "Academic Freedom: Survey, Retrospect, and Prospects," *National Catholic Education Association Bulletin* 64 (August 1967), 67-74; "Freedom and the Catholic University," *National Catholic Education Association Bulletin* 65 (November 1968), 21-29.

[36]"Catholic College and University Presidents Respond to Proposed Vatican Schema," *Origins* 15 (April 10, 1986), 697-704.

[37]This view has been developed in greater detail in Hunt and Connelly.

[38]"Catholic College and University Presidents. . .," *Origins* 15 (April 10, 1986), 699-700.

[39]Quentin L. Quade, Contribution to "Curran, Dissent, and Rome: A Symposium," *Catholicism in Crisis* 4 (May 1986), 20-22.

[40] "Catholic College and University Presidents. . .," *Origins* 15 (April 10, 1986), 697-704.

# CHAPTER THREE
# THE CONTEXT:
# AN EVALUATION

In daily life, one is often carried along somewhat uncritically and unreflectively by the routine events of human existence. The need to make important personal decisions and the pressure of outside events impinging on one furnish occasions to reflect on oneself and what is happening. I see myself as a committed member of the Roman Catholic Church and a Roman Catholic theologian. However, the Congregation for the Doctrine of the Faith has told me that I cannot be called a Catholic theologian and cannot continue to teach in the name of the church. Over the last few years I have had to ponder this entire situation. The overwhelming support of so many theological colleagues, testifying to the fact that I am a respected Catholic theologian in the judgment of my peers, has obviously been a great support. But I personally have had to raise some very significant questions.

In this chapter I want to develop this critical and personal reflection by focusing on a number of different aspects — the attractiveness of the Roman Catholic theological self-understanding, the influences on my moral theology, the development of my theology, a critical appraisal of what I have tried to do, a critical and personal analysis of the present controversy, and my reactions.

## The Attraction of the Catholic Theological Tradition

In a press interview after my situation became public, a reporter was probing me on my claim that I am a committed Roman Catholic and Catholic moral theologian. "Why are you a Catholic?" he queried. I smiled and confessed quite simply that I am probably a Catholic because my parents and family were Catholic! There was no great search, no sudden conversion, no intellectual or religious odyssey. However, as a theologian, I have come to study the Catholic tradition in greater depth and detail and have come to greatly appreciate it. The Catholic faith tradition makes sense to me, and it is precisely the best of the Catholic theological tradition that I see as supporting my theological positions, especially that of dissent from some authoritative, noninfallible hierarchical teachings which are not core and central to the faith.

Karl Barth once said that his greatest problem with Roman Catholicism was its "and."[1] There is no doubt that the "and" has traditionally characterized Catholic self-understanding — Scripture and tradition, faith and reason, divine and human, grace and nature, Jesus and the church, and Mary and the saints. In my perspective it is precisely the Catholic "and" which is very satisfying. There can be and have been problems in the way in which the "and" is understood. Too often the second component of each couplet has been seen as totally independent of the first and thus absolutized. As a result, tradition or church teaching became more important than the Scriptures; the church became absolutized and more important than Jesus. In my judgment the second element is very important, but it is subordinated to the first and understood as a mediation of the first. Thus, for example, the word of God is mediated in and through tradition; grace does not destroy nature but is mediated in and through nature and the human. Jesus is mediated in and through a visible, human church. It will be helpful to develop some of these in greater detail.

The Catholic tradition has rejected the axiom "the Scripture alone." At its best, the acceptance of Scripture and tradition recognizes that the word and work of God must be heard and done in the light of the historical and cultural circumstances of the given time and place. The word and work of God must become incarnate in present reality. The previous chapter pointed out how the development of our christological and trinitarian doctrines in the early church illustrates this Catholic self-understanding. Yes, person and nature are Greek concepts, but the Scriptures must always be understood in the light of the contemporary self-understanding.History reminds us that the church only came to the recognition of the seven sacraments in the twelfth century. For the greater part of its existence the church has not taught that there are seven sacraments. To make the point, I often claim that St. Peter would have flunked a third grade catechism examination. He would have known nothing about persons in the Trinity, natures of Jesus, or the existence of seven sacraments.

The greatest theologian in the Catholic theological tradition is Thomas Aquinas (d. 1274).[2] The genius of Aquinas took the contemporary thought, which was then being debated in the European university world, and used it to explain better the Christian mysteries. Aquinas was not satisfied with just repeating Augustine, Peter the Lombard, and his predecessors. He used the thought of Aristotle, a person who never knew Jesus and probably did not believe in God, in order to understand better the word of God revealed in Jesus.

Aquinas was condemned by church authorities in the thirteenth century. In the late nineteenth and early twentieth centuries Thomas Aquinas was made the patron of Catholic theology and philosophy. Theology was to be taught according to the method, the doctrine, and the principles of Thomas Aquinas. How ironic! If church authority in the thirteenth century insisted that theology be taught according to the method, the doctrine, and the principles of St. Augustine, there never would have been a Thomas Aquinas. The irony is that in the nineteenth and twentieth centuries Thomas was often invoked to prevent meaningful dialogue with the modern world.

The need to make the word and work of God incarnate in the historical and cultural circumstances of particular times and places does not mean that one uncritically accepts whatever is happening at any given time. Especially in dialogue with Protestant theologians, I have learned to give a greater recognition to the presence of sin in our world. The gospel must always be in critical dialogue with contemporary culture. There are many things in our culture that need to be condemned, but at the same time the church can and should learn from what is good in contemporary culture. One of the criticisms of traditional Roman Catholic self-understanding and structures was of its too-strong dependence on Roman political and cultural understandings. The whole church, the hierarchical teaching office, and the theologians are all involved in the continuing task of understanding and doing the word and work of God in contemporary historical and cultural circumstances.

The Catholic insistence on faith and reason at times has given too great and too independent a role to reason. However, I strongly affirm the scholastic vision and axiom that faith and reason can never contradict one another. This statement expresses a great faith in reason. Faith can never be reduced to reason, for faith radically transcends reason. However, faith and reason can never contradict one another. There is no doubt that reason can be deceived and erroneous, but the medieval axiom makes an "in principle" statement. The Catholic tradition, at its best, recognizes the importance and the role of reason. Reason is good and it should lead to the truth. Philosophers and theologians were the first scientists. The first universities were founded under church auspices. In the light of these historical developments, I have been even more insistent to prove that a Catholic university is not a contradiction in terms. In the course of history there have been many times when the church has lost the nerve of these early scholastic theologians. Galileo, evolution, Freud, biblical criticism, Teilhard de Chardin, and many others are examples of the church's failure to appreciate the truths of reason.

In moral theology, reason has traditionally played a very important role. Catholic moral teaching has been substantially based on the natural law, which is understood as human reason reflecting on human nature. By its own admission, Catholic moral theology must always be open to the insights of human reason as it strives to attain truth. There can be no doubt that Catholic theology and Catholic ethics have traditionally given much greater importance to reason than classical Protestant theology and ethics.

The perennial theological problem involves the relationship between the divine and the human. How do you put the two together? The history of theology shows great swings in approaches, which have been either too positive or too negative in their assessment of the human. The Catholic tradition, at its best, has never seen an opposition between the divine and the human, as if by giving more to God you have to take away a corresponding amount from the human. In exalting the human, one does not necessarily downplay the divine. The Catholic tradition with its acceptance of mediation has stressed the idea of participation — the human shares and participates in the goodness and the greatness of God. According to an often cited patristic saying, the glory of God is the human person come alive. According to Thomas Aquinas, the human being is an image of God not by doing God's law but because, like God, the human being is endowed with intellect, free will, and the power of self-determination. The more one directs oneself according to intellect and free will, the more one imitates God and shares in the greatness of God.[3]

The relationship between grace and the natural or the human has been a familiar question in Christian theology. According to the Catholic tradition, grace does not destroy nature. A traditional axiom maintains that grace builds on nature. The human and the natural are not opposed to grace; and grace can in no way take a short cut around the human. The human and the natural are good. The Catholic tradition, at its best, avoided puritanism and pessimism while trying to develop a true Christian humanism. In this connection I have always been fascinated by the difficulty some non-Catholics have in understanding monasticism. Too often the monk is pictured and glorified as the one who flees the world because the human and the worldly are of no value. Such a view is somewhat warped. Why is it that whenever the monks celebrate a great feast they have a banquet of rich food and drink? It is not by coincidence that some of the best wines and liqueurs are named after monks — and they are not used just for medicinal purposes. Again there has been some danger in the past Catholic approach. It was too easy to forget about sin. The supernatural was often seen as something added extraneously to the natural. However, the Catholic tradition has rightly recognized the basic goodness of the human. Thus moral theology is open to a critical dialogue with human experience and the human quest for the truth.

The Catholic understanding of the church well exemplifies the acceptance of the human. The church is not invisible. God is not only in immediate and direct contact with the individual. Catholic theology believes in a visible church which mediates the word and work of God in Jesus through the Holy Spirit. Catholic ecclesiology thus makes a great act of faith in the human. The mystery of the church carries on the basic thrust of the incarnation in time and space. At times the human gets in the way of the divine and does not perfectly mirror the divine, but that is the way in which God chose to reveal God's self. At times we have all experienced the abuses of the human, but Catholic ecclesiology, even and especially in experiencing such abuses, testifies to the importance of the human in the Catholic tradition.

There is a very important characteristic of Catholic ethics which should be mentioned. Morality is intrinsic and not extrinsic. The first question that Thomas Aquinas discusses in his treatment of ethics is the ultimate end of human beings, which is happiness or self-fulfillment. Critics of Aquinas have often pointed out the eudaemonistic nature of his ethic, which is apparently based on self-interest. However, for Aquinas morality is not something extrinsically imposed from outside. Rather morality is the living out of who we are, so that we can obtain our happiness and fulfillment. There is no opposition between the glory of God and human fulfillment and happiness. The glory of God is the human person come alive. Thomas Aquinas can and should be criticized, but he well illustrates the traditional Catholic insistence on an intrinsic morality.

The differences between an intrinsic and an extrinsic morality are illustrated by the answers to the questions — is something commanded because it is good, or is it good because it is commanded? For a Thomist, something is commanded because it is good.[4] In this light, Aquinas defines law as an ordering of reason for the common good. Opponents objected because law should primarily be an act of the will of the legislator, but the Thomistic tradition has rightly seen law as an ordering of reason. Even the legislator must conform oneself to reality, and not the other way around. Thomas has a very simple — in fact, a too simple — approach to civil disobedience. An unjust law is no law and does not oblige in conscience. Authority or the lawgiver must always strive to choose what is reasonable in the light of the common good. What is the gift that Christians traditionally ask God to bestow on their rulers? Wisdom. An intrinsic and realistic morality maintains that something is commanded because it is good. The very fact that authority teaches something, does not necessarily make it good or right. What is commanded depends on what is good. Extrinsicism and authoritarianism put the cart before the horse.

Thus the Catholic insistence on understanding and doing the word and work of God in the particular circumstances of time and place, a critical openness to reason and the human, and an insistence on an intrinsic understanding of morality, are aspects of the Catholic tradition that are most appealing to me. One must readily admit that there are other aspects of the tradition which cannot be ignored. The Catholic Church and its theological tradition often appear to be static, authoritarian, over-centralized, and defensive. There can be no doubt that these characteristics have been present to quite a degree in Catholic life and theology ever since the time of the Reformation. However, I maintain that these characteristics are historical accretions and do not belong to the core of the Catholic theological tradition.

The authoritarian understanding of the church appears to have reached its zenith in the twentieth century. The condemnations of Americanism at the end of the nineteenth century and of modernism at the beginning of the twentieth century well illustrated the overly authoritarian understanding of the church, which was fearful of the modern world and sought security and certitude in the past. Vatican II moved to change all that with its call for dialogue with the contemporary world. There is no doubt that the spirit of Vatican II was a definite break with the immediate past, but it was in keeping with the best and the most central aspects of the Catholic tradition.

In the light especially of some of his more recent comments, including the famous 1984 interview, Cardinal Ratzinger appears to belong more to a pessimistic Augustinian tradition than to the Catholic theological tradition.[5] He appears to be frightened by most of what is happening in the modern world and quite distrustful of human experience, human nature, and human reason. Does Ratzinger really believe that the ethos in the United States is totally opposed to the Catholic ethic? I have pointed out that there is a danger of overoptimism in the Catholic tradition, and we can never forget the reality of sin. However, Ratzinger fails to appreciate the Catholic tradition's critical acceptance of reason and the human.[6]

There is no doubt that we as a faith community will always experience the tension which characterizes the pilgrim church. Mistakes have been made, and mistakes will be made in the future. However, a theological methodology which accepts faith and a critical approach to reason and the human under the inspiration of the Spirit, has the tools necessary to cope with trying to make the word and work of God present in contemporary times. In addition, this pilgrim church will always need that basic Christian love which can put flesh on the famous axiom that must guide the life of the church — in necessary things unity, in doubtful things freedom, in all things charity.

## Influences on My Moral Theology

As the historical section noted, I began my career in moral theology because I was told to do so by my bishop! However, I have come to find moral theology challenging, stimulating, satisfying, and even at times fun.

Bernard Häring has remained the most important influence on my moral theology. Häring was the most significant figure in the change of moral theology immediately before Vatican Council II (1962-65), and he has continued this leadership role. The aim of Häring's moral theology is to be life-centered, in the light of freely responding in the Christian community to the call of Jesus. An older manualistic moral theology was act-centered, and spent most of its time discussing whether or not an act was wrong and the degree of evil involved. The manuals of moral theology were closely connected with canon law, whereas Häring sees moral theology as intimately connected with Scripture, theology, spirituality, and liturgy. However, Häring the sociologist and Häring the pastor also can be seen in shaping his approach to moral theology. For Bernard Häring, moral theology is intimately connected with his own life and ministry and with the church.

In my critical evaluations of Häring I have tried to point out his strengths and weaknesses.[7] The German Redemptorist has courageously spoken out on many controversial contemporary issues, calling for a change in Catholic theology and pastoral practice in many areas. His zeal has taken him to all parts of the world to preach and teach. Truly Häring is a modern Paul, and there is no doubt that no other theologian has spoken to more groups in more places in the world than Bernard Häring. His proficiency in many languages has allowed him to lecture in all parts of the world. His theoretical weaknesses include a failure to systematize and integrate better all the aspects of moral theology, the lack of a consistent philosophical underpinning, an occasionally excessive rhetoric, and a tendency toward the homiletic. Häring has graciously accepted even my negative criticisms. In making these negative criticisms, I am only too conscious that the same weaknesses apply even more to myself as a moral theologian. Bernard Häring has been teacher and role model to me, and I have been constantly sustained by his support and encouragement.

From Bernard Lonergan, I learned the importance of historical consciousness and the significance of the person as subject. As a result, my theology recognizes the historical, the contingent, the changing, and the personal aspects of human existence. Although Lonergan is not a moral theologian as such, these two approaches have been central to my understanding of moral theology and help to explain some of the differences from an older Catholic approach.

One important aspect of the theological scene in the United States since Vatican II has been the ecumenical dialogue. This dialogue opened up a whole new literature to me. In my preparation and study for the doctorate, I had little or no contact with Protestant Christian ethics. In the United States I have had warm personal relationships with many Protestant ethicists and have learned much from the dialogue. I have profited greatly from the important work of James Gustafson and Paul Ramsey. I have come to appreciate Gustafson's great analytic ability and have found very sympathetic vibrations in his constant recognition of complexity. I spent a sabbatical year in 1972 working on Ramsey and published a critical study of his work.[8] Because of his conservative positions on many issues, Ramsey is looked upon by many as a crypto-Catholic. Some Catholics try to dismiss me as a Protestant ethicist. However, the primary difference between our theologial methodologies is that he is in the Protestant tradition and I am in the Roman Catholic tradition. Ecumenical dialogue has not caused me to water down Catholic truth, rather it has helped me to see aspects which tended to be polemically excluded in recent Catholicism and which can only help to fully flesh out the Roman Catholic tradition. Above all, ecumenical dialogue and historical studies have pointed out this danger of polemical exclusion. I have often stated my understanding that problems in theology are caused not so much by positive error as by a failure to recognize all the aspects involved. Protestant and Catholic polemics over the years caused each tradition to exaggerate some aspects and to forget others. Thus, for example, I have pointed out that Catholic ethics needs to give more importance to the reality of sin without, however, denying its basic affirmaiton of the goodness of the human. Protestant ethics often needs to be more positive about the human and the natural.

Moral theology is influenced not only by intellectual currents but also by practical realities. Since moral theology involves systematic and scientific reflection on Christian life and action, the problems and concerns of human existence are going to have a great effect on moral theology. There is no doubt that Vatican II introduced quite a change in the church by its call for a dialogue with the modern world, and thereby it opened up a whole new approach for moral theology. Events in the life of the world and of the church must influence moral theology, and the last two decades have been turbulent times. My moral theology could not help but be affected by these developments, and I have struggled to address these issues. Thus, all of these different factors have helped to shape my own approach to moral theology over the last twenty-five years.

## The Development of My Moral Theology

It is within this general context that my moral theology has developed. By its very nature moral theology has two foci — the methodological understanding and theory of the discipline itself, and the particular issues or questions which are addressed. From the viewpoint of the general understanding and theory of moral theology, I have tried to develop in a somewhat systematic way an approach to a more life-centered moral theology, with a special insistence that moral theology must deal with more than just the morality of particular actions. In an attempt to develop such a theory, I have distinguished four different levels of ethical discourse — the stance, the ethical model, Christian anthropology, and concrete decision-making and norms.[9]

Stance or perspective is logically the first and the most general consideration in moral theology, for it refers to the general perspective or horizon within which the Christian views the world. To carry out its critical function, this stance has to be broad enough to provide a basic perspective for all reality, but pointed enough and specific enough to indicate general directions and orientations. I propose as a stance that the Christian ethicist looks at the world and reality in light of the five-fold Christian mysteries of creation, sin, incarnation, redemption, and resurrection destiny. Such a stance gives the ethicist the basis on which to appreciate and to criticize traditional approaches and methodologies. Lutheran ethics overstressed sin, did not give enough importance to creation and incarnation, and failed to relate redemption and resurrection destiny to what should be done in the world. Liberal Protestantism forgot sin and the fact that the fullness of resurrection destiny will only come at the end of time. Barthian ethics so stressed redemption that it did not give enough importance to creation. Catholic natural law theory rightly stressed creation and incarnation but failed to take account of sin, and did not integrate creation and incarnation with redemption and resurrection destiny. Thus for example, as I reminded the congregation, I "dissented" from the natural law methodology employed in Pope John XXIII's encyclical *Pacem in terris.*[10]

Such a stance gives one a critical vision in looking at the contemporary world. In trying to make the word and work of God relevant in the contemporary society, one needs such a critical stance. Finitude, sin, and the lack of eschatological fullness will always characterize our existence, but likewise incarnation and redemption are already operating in our world. One needs to read the signs of the times critically. Like Ratzinger, I too have criticized the over-optimism of Vatican II.[11] However, I strongly disagree with Ratzinger's criticism of United States culture and ethos as being in total opposition to the Catholic Christian ethos. In my judgment, a proper theological understanding and accurate historical research prove that such an either-or vision is too one-sided and therefore unacceptable. I think the Roman Catholic Church has learned many things from the United States experience, such as the value and importance of freedom, human rights, and justice. On the other hand, the United States should be strongly criticized for its materialism, consumerism, and individualism. In my recent work I have dealt more explicitly with the relationship between being Catholic and being American and have tried to build on this type of critical dialogue. Above all, I pointed out the danger in United States Catholicism before the 1960s of being too uncritical of the American ethos and culture.[12]

The second level of ethical discourse concerns the ethical model which tries to understand and interpret the moral life as a whole. Contemporary ethicists often speak of a teleological model, which understands morality in terms of ends and the means to attain such ends, and a deontological model, which understands the moral life primarily in terms of duty and obligation. Catholic moral theology in its historical development has known both these types. Thomas Aquinas proposed an intrinsic teleological model which sees morality in the light of our ultimate end of human happiness and the means to attain that end. A deontological or duty-based ethics is illustrated by the manuals of moral theology, which explain the moral life in terms of law and obedience to law and use the Ten Commandments for explaining the moral life of the Christian. I propose a relationality-reponsibility model which sees the human person as a subject and agent in the midst of multiple relationships with God, nature, world, and self. This model still needs greater development, but it seems to correspond better to contemporary experience and also to the biblical and early Christian experience.

The third level of ethical discourse concerns Christian anthropology and the person as subject and agent. This level takes seriously the biblical observation that the tree is more important than the fruit. In this connection I have tried to develop the realities of fundamental option and conversion in terms of the growth and development of the person in one's multiple relationships. On this level, moral theology attends to the virtues or dispositions that should characterize the life of the Christian. Here too one sees the role of the Christian story and Christian liturgy in shaping the reality of the person as a member of the community of the disciples of Jesus.

Finally, on the fourth level one deals with norms and concrete decision making. Too often this has been the only consideration in moral theology. These are important issues, but the moral life and moral theology must concern themselves with much more than just norms and specific actions.

In the course of developing this rather broad understanding of moral theology, there are many other methodological questions with which I have dealt — the role and use of the Scripture; the role of the empirical sciences and technology; the ethical ramifications of such theological concerns as Christology, ecclesiology, eschatology, and anthropology.

The second important focus of moral theology concerns the specific issues which are facing the church and society. In my moral theology it is only natural that I would have been grappling with these issues. The primary issue facing the Roman Catholic Church in the mid-1960s was artificial contraception. In retrospect, the two underlying issues in the artificial contraception discussion continued to surface again in many future discussions. These two primary questions were the existence of absolute moral norms which do not admit of exceptions and the teaching authority of the hierarchical magisterium.

My problem with the official Catholic teaching on contraception was often phrased in terms of physicalism or biologism. The human was reduced just to the physical or the biological dimension. The physical act of depositing male semen in the vagina is sacrosanct and can in no way be interfered with. The natural law basis for such a position absolutized the physical or the biological at the expense of the total person. In most other cases Catholic moral theology never absolutized the physical aspect of the act. Thus, for example, we never said that all killing is wrong — only murder is always wrong. Murder is a moral act, whereas killing is a physical act. The natural law itself is not primarily the given natural or biological order but right reason. In the name of right reason, one can and should interfere with physical and biological structures. A poor anthropology tended to absolutize animal and biological nature by just adding human rational nature on top of an already existing animal and biological nature. I insist that at times reason can and should interfere with the biological. Thus in my judgment the arguments against artificial contraception were not convincing, and the natural law and anthropological basis of such arguments were erroneous.

The insufficiency of the arguments against artificial contraception was supported both by contemporary experience and by historical considerations. As a very young moral theologian, I was grappling with the problem of artificial contraception. Many friends of my age were personally experiencing that problem. I also had a study and prayer group with young married couples which discussed this and other subjects. I was also often asked to counsel people on this question. There is no doubt that I learned from and was influenced by the experience of generous and good Catholic wives and husbands. Their own experience moved me to question and ultimately to disagree with the arguments proposed to condemn artificial contraception.

My doctoral dissertation at the Gregorian University had been on the prevention of conception after rape.[13]Little did I realize then how relevant was my research into the development of the biological knowledge of human reproduction. In their correspondence with me, the congregation still maintains the position that every sexual act must be open to procreation. My study of the historical development of biological knowledge indicated how late we came to appreciate and understand the whole female component in human reproduction. In 1672 DeGraaf discovered the female ovaries and the follicle which now bears his name, but he made the mistake of identifying the ovum with the entire follicle. Only in the nineteenth century was the theory of DeGraaf revived and cor-

rected by the realization that the ovum is contained within the follicle. In 1875 Oscar Hertwig showed that fertilization was effected
by the union of the nucleii of ovum and sperm. The classical scholastic moral theologians believed, on the basis of their inadequate
knowledge of human reproduction, that every sexual act was
biologically open to procreation. Today we know that is not true.
The woman is fertile only for a comparatively short time during her
menstrual cycle. The condemnation of artificial contraception was
originally supported by the erroneous biological contention that
every single act of sexual relations is open to procreation.

The same two underlying issues of physicalism and the teaching
authority of the church were also involved in the church teaching
that masturbation is always objectively a grave evil. In 1966 I challenged this particular teaching and again appealed both to human
exprience and to history to indicate the inadequacy of the arguments behind the official church teaching.[14]

Contraception, sterilization, and masturbation are good illus-
trations of the fact that the morally condemned action is described
only in terms of the physical aspect. However, I also pointed out at
the time the complexity of the question by showing that in some
cases we do understand the human and the moral in terms of the
physical. The best illustration is the meaning and the test for
death. Human beings are dead when the body is dead, and the test
for such death is based on physical realities such as breathing, a
heartbeat, or brain waves.

The problem of physicalism existed above all in sexual and medical ethics. The problem did not exist in social ethics. In social
ethics there had not been the identification of the human or moral
aspects of the act with the physical. Injustice is always wrong, but
injustice is not defined primarily in terms of the physical structure
of the act. In accordance with Catholic understanding, theft is always wrong, but our tradition justified the physical taking of something that is not one's own if there is extreme need or danger. Thus
the physical act was not condemned as always wrong. I addressed
most of the individual questions in sexual and medical ethics in
which the problem of physicalism appeared. But other theologians,
especially Richard McCormick, have advanced in much greater
depth a theory to explain how norms should function in these
areas. This theory is generally called proportionalism, and maintains that physical or premoral evil can be done if there is a propor-

tionate reason.[15]

By the early 1970s, I had addressed the issues subsequently mentioned in my correspondence with Rome — contraception, sterilization, masturbation, premarital sexuality, homosexuality, abortion, and the indissolubility of marriage. I never did an in-depth article on euthanasia and merely mentioned it in passing on a couple of occasions. Also my discussion of premarital sexuality was usually included as part of a discussion of sexuality in general. I have occasionally continued to write in these areas in the intervening years, but they no longer were the primary focus of my interests. In early 1976, for example, in response to the "Declaration on Sexual Ethics" of the Congregation for the Doctrine of the Faith, I wrote a critical commentary which appeared in French in *Le Supplément* and in English in the *Linacre Quarterly*.[16]

Throughout the 1970s I maintained some interest in medical ethics and wrote articles on such subjects as human experimentation, genetics, in vitro fertilization, aging, and biomedicine in general. I also contributed the articles on abortion and Catholic medical ethics to the *Encyclopedia of Bioethics* which was published in 1978.[17]

I had occasionally done some work in social ethics in the early 1970s, but I began writing and teaching more and more in the area of social ethics in the mid-1970s. Here again it was my perception of the pastoral needs of the church which was paramount. I had already addressed most of the controversial issues in personal morality, especially those in the areas of sexual and medical ethics. I wrote in 1975 that in my judgment the most pressing problem facing the church and its members is a more just distribution of the goods of this world.[18] We must raise consciousness about this fact especially in the United States, with our consumer-oriented society. I was already beginning to do some work on the historical development of Catholic social ethics in the United States. There had been a considerable amount of writing in this area, to the credit of those who had gone before us; but such teaching was generally not found in the pulpit and in the general Catholic consciousness. The historical record of the Catholic Church in the United States with regard to the poor was quite good, but one must recognize that it was much easier to defend the poor when we were the poor. Since the Second World War, Catholics have entered the mainstream of United States life and passed into the middle class. As a result, we tended to lose sight of the needs of the poor. Today the problem is world-wide, and we as the richest nation in the world have great responsibilities. I closed this short discussion in 1975 on the importance of social issues by saying, "I am also aware that our efforts in this area will not be as dramatic and as attention-catching as our criticism of particular past teachings of the church, but they are even more important than those earlier efforts."[19]

After 1975, I concentrated my writing and research in the area of official Catholic social teaching and of Catholic social ethics in the United States, and addressed such specific problems as the just distribution of health care and the responsibilities of the present generation to the aging. A number of articles also dealt with the social mission of the church and the question of how specific church teaching should be in political and economic areas. I also dealt with the relationships between law and religion and between law and morality. These questions were raised by the 1973 Supreme Court decision overturning restrictive abortion laws. In light of the understanding of law found in the Declaration on Religious Freedom of Vatican II, I developed a theory about the coercive use of law in a pluralistic and democratic society. On the basis of this theory, I came to the conclusion that there should be no effort on the part of Catholics at the present time to work for a constitutional amendment to change the Supreme Court rulings. Such a position was strongly opposed by many Catholics and by the right to life movement. In 1982 the University of Notre Dame Press published my *American Catholic Social Ethics: Twentieth Century Approaches,* and in 1985 the same press put out some of my collected articles under the title *Directions in Catholic Social Ethics.* I was very pleased that the United States bishops were taking a more active teaching role in social and political morality with their two pastoral letters on peace and the economy. I was one of many consultants called by the two committees of the United States Catholic bishops who drafted these pastoral letters. This marked the first time I had ever been asked by any church officials to do anything formally for or in the name of my church.

All that time, in my writing and research on social ethics, it was becoming more evident that there was a growing split between Catholic social ethics and Catholic personal or sexual ethics. The official Catholic social teaching had accepted and embraced historical consciousness, a more inductive methodology, and the freedom and dignity of the human person as subject and participator in social life. Catholic sexual ethics has not yet accepted these methodological approaches, which in my judgment would necessarily call for the type of changes I have been advocating in Catholic sexual ethics.

I have also written in other areas. In 1972 I published a small paperback, *The Crisis in Priestly Ministry,* which tried to address some aspects of the crisis from a theological and spiritual perspective. Since my appointment to the faculty of Catholic University in 1965, I have been interested in the question of academic freedom in Catholic institutions and theology. This area of research was very important at the time of the inquiry at Catholic University after *Humanae vitae* and again in the last few years with the new Vatican norms for ecclesiastical faculties, as well as the new Code of Canon Law and the proposed schema for all Catholic institutions of higher learning.[20]

Since 1966 I have published sixteen books, most of them being collections of previously published articles. The first volumes were published by Fides Publishers, but beginning in 1976 the University of Notre Dame Press has been my publisher. The articles I have written for different theological journals and conferences have ultimately appeared in these books. Since 1979 Richard McCormick and I have edited five volumes for Paulist Press, in an ongoing series *Readings in Moral Theology.* We have gathered together previously published articles trying to make available to a wider audience both sides of the most significant disputes in contemporary moral theology — the existence of universal norms, the distinctiveness of Christian ethics, the magisterium and morality, the use of Scripture in moral theology, commentaries on official Catholic social teaching.

The congregation's condemnation concerns my writings on sexuality. In reality I purposely made a decision in 1975 to move away from that field and to concentrate more of my focus on social ethics. I have done little work in sexual ethics for over ten years. Yet as a result of the Vatican's action, many people think that I specialize in sexual ethics and am an expert in the field. However, that is no longer the case.

## Critical Assessment

Reflection on the development of my moral theology also furnishes the opportunity and the need for a critical assessment. In my work with graduate students in moral theology I try to emphasize the importance of developing critical skills. All of us need to be self-critical about our own work. I am frequently referred to as one of the leading figures in Catholic moral theology in this country, but I am also conscious of my limitations.

As a moral theologian teaching in a university, I feel myself involved in both the church and the academy. I have enjoyed my work, which relates to both the church and the academy. At times I have been frustrated with both, for both have their own entrenched bureaucracies. I have been disappointed at the lack of interdisciplinary discussion and collaboration within the university, but the atmosphere of the academy at its best is stimulating and provocative. I have directed much time and effort to participating in the life of the academic community and have served on numerous committees. However, while I enjoy and appreciate my work in the academy, I still see this as secondary to my role in the church. My theology is done primarily for the church. Some theologians would be properly classified as doing their theology for the academy, but that is not my role. I have stayed at Catholic University, despite numerous offers and feelers to go elsewhere, because I wanted to do theology for the Catholic Church. There could be no better place to exercise that role than at the Catholic Univerity of America. Yes, over the years there have been numerous tensions created for me by my presence at Catholic University, but I decided to stay and do my theology at Catholic University because of the role it gave me in the life of the Catholic Church.

Moral theology by its very nature is more practical and pastoral than so-called systematic or dogmatic theology. We moral theologians do not deal with the deep speculative problems of the meaning of God, but with the more practical problems and issues of daily life. In a sense moral theologians will probably never produce "classics," which will last for centuries and influence future generations of scholars and students. Also, my own approach to moral theology has been more pastoral than scientific. I see my whole life and all that I do in terms of a broader ministry in the service of the church. I believe that my original intent to be a diocesan priest still comes through in my pastoral approach to moral theology. My moral theology is aimed at serving the needs of the People of God.

I still have many pastoral contacts with people experiencing problems and pain in living out their Christian lives. My writings on the problem areas in the '60s and '70s were definitely stimulated by my sharing the struggle of Christian people in their daily lives. I do not do moral theology only in the library or in my study. I strive for academic and scientific rigor in my work, but my whole optic is pastoral.

Even in the midst of sharing the pain and the struggles of Christian people in their daily life, one cannot lose a critical sense. In my own development I have tried to recognize the dangers present in our American society and also the need to deal with the difficult social problems of our day and not just with personal problems. As a consequence I was taken aback by Cardinal Ratzinger's remark in April 1986 that the widespread dissent in the United States on sexual questions is the expression of a "bourgeois Christianity."[21] Most United States Catholics would be deeply insulted by such a remark.

Moral theology has had many significant issues to grapple with in the years since the close of the Second Vatican Council in 1965. In the midst of all these issues, some moral theologians have opted to specialize in a particular area such as medical ethics. I purposely decided to remain more broadly focused, even though over the years I have put more emphasis on some areas than others in moral theology. As a result I have dealt with a great number of issues facing the contemporary church and world. There is always a tradeoff between breadth and depth. One who does not specialize in a particular area will always be conscious of a lack of depth. My own pastoral instincts have influenced my decision to remain more of a generalist and to be open to all the problems and issues that arise. However, there is a price to be paid for such a choice. I am the first to admit the dangers of being stretched too thin. It seems to become increasingly more difficult to keep up in so many different aspects of moral theology. Perhaps in the future I will have to opt for greater specialization. By responding to the pastoral problems facing church and society, I have not had the opportunity to develop a more systematic approach to moral theology.

Almost from the beginning of my work in moral theology, I thought of myself as a transitional or bridge figure — moving from the older manualistic moral theology to newer approaches. I greatly appreciated the Catholic tradition but acknowledged the weaknesses of the manuals and the need to change them. However, I did not think that I was in a position to come up with a systematic new approach to moral theology, without more time and study. It seemed to me that the development of more systematic approaches to moral theology would rest with the generation of moral theologians who would come after my generation. My generation has been so busy dealing with the pressing problems of the present that we have not had time to develop entirely new systematic approaches. However, my original thinking might need to be revised. I am becoming increasingly alarmed by the fact that there are fewer and fewer moral theologians coming along. I am afraid that, in light of all the tensions and problems faced by people trying to do moral theology in the Catholic Church today, many have decided not to enter this field in the first place. My own condemnation by Rome will only increase this reluctance. The future of Catholic moral theology at this moment cannot be called bright. However, I am impressed by some of the people who are now working in the discipline and especially by a number of women theologians. Yet we need many more theologians to develop the discipline.

Reflecting on my own experience, I recognize that one of the problems has been that I did not have the time or opportunity to develop my moral theology because there were so many controversial issues that needed to be attended to. And there were so few others around to help. Many of the older Catholic moral theologians were trained in the neo-scholasticism of the older manuals and had difficulty coping with the changes of Vatican II. Leadership in this field fell on the few of us who were in a position to respond to these changes and the contemporary needs. I was only 34 years old when *Humanae vitae* came out and I acted as spokesperson for the group of theologians dissenting from that encyclical. As a result, I did not have the time or the opportunity most younger scholars have, to develop their own discipline in a somewhat quiet and tranquil atmosphere. I was on the firing line coping with the important issues facing church and society and attempting to develop a moral theology which meets these needs.[22]

In the light of critical reflection, I am conscious of the shortcomings and weaknesses in my theologizing. At times there is the problem of being stretched too thin and trying to cover too many areas. By definition such work cannot have the depth of one who specializes in a particular area. The genre of my writing has been primarily the theologial essay and not the monograph. I have not developed a coherent systematic moral theology or even attempted to write a *magnum opus*. I do not pretend to have any in-depth knowledge of the empirical sciences that could and should be dialogue partners with moral theology — psychology, sociology, economics. My own philosophical approach is eclectic, and I have not produced a sustained philosophic basis for moral theology. Perhaps in the future I will be in a somewhat different situation and will be able to expend more time and effort in dealing with these shortcomings and weaknesses.

## Personal Reactions

I have explained the historical development of the present controversy and have reflected on it from the viewpoint of theology as such and from the perspective of myself as a moral theologian. How have I personally reacted to these events? I am not accustomed to discussing in public or writing my own personal feelings. In my writings I have always worked for an objectivity that tries to deal with the issues involved and to fairly represent all sides. In my classes I have made it a point never to bring up my personal situation or the controversies in which I have been involved. However, I will now briefly try to indicate my personal reaction to my work as a moral theologian and to the present controversy.

As the historical chapter indicates, I have been involved in a number of controversies over the years and have often been attacked in the right-wing Catholic press. Yet, I have enjoyed what I have been doing and have made, and frequently reinforced, the decision to continue doing moral theology at The Catholic University of America. I do not go out of my way to look for controversy, and I am a person who generally gets along quite well with most people. Although I have been involved in more than my share of controversy, the controversy has usually existed "out there," and I have found very congenial circumstances for my own work with my colleagues in theology and throughout the university and with my students. In addition, I am not a brooder and tend to forget about the past and move on. Today and tomorrow are too important to be overly concerned about what happened in the past. I can forget past differences of opinion with others and work with the same people on different projects in the future.

But the present controversy is somewhat different. The Vatican is saying that I am not a Catholic theologian and cannot teach in the name of the church. I think their judgment is erroneous, and harmful to the good of the church, and the judgment and the process have been unfair and unjust in many ways. Without a doubt I have been personally hurt, but I still believe in the Catholic Church and find strength, support, and challenge from many of the various communities that make up the church. I remain convinced that in the end the hierarchical magisterium will definitely recognize the possibility of legitimate pluralism in these areas and ultimately will modify its teachings. I am aware of the temptation to both bitterness and arrogance, and I pray that I might avoid such responses. I want to remain a believing Catholic. Why?

As I mentioned above, the Catholic theological tradition makes sense to me. There is no doubt that the church will continue to make mistakes, but the Catholic theological tradition has the tools to ultimately overcome these mistakes and challenge them. The realization that the word and work of God must become incarnate in contemporary realities, the critical openness to reason and to the human, and the insistence on an intrinsic morality, all provide ways of continuing to be critical and to avoid and/or correct possible errors and mistakes. Above all, steadfast in the church is the presence and the gift of the Spirit, which ensures that the church has the resources to arrive at the truth.

However, there is also the human element in the church. The Catholic tradition has taken the human very seriously, but this also brings with it some problems. I have been tempted in the past, but not for long, to think that belief in God would be so much easier if it were not mediated in and through the human as in Catholic ecclesiology. However, the human aspect is so important, even though at times it can get in the way. My six years of study in Rome were basically very happy years, but for a period I did go through some doubts and questioning brought on by the very visible, and at times troublesome, human element in the church.

The church is not only human but it is also sinful. From the beginning of my teaching theology in 1961 I have often mentioned that there are five marks of the church — one, holy, Catholic, apostolic, and sinful. There is no doubt that the human church is also a sinful church. Yet the Holy Spirit is God with us in the church. In recognizing the sinfulness of the church we must be conscious of the danger of our own self-righteousness, for we too are sinful human beings who never respond fully to the gospel. There will always be tensions in this pilgrim church, and theologians and hierarchs are bound to be involved in this tension. All of us at times exacerbate these tensions. So with this realistic understanding of the church, I am able to accept what is happening to me. One Protestant colleague once said to me that the Protestant Church could care less about what its theologians say and teach, whereas the Catholic Church is very concerned about its theologians. This is true and I welcome it, but I could do with a little different type of concern at the present!

History also gives me hope and optimism for the long run. Theological tensions and disputes have constantly existed in the church. Theologians have been under shadows and suspicions but have later been proved right. The recent history of the Second Vatican Council indicates that theologians who were in disfavor and were even under some type of church punishment or censure became the leading figures at the Council itself. History seems to validate the understanding that Catholic ecclesiology and theology have the tools ultimately to correct errors and to find an exit from "dead-end streets." However, sometimes the corrections and changes are a long time coming.

There is also another aspect to be considered. Theologians in the past have been wrong and made mistakes. Some who were right were never vindicated in their lifetimes. I too must recognize that I might be wrong. There is comfort from the overwhelming support of my theological colleagues, but numbers do not necessarily make something right or wrong. I am personally convinced that I am right, but I too must remain always self-critical and conscious of my own limitation, finitude, and sinfulness. In this light I can be somewhat patient and allow the future to ultimately decide. Thus I remain a Catholic.

Am I a radical and/or revolutionary? In the eyes of some I am dangerous and bent on destroying and harming the church. Some of my friends like to remind me of the conservative Catholic editor who a few years ago called me "the aging enfant terrible." There might be some possible justification for these judgments. I have been involved in a number of public controversies. The only thing some people know about me concerns the fact that I have stood up to church authority on a number of different occasions.

In reality I am neither a radical nor a revolutionary. It is not even necessary to take my word for that judgment. My colleagues and my students, the people who know me best, have pointed out repeatedly that I am not a radical, but a moderate.

From an intellectual perspective, I am no radical. How can one who emphasizes tension and complexity be a radical? My inclination to go always for the "both-and" solution and my innate unwillingness to accept "either-or" solutions are totally incompatible with being a radical or a revolutionary. My ecclesiology is not radical. One of my favorite remarks is, "My church is a big church and my God is a big God." There has to be room in the church for greater diversity and pluralism. By recognizing the possibility of dissent, I must logically conclude that within the church there can be a variety of approaches to specific issues. In social ethics I have resisted the attempts by some to say that the church must adopt one rather radical position, such as that of pacificism, as the only possible approach. I thank God there are pacifists in the church, but I do not think the whole church can ever be pacifist. In the light of the complexities and the tensions of our existence in this world short of the fullness of the eschaton, one cannot absolutely do away with the possible recourse to violence. Many times we will disagree with people on issues, but we should be loathe to exclude someone from the church community because of their position on specific, complex moral issues. Our big church must have room for many people, even those with whom we disagree on very specific issues.

Within this intellectual understanding I have tried to promote dialogue with those who disagree. Some more conservative Catholic theologians in 1977 founded their own organization, the Fellowship of Catholic Scholars. I have publicly called for and worked for greater dialogue and discussion with these different positions in moral theology.[23] In my classes I make sure that my students are acquainted with all sides of an issue. One newsperson, after an indepth interview, wrote me later to say that what impressed him most was my intellectual honesty. It was only because I reminded the reporter that he should talk to people who disagreed with me and I gave him the names of the people to contact. I have been humbled by the commendations that many have made about me, but I was particularly pleased by the remark one anonymous student made to the press. This student, identifying himself only as a conservative Catholic, said he disagreed with me on numerous issues but has an enormous respect for me.[24]

Not only from an intellectual position but also from a personal perspective, I am neither a revolutionary nor a radical. I usually do not make quick decisions but take my time and seek advice and counsel from many others. My intellectual insistence on complexity is probably rooted somehow or other in a personality which can accurately be described as careful and cautious. I seldom see things in either black or white. I am very much at home in the grays of human existence. In fact, at times I have to remind myself of the famous saying of Karl Barth that even in the dark of night not all cats are gray. Even though things are complex and there can never be 100% certitude, as human beings we have to make decisions and cannot just sit back and do nothing.

My pastoral bent has always made me pay attention to people and their needs. I have seen and heard the stories of many people who I judged to be trying hard to live out their Christian life in the midst of difficult personal situations. I am quite tolerant and respectful of other persons. Such tolerance and respect make it difficult if not impossible to write off other people, even if I do disagree with them on particular issues. People are always more important than issues.

I dealt with this question of my own radicalness or lack thereof in the past, and I can only repeat what I wrote in 1975:

> As for being a radical, no one who stresses complexity can really be a radical. In life and in theory, I am not a radical, but there are times when the simplicity of the radical does appeal to me. This is probably why I say that at times I wish I were more radical, but "common sense" or is it "common nonsense" and a sense of practical reality usually win out. My fear is that an acceptance of sin and complexity will at times make my theology too middle-of-the-road.[25]

Why do I become involved in so many controversies? A good question! At the very minimum, I think that these controversies must be put into a proper perspective. Most of my life is not involved in such controversies. Even in my teaching and in my writing most of the time I am not dealing with these controversial issues. Recall that I have not even taught the course in sexual ethics here at Catholic University in the last fifteen years. However, I do believe in the need to stand up for what one believes in. I have always tried to address problems in a clear and straightforward manner. I am not a person who can pretend or hide my true feelings or positions. Also, I must recognize there is some stubborness in me that makes me want to stand up for what I believe in. At the same time I also have enough Irish genes to enjoy a skirmish and the strategies involved in such disputes. But by temperament I am not contentious or assertive.

On a number of occasions it has been suggested that I might be hurting my own cause by labeling my positions as dissent.[26] However, I want to be clear and responsible. As a Catholic theologian I should always explain the official Catholic teaching and then show how I relate to it. Clarity, honesty, and truth require that positions be labeled as dissent when they are such. However, as mentioned above, my theological endeavor is in no way totally identified with dissent. The primary function of the theologian is to interpret, explain, and understand. The vast majority of the times this does not involve any dissent. However, on occasions the interpretive function of the theologian will result in a dissenting position. A responsible theologian should never try to hide or dissimulate dissent. Dissent is dissent and not just dialogue.

One aspect of the controversies I have been involved in does call for more comment. I have been accused of using the public media and organizing dissent. In one sense there is some truth to this charge. As a Catholic theologian I have always recognized that we are by nature social and called to work together, and not just as individuals. In the Catholic tradition, politics is not a dirty word or game but the art of making the city a just and fitting place in which to live. Academic faculties often act in a corporate manner, as a group. Theologians belong to the same college or group. In the past Catholic faculties of theology by acting corporately have had a very powerful role in the teaching of the church. Organization in itself is not necessarily something bad. I have written appreciatively about the community organizing methods of Saul Alinsky.[27]

I do not think that the public media is something bad. Modern human beings, including church officials, use the popular media all the time. I am, nevertheless, quite conscious of its limits and have often paraphrased the biblical statement — "those who live by the media will die by the media." At times it is necessary to use the media, but in the midst of controversy I always try to see this use as a last resort. I tried for a very long time in the present controversy to find a solution to my problem by using every private channel that was available to me. From 1979 until 1986, I purposely refrained from any public statements about my investigation by the Vatican. After receiving the September 17, 1985 letter from Cardinal Ratzinger, I realized that sooner or later this whole matter would become public, no matter what I did. I decided that it was most important for me to control the way in which it was presented to the public. I wanted it to be a teaching moment and to avoid any bitterness, disrespect, or namecalling. The public media would provide me an opportunity to make people in the church and the general public more familiar with the whole understanding of the teaching function of the church. In retrospect, and with great gratitude to FACT and others, the whole matter was presented publicly as a teaching moment without rancor or disrespect.

I suppose something should be said about my reactions to the very negative things that are occasionally printed about me in parts of the extreme Catholic press, and also the negative letters and hate mail that I receive. I do not think any of us enjoys these things. However, even here we must keep our sense of humor. Very often the most negative letters tend to go on and on; people frequently write in the margins; underlining is often done with red or yellow markers; last minute comments are made and even marked on the envelope. One letter I received stands out all the more. There was neither a date nor a salutation but simply the message: "You are dead ass wrong." I do not enjoy seeing these things in the press nor receiving this type of mail. However, once again, it is possible for me to do my daily work without any real interference caused by such comments or mail. What I must always be conscious of is the danger of hurting people and causing them unnecessary pain. I realize that some Catholics are hurt by what I have done, but I have tried to do it in such a way as to avoid as much pain as possible. We who recognize that tension will always be a part of the church, must also do everything possible not to exacerbate those tensions. However, at times what we do is bound to cause hurt and pain to others. We will always know and experience both the suffering and tension of trying to do the truth in love.

## My Analysis of the Situation

One should always try to understand the situation in which one finds oneself. I have tried to analyze the present situation and have wondered about the future. As for the present, there can be no doubt that the primary issue in my case is that of dissent and church authority. This is a very complex reality, and I am sure that there are many factors involved, including all those aspects which touch on power and authority. I am convinced that the church must change its position on dissent and also its hierarchical teaching on these issues, but the official church seems unwilling to recognize the possibility of dissent and to change any teaching. Change is always threatening, but change in the area of official church teaching is very threatening. I have tried to put myself in the shoes of those who disagree with me.

The problem of change is well illustrated by a conversation I had with a well-known Catholic moral theologian in the mid-1960s on the issue of contraception. He was defending the existing church teaching, while I was calling for change. After a long private conversation, and as the evening wore on, he moved from the intellectual reasons to what could only be called the more existential and personal reasons. He had dedicated his whole life to Catholic moral theology as a priest and religious. His life was dedicated to the service of God, the church, and God's people. On many different platforms throughout this country, he had publicly explained and defended the teaching of the church on birth control. If this teaching were wrong, it would mean that instead of helping others, his whole life would have been a hindrance to others. Could God allow such a thing to happen? Could God allow the Catholic Church to be wrong on such an important matter and thereby see its teaching role as harming rather than helping people? I think this was probably the same question that Pope Paul VI grappled with before deciding to reaffirm the ban on artificial contraception in the encyclical *Humanae vitae* in 1968.

One can and must appreciate the force of this argument, but perhaps the problem comes from too triumphalistic a notion of the teaching office of the church in some noninfallible areas. To recognize officially the possibility of dissent and to admit that Catholic teaching in this area has been wrong are very difficult and painful choices. Theological history shows how difficult it has been for the Catholic Church, especially since the time of the Reformation, to come to grips with the possibility of change in its life and its teaching. However, truth must be the primary consideration.

Another factor also enters in. Where do we draw the line? There are people calling for change in many areas of the church's noninfallible teaching. Perhaps this is why the birth control issue has become so important today. All must recognize that most Catholic couples have already made up their minds on this issue. It has not been a burning question or problem, even on the pastoral level, for the past decade or so. However, the issue is now symbolic. If the church can change on birth control, the church can change in many other areas as well. If the church does not change on artificial contraception, it is a very strong indication that the church will never change on all these other issues. Even someone with my perspective must recognize that there are many legitimate and significant questions to raise about the limits to dissent and to change within the church.

There is no doubt that the changes in the church sparked by Vatican II's call for dialogue with the modern world have been stressful for many people precisely because, in the decades and centuries immediately before Vatican II, the church saw itself as an unchanging bastion in the midst of a changing world. For all the reasons that have been discussed, I think that the church must recognize the validity of dissent in these areas, and also ultimately even change its hierarchical teaching. However, I can also appreciate why dissent and change are such difficult issues for the Catholic Church.

Why you? I have been asked this same question hundreds of times. There are many theologians who hold similar positions and even positions much more radical than mine both in this country and abroad. Why have I been singled out? I have no definitive answer to that question but I have tried to grapple with it.

First of all, I am an American. There are great stresses now in the Vatican's relationship with the church in the United States. Look at what has been happening. Rome has formally investigated two United States bishops as well as seminaries and religious orders of women in our country. The newer appointments being made to the posts of diocesan bishops and archbishops are of a very conservative theological bent and are markedly different from the appointments that were being made ten years ago. The newly proposed regulations for Catholic colleges and universities, with their aim of greater direct control of theologians, appear aimed at the United States precisely because we have more Catholic institutions of higher learning than all the other countries in the world. Cardinal Ratzinger sees the United States' ethos and culture as opposed to the Catholic ethos and culture. I see the action against me as a part of this continuing trend of Vatican concern about what is happening in the United States.

I think the past actions by the Vatican against theologians have also had more than a theological dimension. The Vatican has also been gravely concerned about what is happening to the church in Holland and in Brazil. The theological investigations of Schillebeeckx and Boff were concerned with more than just theology. Boff was not the most radical of the liberation theologians, but Brazil was a country in which the local bishops were showing some independence from Rome. So too, in my case, the fact that I am an American has something to do with the Vatican's threatened action against me.

A second reason for singling me out comes from the subject matter involved. Sexuality is always an area of great concern. When sexuality and authority are joined together, it is a very neuralgic situation. As already mentioned, actions have previously been taken against United States theologians writing in the area of sexuality. Rome forced the Archbishop of Seattle to take away the *imprimatur* from Father Philip Keane's book *Sexual Morality*. At the request of the congregation, one other archbishop forbade this book to be used as a text. Father John McNeill, who wrote *The Church and the Homosexual,* was forbidden by his Jesuit superiors, on orders from Rome, to speak or write any more in the area of homosexuality. Not only the Doctrinal Committee of the United States bishops, but also the Congregation for the Doctrine of the Faith negatively criticized the book *Human Sexuality: New Directions in American Catholic Thought,* which was a publication by a committee appointed by the Catholic Theological Society of America. The congregation also made sure that the principal author, Father Anthony Kosnick, was no longer allowed to teach sexual ethics at Sts. Cyril and Methodius Seminary in Michigan. The fact that I have written a good number of articles on sexual issues made me a logical target in the light of the actions which Rome and the Congregation for the Doctrine of the Faith, even before Cardinal Ratzinger became prefect, had been taking against those advocating changes in the sexual teaching of the church.

A third partial response to the question, "Why me?" comes from my visibility. I have written at great length in moral theology. I teach at The Catholic University of America, which was founded by and is supported by the United States bishops. The university has a canonically erected and approved faculty of theology. The faculty and student strike at Catholic University in 1967 and my role in theological opposition to *Humanae Vitae* in 1968 were well known. The historical section has documented how the conservative Catholic press has been after me for many years and has constantly urged my removal from Catholic University. Thus, all these reasons taken together at least give some indications why the Vatican chose to take action against me rather than against others.

## The Future

Predicting the future is always difficult. It is even harder in volatile circumstances such as those existing at the present. It is safe to say that recently there has been a marked and significant shift within the Catholic Church in general, and within the church in the United States in particular, toward a more conservative theological and institutional posture. The liberal documents of the United States bishops on nuclear war and the economy are a part of the more liberal official social teaching and in no way call into question church teaching or structures. The fact that the Vatican is now willing to place itself in opposition to the great majority of the Catholic theological community seems to be a significant step in a more conservative and even repressive direction. These pages have already pointed out many other indications of a "crackdown."

From the viewpoint of Catholic theology I do not think that there will be a wholesale purge of liberal or dissenting theologians. At the very minimum, however, the actions already taken will produce an intimidating effect on the work of Catholic theology in general, and especially on Catholic moral theology in dealing with questions of dissent and sexuality.

The Theology Department of The Catholic University of America will suffer greatly in the short run, if I am dismissed from the faculty. Gerard Austin, the Chair of the Department, in his annual report for 1985-86 sees "the very future of the department at stake" as a result of my case and others. In the future, good, new faculty are not likely to come to this department. Graduate students, who are looking for challenging education now and jobs in the future, will definitely not be attracted by such an institution. Many of the better faculty now teaching in this department will leave. The reputation of the department in the broader United States academic and theological communities will be severely tarnished. I am sure there will always be students and faculty, but no one will expect such an institution to make any real theological contribution.

If the proposed schema of norms for Catholic institutions goes through (and it probably will because the basic legislation is already present in the new Code of Canon Law), the machinery will be in place to enforce the understanding that the Catholic theologian teaches by reason of deputation from the local bishop. Thus there will be stifling structures as well as a stifling atmosphere. The next few years will probably see more and more Catholic theologians doing their work at non-Catholic institutions. In one sense, I see nothing at all wrong with such a situation. However, it is both ironic and very short-sighted that the pope and the bishops are driving Catholic theologians out of Catholic institutions. Thus there are many clouds on the horizon for Catholic theology and Catholic theologians.

Only a learned sociologist could try to give an accurate view of what is happening now in the church at large and to indicate future trends. I lack any such expertise. However, one does not need a crystal ball to realize where the greatest tension will arise in the next decades in the life of the Catholic Church in the United States. The church will find its women members becoming more hostile and alienated. The Catholic Church must find a way to give equality and justice to women. Yes, this means the ordination of women, but it means so much more than that. Already the tension between religious women in the United States and official church authority structures has burst into the open on a number of specific occasions. There will be more and more such occasions. Intelligent and committed women are becoming more disillusioned with the church and its structures.

In the last few years I have seen the change of attitude in many women as they have deepened their own theolgical knowledge and expectations of what it means to belong to the community of equal disciples of Jesus. A good number have become alienated and left the church. A few are bitter. Many are holding on but are not sure about the future. In the light of all that is happening at the present time, I am afraid that there is going to be much anger, alienation, and frustration among women who are working to make the church a community of equal disciples.

I have seen one of my own functions in the last few years to be that of giving whatever assistance I can to help change the role of women in the church. Yes, there are occasionally some aberrations in the women's movement within the church, but the problem for many of us is that the church itself is failing to live up to its gospel call and commitment and thereby is alienating some of its best members. We have such a long way to go. Take even the matter of sexist language. One secular columnist picked up on the fact that in my March 11, 1985 press conference I referred to God as mother and father.[28] The role of women in the Catholic Church in the next decade or two is not going to be an easy one, and the present climate will make it all the more difficult.

Yes, there are indications that in the future there will be some bitter and acrimonious struggles in the Catholic Church. From my perspective the outlook for the immediate future is rather bleak. However, for the many reasons mentioned earlier, I remain hopeful for the long run.

As for myself, there will be some changes and some hurt. However, I must put my own problems into a proper perspective. When I see all the sufferings and difficulties in the lives of so many other people, my problems are minor in comparison. My knowledge of history and the support I have received from so many in the church give me great strength. I am sure that I will find ways of continuing my theological teaching and writing. I continue to pray that I can avoid both arrogance and bitterness. All in all, I still hear in my mind the words of Bernard Häring after our meeting with Cardinal Ratzinger — "Christians are people who have hope."

Notes

[1]From a Catholic perspective, see Hans Urs von Balthasar, *The Theology of Karl Barth* (New York: Holt, Rinehart, and Winston, 1971), pp. 40, 41.

[2]The best study of Aquinas is James A. Weisheipl, *Friar Thomas D'Aquino: His Life, Thought and Works* (Washington: Catholic University of America Press, 1983).

[3]Thomas Aquinas, *Summa Theologiae,* Ia IIae, prologue.

[4]The best in-depth treatise on Thomas Aquinas' intrinsic approach to law is Thomas E. Davitt, *The Nature of Law* (St. Louis: B. Herder, 1951).

[5]Vittorio Messori, colloquio con il cardinale Joseph Ratzinger, "Ecco Perchè La Fede e in Crisi," *Jesus,* Novembre 1984, pp. 67-81.

[6]For similar assessments and criticism of Ratzinger's approach, see "Ratzinger on the Faith: A Response Written by a British Group of Catholic Theologians," *New Blackfriars* 66 (1985), 259-308.

[7]Charles E. Curran, *Critical Concerns in Moral Theology* (Notre Dame, IN: University of Notre Dame Press, 1984), pp. 3-41.

[8]Charles E. Curran, *Politics, Medicine, and Christian Ethics: A Dialogue With Paul Ramsey* (Philadelphia: Fortress Press, 1973).

[9]I have brought together my articles on these different levels and aspects of moral theology in *Directions in Fundamental Moral Theology* (Notre Dame, IN: University of Notre Dame Press, 1985).

[10]Charles E. Curran, *Catholic Moral Theology in Dialogue* (Notre Dame, IN: Fides Publishers, 1972), pp. 111-149; paperback edition, (Notre Dame, IN: University of Notre Dame Press, 1976).

[11]*Ibid.,* pp. 130-134.

[12]Charles E. Curran, *American Catholic Social Ethics: Twentieth Century Approaches* (Notre Dame, IN: University of Notre Dame Press, 1982).

[13]Charles E. Curran, *The Prevention of Conception after Rape: An Historical Theological Study* (Rome: Pontifical Gregorian University, 1961).

[14]Charles E. Curran, "Masturbation and Objectively Grave Matter: An Exploratory Discussion," *Proceedings of the Catholic Theological Society of America* 21(1966), 95-112.

[15]Richard A. McCormick and Paul Ramsey, eds., *Doing Evil to Achieve Good* (Chicago: Loyola University Press, 1978). The most systematic and comprehensive theory supporting the older teachings on these questions is proposed by Germain Grisez, *The Way of the Lord Jesus*, I: *Christian Moral Principles* (Chicago: Franciscan Herald Press, 1983).

[16]Charles E. Curran, "Ethique Sexuelle: Réaction et Critique," *Le Supplément* 118 (September 1976), 390-411; "Sexual Ethics: Reaction and

Critique," *Linacre Quarterly* 46 (1976), 147-164.

[17]Warren T. Reich, ed., *Encyclopedia of Bioethics,* 4 vols. (New York: The Free Press, 1978).

[18]Charles E. Curran, *Ongoing Revision: Studies in Moral Theology* (Notre Dame, IN: Fides Publishers, 1975), pp. 290, 291.

[19]*Ibid.,* p. 291.

[20]Charles E. Curran, *Moral Theology: A Continuing Journey* (Notre Dame, IN: University of Notre Dame Press, 1982), pp. 11-32.

[21]*National Catholic Register,* May 11, 1986, p. 5.

[22]At the invitation of Gregory Baum I contributed to a book in which different theologians wrote about their journeys — Gregory Baum, ed., *Journeys* (New York: Paulist Press, 1975), pp. 87-116; also in my *Ongoing Revision,* pp. 260-294.

[23]*Moral Theology: A Continuing Journey,* p. 68.

[24]*Washington Times,* March 12, 1986.

[25]*Ongoing Revision,* p. 294.

[26]E.g., Kevin Kelly, "Obedience and Dissent, II: Serving the Truth," *The Tablet* 240 (June 21, 1986) p. 647.

[27]*Critical Concerns in Moral Theology,* pp. 171-199.

[28]Colman McCarthy, *Washington Post,* March 23, 1986, Style, p. 2.

# Part Two
# Documentation

# I
# THE FIRST EXCHANGE
# (1979)

July 13, 1979.    Letter from Cardinal Franjo Seper, Prefect of the Congregation for the Doctrine of the Faith informing Curran that he is under investigation, enclosing 16 pages of "Observations" and the procedures of the congregation. Handed to Curran on August 2.

August 28, 1979.    Short letter from Archbishop Jerome Hamer, Secretary of the Congregation for the Doctrine of the Faith, to Curran recognizing the need for delay in responding.

August 29, 1979.    Curran to Seper raising some questions and including bibliography and Hamer letter to Bishop Sullivan of Baton Rouge.

October 4, 1979.    Hamer to Curran acknowledging receipt of earlier letter.

October 26, 1979.    Curran's response of 21 pages to the "Observations" concentrating on the "fundamental observation."

SACRA CONGREGATIO
PRO DOCTRINA FIDEI
00193 Romae
Piazza del S. Uffizio, 11

Prot. N. 48/66

July 13, 1979

Dear Father Curran,

After having several of your articles and books called to its attention, the Congregation for the Doctrine of the Faith has judged it necessary to examine some of these writings in accord with its procedure "Nova agendi ratio in doctrinarum examine" (A.A.S. 63, 1971, pp. 234-6; copy enclosed).

The first stage of this procedure has now been completed, and I am sending you the enclosed "Observations" detailing the principal errors and ambiguities which have been found in the writings examined. I would ask your attentive consideration of these "Observations", which our mission in the service of moral truth requires us to send to you, with a view to preparing a response as indicated in the above-mentioned "Ratio agendi" (n. 13), in order to provide the appropriate explanation or correction of the points indicated.

As you will notice, the "Ratio agendi" suggests that you furnish your response within a "working month." Should this time prove too short for the response indicated, I would be grateful to you for sending to the Congregation an indication of when you think you will have the response ready.

This intervention has been made through Cardinal William Baum, Chancellor of the Catholic University of America, and Ordinary of the Archdiocese of Washington, in which you reside and teach. Your own Ordinary, Bishop Matthew Clark, has also been informed of this procedure.

Sincerely yours in Christ,
Franjo Cardinal Seper, Prefect

## "New Procedure in Doctrinal Examination (S.C. Doct. Fid., 15 Jan. 1971) AAS 63-234.*

In accordance with n. 12 of the apostolic letter *Integrae servandae,* issued *motu proprio* on 7 December, 1965,[1] the Sacred Congregation for the Doctrine of the Faith has established the following "Procedure in Doctrinal Examination" and makes it part of the public law.

1. Books and other publications or conferences whose contents pertain to the Sacred Congregation for the Doctrine of the Faith, are referred to the staff which is composed of superiors and officials and which meets every Saturday. If the opinion subjected to examination clearly and certainly contains an error in faith and if at the same time, as a result of its diffusion proximate harm is threatened for the faithful or already exists, the staff can stipulate that the matter proceed in an extraordinary manner, namely, that the Ordinary or the Ordinaries concerned should be informed at once about the matter and the author should be invited through his own Ordinary to correct the error. After the response of the Ordinary or Ordinaries has been received, the regular meeting of the staff will take appropriate steps according to the norm of the following articles 16,17,18.

2. The staff meeting likewise decides whether there is need to investigate more closely in the regular procedure certain writings or conferences. And if it seems it should, the staff itself will designate two experts, who are to prepare opinion studies, and a reporter "for the author." Moreover, the staff meeting will decide whether the Ordinary or Ordinaries concerned should be informed at once or only after the investigation has been completed.

3. Those to whom has been entrusted the task of drawing up "opinion studies," for that purpose inquire into the authentic work of the author to see if it squares with divine revelation and with the Church's magisterium. Thus they form a judgment on the doctrine therein presented and, if the case warrants it, recommend what must be done.

4. The cardinal prefect, the secretary and, if these are absent, the subsecretary have the power, if the matter is urgent, to entrust the opinion study to one of the consultors; however, only the staff designates an expert "out of a special commission."

5. The opinion studies are set up in print together with the office

report in which are recounted all the details useful for evaluating the proposed matter as well as the prior acts which are pertinent to the issue.

6. The report together with the aforesaid opinion studies is given to the reporter "for the author." Furthermore, he may look into all the documents which exist on this matter in the files of the S. Congregation. The task of the reporter "for the author" is: to point out, in the spirit of truth, the positive aspects of the doctrine of the author and his merits; to cooperate for the correct interpretation of the genuine meaning of the opinions of the said author in their general and their theological context; to respond to the observations of the other reporters and consultors; to express a judgment on the influence of the author's opinions.

7. The same report together with the opinion studies and other documents is turned over to the consultors at least one week before discussion is had on it in the consultors' meeting.

8. The discussion in the meeting begins with an exposition by the reporter "for the author." Following him, each consultor, orally or in writing, gives forth his opinion on the matters contained in the text under examination; then the reporter "for the author" can request the right to speak in order to respond to the observations or to explain the issues more clearly; and, lastly, he leaves the conference room while the consultors make known their own opinions. Finally, when the discussion has been completed, these opinions are read and are approved by the consultors themselves.

9. Then the total report together with the opinions of the consultors, the report "for the author," and the summary of the discussion is distributed to the regular session of the cardinals of the Sacred Congregation for the Doctrine of the Faith at least a week before it is discussed by the members of the Congregation. Each one of the seven member-bishops living outside the city can take part with full right in the regular session.

10. The cardinal prefect presides over the regular session, sets forth the issue itself, and declares his mind on it; the others follow in order. Their opinions are collected by the subsecretary and committed to writing in order that after the discussion and show of votes they may be read and approved.

11. The cardinal prefect or the secretary, when one or other of them next has an audience with the Supreme Pontiff, proposes these decisions to him for approval.

12. When no erroneous or dangerous opinions in the sense defined above in article 3, are detected in the examination, this outcome is brought to the notice of the Ordinary if he was previously informed of that examination. Contrariwise, if in the course of the examination false or dangerous opinions are found, that is announced to the author's Ordinary or to the Ordinaries concerned.

13. The propositions which have been declared to be considered false or dangerous are made known to the author himself so that within a month of available time he can transmit his written response. Furthermore, if there should be need of a conference, the author will be invited to meet and confer with persons deputed by the Sacred Congregation.

14. The said delegated persons must write up, at least in summary form, the conference which was held and, together with the author, must sign the sheet on which this conference is written up.

15. Both the written response of the author and the summary of the conference, if one happened to be had, will be presented to the regular session so that it can decide the matter. If, however, that written response of the author or the conference shows new doctrinal topics which should be examined more subtly, that response or summary of the conference is first of all set forth before the meeting of the consultors.

16. If, on the other hand, the author shall not have responded or, having been invited to a conference, does not come, the regular session will take appropriate steps.

17. The regular session also determines whether and in what way the outcome of the examination should be publicized.

18. The decisions of the regular session are submitted to the Supreme Pontiff for approbation and are then communicated to the Ordinary of the author.

The Supreme Pontiff, Paul VI, in the audience granted on the 8th day of January, 1971, to the undersigned cardinal prefect of this Sacred Congregation, confirmed and approved these regulations and ordered that they be made part of public law.

From Rome, the 15th day of January, 1971.

*(N.B. Cardinal Seper sent Curran the Latin document as found in *Acta Apostolicae Sedis*. This translation is from *Canon Law Digest* vii, pp. 181-184).

Prot. N. 48/66                                              July, 1979

## OBSERVATIONS

of the Sacred Congregation for the Doctrine of the Faith
on some writings of
Father Charles CURRAN

-------------------------------

The fundamental observation to be made regarding the writings of Father Charles Curran focuses upon his misconception of the specific competence of the authentic magisterium of the Church in matters *de fide et moribus*. The assistance of the Holy Spirit, in which the Church believes, moves the faithful to accept every authentic teaching, in the absence of valid and certain arguments to the contrary. Father Curran minimizes or even denies the specific value of the noninfallible magisterium, which enjoys the presumption of truth grounded in the above-mentioned assistance of the Holy Spirit. Insofar as the individual theologian does not have reasons which appear to be clearly valid to him and which derive from his competence in the matter in question to suspend or refuse assent to the teaching of this authentic magisterium, he must heed its teaching, even while recognizing that it might in an exceptional case be mistaken, since it does not enjoy the guarantee of infallibility. But this suspension of assent does not provide grounds for a so-called right of public dissent, for such public dissent would in effect constitute an alternative magisterium contrary to the mandate of Christ given to the apostles and constantly exercized through the hierarchical magisterium in the Church.

The ordinary member of the faithful, lacking expertise in a particular question, could not prudently trust himself to human wisdom or theological opinion in making a decision, in the face of the authentic teaching of those who "by divine institution . . . have succeeded to the place of the apostles as shepherds of the Church," so "that he who hears them, hears Christ, while he who rejects them, rejects Christ and Him who sent Christ (Cf. Luke 10:16)" [*Lumen gentium,* 20]. The teaching of *Lumen gentium* (cf. particularly n. 25) confirms the traditional teaching of the Church in the following documents: CLEMENT XI, DS 2390; PIUS IX, DS 2875-80; BENEDICT XV, DS 3625; PIUS XII, AAS 42 (1950) 569-578; 756-757; 46 (1954) 666-667; JOHN XXIII, AAS 54 (1962) 790-793; PAUL VI, AAS 56 (1964) 363-367; 58 (1966) 889-896; 877-881; 59 (1967) 960-963; 61 (1969) 713-716; 67 (1975) 39-44.

The following observations do not intend to single out every text in which Father Curran gives opinions contrary to this teaching of the Church. Nevertheless, these citations may usefully serve by way of illustration:

Curran seems to presume, for example, that there can be no secure teaching of morality by the authentic magisterium:

"The believing Catholic recognizes the God-given role of the hierarchical magisterium but also realizes that the teaching on specific moral questions cannot absolutely exclude the possibility of error. The prudent person will pay significant attention to this teaching and only act against such teaching after a careful and prayerful investigation. . . . Even recognizing newer theological methodologies and following an ecclesiological search for moral truth as described in the documents of the Second Vatican Council, the authoritative, noninfallible, hierarchical teaching on specific issues can never claim to exclude the possibility of error. The Catholic can never hope to have that type of certitude because of the complexities involved in specific moral questions but must be content with the moral certitude and risk involved in such specific decisions. The Catholic should gratefully receive the teaching of the hierarchical magisterium and only for serious reasons and after commensurate reflection make a conscience decision in opposition to it." ("Pluralism in Catholic Moral Theology," in *Ongoing Revision in Moral Theology,* pp. 64-65.)

Hence Curran moves immediately from the *possibility* of error by the non-infallible magisterium to the justification of his theory of dissent and of plurality of (supposedly equivalent) magisteria:

"If the hierarchical magisterium can be wrong in noninfallible matters then it follows that the hierarchical magisterium cannot be the only way in which the Church teaches. Historical studies have indicated that the Catholic Tradition recognizes this reality, especially in the context of the authoritarian Catholicism of the twentieth century. In the last decade most theologians have recognized that the hierarchical magisterium does not constitute the total magisterial activity of the Church . . . There are many magisteria in the Church — papal and episcopal magisteria, the authentic magisterium of laity and the magisterium of theologians. Each of these has a creative service in the Church." ("Ten Years Later," in *Commonweal,* 4 July 1978, p. 427).

With regard to the prophetic office in the Church, Curran fails to recognize the decisive role of the bishops in discerning the truth of Catholic doctrine:

The possibility of dissent from authoritative, authentic, non-infallible Church teaching rests on the theological reality that all the baptized share in the gift of the Spirit, and the hierarchical, non-infallible teaching office in the Church has never claimed to have a total monopoly on the Spirit . . . The role of the prophet exists in the Church and is not always identified with the hierarchical teaching function. The prophets both in the past and in the present have continuously taught the whole Church. There arises the difficult question of the discernment of the true prophet. But at least one has to admit that the acceptance of the authoritative, noninfallible teaching of the hierarchical magisterium cannot always be an ultimate test of the true prophet, although the prophet, like all others, must give due weight to this consideration." (*Ongoing,* 47; cf. also pp. 51-62).

Curran appeals to a mistaken concept of pluralism in Catholic theology and practice to justify dissent, not only private but even public:

"The negative reaction of theologians and even of bishops to the papal encyclical on artificial contracep-

> tion . . . brought to the attention of all Catholics . . .
> the right to dissent from authoritative, noninfallible,
> papal teaching when there are solid reasons for so doing
> . . . Even when the hierarchical magisterium has spo-
> ken on a particular issue, there can still be a pluralism
> of Catholic thinking on this issue. Thus from the view-
> point of a proper understanding of the moral teaching
> office of the hierarchical magisterium, it will be impossi-
> ble to speak about the Roman Catholic position on a par-
> ticular moral issue as if there could not be any other pos-
> sible position" ("Catholic Moral Theology Today," in
> *New Perspectives in Moral Theology,* 26-27).

He fails to recognize that pluralism in moral theology classically
involved disputes among theologians, not between the theologian
and the magisterium, when he states, "There has been a contradictory pluralism on many important specific moral questions within
Roman Catholicism. There is a tendency today to extend this
pluralism to a comparatively few other areas where it did not exist
before, but the same epistemological reason justifies the pluralism
in these new areas just as it did in the more numerous areas where
pluralism has existed in the past" (*Ongoing,* 52).

Finally, Curran promotes public dissent from the teachings of
the authentic magisterium:

"*Humanae vitae* is important because for the first time in recent
history it has been widely proposed and accepted that one can dissent from authoritative, noninfallible hierarchical teaching and
still be a loyal Roman Catholic. From the very first reaction to the
encyclical, I was among those who insisted that the basic teaching
condemning all artificial contraception for married couples was
wrong and that a Roman Catholic could dissent in theory and practice from such a teaching." (*Commonweal,* 425). "There are two ultimate theological reasons justifying the possibility of dissent.
First, specific moral teachings are not that intimately connected
with faith . . . A second reason justifying the possibility of dissent
from specific moral teachings rests on epistemological grounds . .
. The greater the particularity and specificity, the more difficult it
is to claim for one's solution a certitude that excludes the possibility of error." (*Commonweal,* 427-8).

And finally, "The reasons briefly mentioned justifying the possibility of dissent from authoritative, authentic, noninfallible Church teaching are also present with regard to the possibility of dissent on abortion and on euthanasia. Legitimate dissent in these areas remains a possibility because of the complexity and specificity of the material with which we are dealing and the fact that one cannot obtain the degree of certitude that excludes the possibility of error. One can, and in my judgment must, apply to those denying the hierarchical teaching on abortion and euthanasia what the Canadian bishops said about those dissenting from *Humanae vitae:* "Since they are not denying any point of divine and Catholic faith nor rejecting the teaching authority of the Church, these Catholics should not be considered, or consider themselves, shut off from the body of the faithful." For this reason I have urged that ultimate Roman Catholic identity cannot be sought in terms of absolute acceptance of specific moral teachings including the teaching on abortion and euthanasia.

"Although dissent from specific moral teachings always remains a possibiltiy for the Roman Catholic, this does not mean that such dissent is always justified and right. There must be reasons to justify the dissent, but this does not limit dissent only to theologians. Theology by definition operates on the level of the systematic, the thematic and the reflexive, but every Christian can and must arrive at ethical judgments. The ordinary Christian makes decisions in a nonthematic, nonreflexive, and nonsystematic way, but these are not pejorative terms. One does not have to be a theologian in order to be able to dissent from hierarchical teaching, but prudence calls for one to seek out how theologians and other people in the Church have approached the particular point in question." ("The Catholic Hospital and the Ethical and Religious Directives for Catholic Health Facilities," in *Linacre Quarterly,* February, 1977, p. 28-29).

The above-mentioned fundamental flaw in understanding the role of the Church's authentic magisterium, with its consequently mistaken justification of a right to public dissent, is based on a faulty concept of ecclesiastical magisterium. Furthermore, it does not seem able to be reconciled with the responsibilities of a Catholic theologian as outlined in *Optatam totius,* n. 16. The following list will indicate the more important errors and ambiguities found in these writings of Father Curran, giving examples which are intended to be illustrative rather than exhaustive. This list does not intend to identify any order or priority among these points, nor does it imply a judgment about the doctrinal note which may accompany the Church teaching in question.

1) Father Curran gives an ambiguous presentation of the notion of fundamental option, implying that a single, personal act will not normally be able to be called mortal sin.

He maintains,

> "The personalist influence in contemporary moral theology is readily seen in the reconsideration of human acts and especially sin. Sin is not primarily an act in violation of a law, but the fundamental option theory views sin in terms of the basic personal decision directing and guiding one's life. The fundamental option gives meaning and intelligibility to the whole life of the person." (*Ongoing Revision,* p. 99).

It is difficult to know from Curran's comment on "Persona humana" (n. 10) whether he intends to affirm the Catholic tradition that permits a judgment about whether or not a particular act has been mortally sinful:

> "The discussion on mortal sin and the fundamental option tends to be a caricature of what is generally accepted teaching in contemporary Roman Catholic theology and has strong roots in Thomistic thought itself. The document describes the opinions of some who see mortal sin only in a formal refusal directly opposed to God's call and not in particular human acts (no. 10). To my knowledge no reputable Catholic theologian holds such a position because our relationship with God is mediated in and through our relationship with neighbor and self. However, as the theory of the fundamental option rightly points out, mortal sin is a much less frequent occurrence in the lives of Christians than was recognized in an older understanding of mortal sin. Why?
>
> An older theology understood mortal sin in terms of an act against the law of God, but my theory of fundamen-

tal option sees mortal sin not primarily in terms of acts
but ultimately in terms of breaking the relationship of
love with God, neighbor and the world. The external act
involves mortal sin only if it signifies and expresses the
breaking of the fundamental relationship of love wih
God. Moral theology can and should describe certain
acts as right or wrong — e.g., murder, adultery, lying,
etc.; but one can never know just from the external act
alone whether or not mortal sin is present. The fundamental option basically involves the relationship of love
by which the person is linked to God. In the words of the
manuals of theology mortal sin involves one's going
from the state of grace to the state of sin and is not just
the external act as such. The relational understanding
of fundamental option recognizes that this relationship
is always mediated in and through particular actions,
but the external act in itself cannot be determinative of
the existence of mortal sin." (Sexual Ethics: Reaction
and Critique" in *Catholic Mind,* Jan. 1977, p. 52)

2) Through Curran's theory of compromise the objective moral
order is so affected by sin that the Christian is no longer held to its
full observance:

"To deal with some conflict situations I have proposed a
*theory of compromise* which is based on the recognition
of the reality of sin in all its ramifications. Sin is present
in life and society, and the Christian is called upon to
overcome sin; but sin will not be fully overcome until the
end of time. One could interpret the traditional Catholic
teaching that something could be wrong in the objective
order but not subjectively sinful as a recognition of the
fact that human limitation and even human sinfulness
can somehow or other affect the subjective realm but not
the objective realm. The theory of compromise recognizes that sin affects the objective order as well as the
subjective order. However, compromise also recognizes
that the Christian is called to attempt to overcome the
reality of sin as well as acknowledging that sin will
never be completely overcome this side of the eschaton.
Meanwhile, the presence of sin occasionally forces us to

do things which under ordinary circumstances we would not do. The word compromise tries to indicate the tension involved in recognizing even in the objective order the fact that sin is present and the Christian tries to overcome it, but at times the Christian will not be able to overcome sin completely." (*Ongoing Revision,* p. 186; cf. also "Catholic Moral Theology in Dialogue," pp. 216-218).

Such a theory, moreover, does not seem able to be reconciled with the constant teaching of the Church that God wills the observance of the moral order and does not command what is impossible (cf. DS 1536, AAS 22, 1930, p. 561-2; AAS 43, 1951, p. 846-7; AAS 36, 1944, p. 73-4; PH, 10.)

3) Furthermore, Father Curran mistakenly accuses St. Thomas Aquinas, contrary to S.T. 1-2, 94c, and Catholic moral teaching of "physicalism" (cf. for example his critique of "Persona humana" on this point; "Sexual Ethics," *Catholic Mind,* p. 50). He ignores the declaration's careful attempt to present sin in sexual matters in the context of a violation of the moral order, which involves the constitutive elements (ethical, psychological, spiritual, as well as physical) and essential relationships of the human person (the primary of which is with God).

So, for example, Curran states, "In my judgment the areas of questioning today in Catholic moral theology are especially those areas in which the human moral act has been identified with the physical structure of the act itself" (*Ongoing Revision,* p. 44). And again,

"All of these approaches to the evaluation of the moral act differ from the approach of the past which often spoke of intrinsically evil actions in terms of the physical structure of the act itself. These contemporary approaches differ among themselves, but they agree in proposing an evaluation of the human moral act which includes so many other considerations that one cannot identify the human moral act and the physical structure of the act with such certitude that the possibility of error is excluded." (*Ongoing Revision,* p. 43).

As a result of this sort of argumentation, Curran denies that one
can arrive at a clear understanding of absolutes in the matter of
wrong or sinful human behavior.

> "In the context of the situation-ethics debate in the
> 1960's Catholic theologians have reexamined the role
> and place of absolute norms in moral theology. I agree
> with an increasing number of Catholic theologians who
> deny the existence of negative moral absolutes: that is,
> actions described solely in terms of the physical struc-
> tures of the act (a material piece of behavior) which are
> said to be always and everywhere wrong. There are a
> variety of reasons for such a denial, including both a re-
> examination of the teaching of the past, which does not
> appear to be as absolute as presented in the manuals,
> and newer methodological approaches to meet our
> changing understandings of man and reality. Obvi-
> ously, such a denial stems from a more inductive, rela-
> tional, and empirical approach to moral problems."
> ("Moral Theology: the present state of the discipline," in
> *Theological Studies* 34, 1973, p. 454-5).

In applying these ideas to particular questions of morality, Curran maintains,

> "The more historical and relational approach that
> characterizes contemporary moral theology is more
> willing to see exceptions in absolute norms. I personally
> do see occasions where sexual intercourse outside mar-
> riage would not be wrong, but the exceptions are quite
> limited. Others have argued that sometimes sexual re-
> lations for the engaged couple would not be wrong, but
> it seems to me that such people may already have made
> the total commitment to one another even though they
> have not publicly expressed this commitment in the
> marriage ceremony. In the theory of compromise one
> could imagine certain situations in which sexual re-
> lationships outside marriage would not be wrong. Also
> in view of proper medical experimentation and knowl-
> edge, sexual intercourse outside marriage would not
> seem always wrong (although by no means do I intend

to justify all that is presently being done along these lines)." (*Contemporary Problems in Moral Theology,* p. 179-80).

"The principal areas of practical differences between some situationists and the teaching found in the manuals of moral theology are the following: medical ethics, particularly in the area of reproduction; conflict situations solved by the principle of the indirect voluntary, especially conflicts involving life and death, e.g., killing, abortion; sexuality; euthanasia; and divorce.

The major points of disagreement have one thing in common. In these cases, the manuals of Catholic moral theology have tended to define the moral action in terms of the physical structure of the act considered in itself apart from the person placing the act and the community of persons within which he lives. A certain action defined in terms of its physical structure or consequences (e.g., euthanasia as the positive interference in the life of the person; masturbation as the ejaculation of semen) is considered to be always wrong. I have used the term 'negative, moral absolute' to refer to such actions described in their physical structure which are always wrong from a moral viewpoint. Thus the central point of disagreement in moral theology today centers on these prohibited actions which are described primarily in terms of their physical structure.

"In the area of medical ethics certain actions described in terms of the physical structure of the act are never permitted or other such actions are always required. Artificial insemination with the husband's semen is never permitted because insemination cannot occur except through the act of sexual intercourse. Contraception as direct interference with the act of sexual intercourse is wrong. Direct sterilization is always wrong. Masturbation as the ejaculation of semen is always wrong as a way of procuring semen for semen analysis. Frequently in such literature the axiom is cited that the end does not justify the means. However, in all these cases the means is defined in terms of the

physical structure of the act. I believe in all the areas
mentioned above there are circumstances in which such
actions would be morally permissible and even necessary." (*Contemporary Problems in Moral Theology,* p.
142-3).

Further Curran appeals to "personalism" to justify a departure
from objective moral truth:

"Personalism has become a very important normative
criterion in contemporary moral theology. The category
of person has often taken over the primacy which the
older manualist approach gave to the concept of nature.
The person does not totally conform in a passive way to
a given nature, but rather all things are to be integrated
into the good of the person. Many changes in contemporary thought illustrate the importance of personalism.
The Declaration on Religious Freedom bases its teaching on the dignity of the human person as this dignity is
known through the revealed word of God and by reason
itself (no. 1, 2). No longer is objective truth the ultimate
and controlling factor although it does have some importance. The call to reform canon law recognizes the
danger of a one-sided emphasis on the institution and
tries to safeguard the dignity and rights of persons in
the Church as well as the participation of all persons in
the life of the Church. A criterion of person rather than
nature has been at the heart of the call for change in the
traditional Catholic teaching on contraception and
sterilization." (*Ongoing Revision,* p. 97-8).

This appeal to the "Declaration on Religious Freedom" in support of the argument from human dignity seems to ignore that
document's clear statement that "in the formation of their consciences, the Christian faithful ought carefully to attend to the sacred and certain doctrine of the Church. The Church is, by the will
of Christ, the teacher of the truth. It is her duty to give utterance
to, and authoritatively to teach, that Truth which is Christ Himself, and also to declare and confirm by her authority those principles of the moral order which have their origin in human nature
itself." (*Dignitatis humanae,* 14).

4) Father Curran's use of Scripture as containing ethical teachings which represent an ideal or goal of the quest for Christian perfection, rather than a concrete obligation for moral living, even in those cases in which Church tradition has given a definitive interpretation about the presence of such an obligation, gives evidence of a faulty methodology in the understanding and use of Scripture in moral theology. For example, Curran says,

> "I opt for the opinion that one can partially understand some of the strenuous ethical teachings of Jesus in the Sermon on the Mount as a goal or ideal toward which the Christian must strive without always being able to attain the ideal. In the light of these and other reasons, I propose that indissolubility remains a goal and ideal for Christian marriage; but Christians, sometimes without any personal fault, are not always able to live up to that ideal. Thus the Roman Catholic Church should change its teaching on divorce." (*Issues in Sexual and Medical Ethics,* pp. 15-16)

5) Curran contradicts Catholic moral teaching on cooperation when he suggests that the person cooperating is not responsible for a personal moral judgment, but can rely on the intention of the principal agent:

> "I disagree with the fundamental basis for saying that immediate material cooperation is wrong because my action is intrinsically evil and not indifferent. One does not immediately materially cooperate with an act which is intrinsically wrong but rather with a person who has a right to act in accord with one's conscience provided that other innocent persons or the public order are not hurt." (*Ongoing Revision,* p. 192).

> "Roman Catholic moral theology in general has rightly been criticized for the fact that its moral teaching in the last few centuries has given so much emphasis to the objective and even the physical that it has not given enough importance to subjectivity and freedom. The newer approach to religious liberty recognizes this fact and indicates a dimension that had not heretofore been considered. In the case of cooperation it seems that

one must also consider the right of the individual person
to act in accord with one's own decision of conscience.

"The older approach to cooperation understood the action of the cooperator as concurring with the will or the
act of the other person. If the will was bad or if the act
was bad, then there was either formal or material cooperation. But is it adequate to describe the action merely
as cooperating with a bad will or a bad action? This could
be a partial explanation but a more adequate description understands cooperation as concurring not primarily with will or with an act but with a person. The person, however, may have a bad will (e.g., a criminal planning a robbery) or may do a bad act (needlessly hurt an
innocent person). The point is that the full understanding of cooperation must take account of the dignity of the
other person and that person's right to act in accord with
one's own responsible freedom. Nevertheless, one cannot ignore the elements of a bad will or a bad act which
have been part of the consideration in the past.

"There is another factor which should also change
somewhat the traditional teaching on cooperation. As
mentioned, one of the most important parts of the
Roman Catholic teaching has been the fact that one cannot cooperate with an action which is intrinsically
wrong. However, there is much dispute today within
Roman Catholic theology about the whole question of
what, if anything, is intrinsically wrong." (*Ongoing Revision*, p. 219-220).

6) Curran's position on Christian marriage — its indissolubility
and the pastoral practice resulting from this — contradicts the
teaching and practice of the Church. For example, in his article
"Divorce: Catholic Theory and Practice in the United States" (*New
Perspectives in Moral Theology*), in commenting on tribunal practice in the United States, Curran says:

"I agree with the judgment that matrimonial tribunals
are not an adequate institution to achieve the purpose
of the Church in safeguarding Christian marriage and
even in upholding the indissolubility of marriage as well

as in providing a means of justice for Catholics. My personal conviction that the Church should change its teaching and practice on the indissolubility of Christian marriage obviously influences such a negative judgment on the tribunal system, but the arguments against the existence of the tribunal system still have validity apart from the contention that the Church should change its basic teaching." (p. 233-4)

In discussing various pastoral practices proposed for a Church celebration of a second marriage after a divorce, Curran recommends his own practice based on his proposed change in Church teaching on indissolubility:

"In the second case in which there was a true previous marriage, there is no difficulty in proving that Catholics can at times enter new marriages, and that priests can so advise if one accepts, as I do, that the Church should change its teaching on indissolubility and see it as a goal or ideal which is not always to be attained. In practice I also have a small Eucharistic celebration and an exchange of vows after a civil ceremony in this case." (p. 247)

And again, in his conclusion to his article, he states,

"On the basis of the foregoing evidence I conclude that the Roman Catholic Church should change its teaching and practice on divorce. Divorce and remarriage must be accepted as a reality in our world that at times can take place even without personal guilt on the part of the individuals involved. Indissolubility or permanency is a radical demand of the gospel that is seen as a goal but not an absolute norm." (p. 271-272)

This fundamental departure from Church doctrine is further exposed in Curran's subsequent article "Divorce in the Light of a Revised Moral Theology" (in *Ongoing Revision*):

"If the above reading of the signs of the times is accurate, there will soon be a change in the pastoral practice of the Catholic Church concerning the participation of divorced and remarried Catholics in the sacramental life of the Church. Even without any hierarchical sanction, today many Catholics in this situation are participating in the sacramental life of the Church. It seems that this will become the regular practice whether it is officially sanctioned by the hierarchical Church or not.

"How then should one evaluate such a fact from the perspective of contemporary moral theology? In my judgment such a pastoral approach does not go far enough. I believe that the Catholic Church should change its teaching on the absolute indissolubility of marriage. Perhaps it could be argued that from a logical viewpoint one could propose an argument for a change in the pastoral practice towards divorced and remarried Catholics which does not involve any change in the teaching of the indissolubility of marriage. However, in the light of the data on the question of divorce itself and in the context of the self-understanding of contemporary Catholic moral theology, I argue that a change in the pastoral practice really involves and should lead to a change in the teaching on the absolute indissolubility of marriage." (p. 75)

and further:

"An eschatological perspective which tries to account for the tension which comes from our living between the two comings of Jesus argues against an approach which wants to maintain in paradoxical tension the teaching on the absolute indissolubility of marriage and a pastoral practice tolerating second marriages after divorce. The limitations coming from the fact that the fullness of the eschaton is not yet here need to be expressed in more than just the toleration of a pastoral practice. This limitation of the present affects the objective understanding of marriage in the only world that we know. Indissolubility of marriage in such a perspective can only be the goal which is imperative for all and which the couple promises to each other in hope; but which, without their own fault, might at times be unobtainable." (p. 105) and still more recently, Curran touches upon the same theme:

> "In the present situation the role of institutional structures and of the hierarchical office is being steadily eroded. Take, for example, the question of remarriage after divorce. Many Catholics decide, often with the advice of a priest, to remarry and to continue celebrating the sacraments of the Church. Such a situation is basically good, but there are dangers of harm and injustice to innocent people which call for some official guidelines. There is a proper place and a need for the hierarchical office to regulate aspects in the life of the church, but today many things are developing outside and beyond the official structure. Such a situation cannot and should not continue for too long a period of time. . . .
>
> "In the eyes of many Roman Catholics there must be important insitutional changes in the church. Issues such as divorce and remarriage, women priests, and clerical celibacy call for a change. In a sense *Humanae vitae* has become symbolic. If the hierarchical church refuses to change here, there will probably be no change on other issues."
>
> ("Ten Years Later," in *Commonweal,*
> 7 July 1978, p. 430.)

7) On the questions of abortion and euthanasia, Curran advances positions at least partially in conflict with Church teaching:

> "My own teaching constitutes a dissent from the authoritative Church teaching on the two questions of when does human life begin and how can one solve conflict situations, but my dissent is not all that great. Others might propose a more radical solution."
>
> (*Ongoing Revision,* p. 157)

> "What about euthanasia or the active and positive interference to bring about death? Traditionally Catholic teaching and the hierarchical teaching authority have

opposed euthanasia. Two reasons are frequently given. First, the individual does not have full dominion but only stewardship over one's own life and therefore cannot directly interfere with life. Second, there is a great difference between the act of omitting an extraordinary means and the positive act of bringing about death. To allow one to die is not the same as positively interfering to cause death especially as it concerns the intention and act of the person performing the deed.

"Those two arguments in my judgment are not absolutely convincing in all cases. Human beings do have some dominion over life and death, for example, by refusing extraordinary means one can intend to die and efficaciously carry out that intention. I grant there is an important difference between the act of omission and the positive act of killing, but in my judgment at the point in which the dying process begins there is no longer that great a difference between the act of commission and the act of omission. I acknowledge problems in determining when the dying process begins (some could argue it begins at birth), so I practically identify the dying process with the time that means can be discontinued as useless but having in mind such means as respirator, intravenous feeding, etc. In practice there will always be a difficulty in determining just when the dying process begins so that one must recognize the potiential problem of abuse that can arise and the difficulty in determining laws in this matter. Now and in the future one can expect some others to dissent from past Catholic teaching in this case. Again, despite all the dangers involved, dissent remains a possibility for the Catholic. The matter is so complex that the present teaching as proposed by the authoritative, noninfallible magisterium cannot claim and, to its credit, does not claim to exclude the possibility of error."

("*Ongoing Revision,*" p. 160-161)

8) Father Curran has frequently sustained positions in contrast with the teaching of the Church's magisterium on questions of sexual morality. In a recent summary of his positions on masturba-

tion, homosexuality, and premarital sexuality, he first calls to mind "the distinction between sin and right or wrong. . . . Sin thus considers the action in relationship to the responsibility and personal involvement of the one placing such an action. . . . The human act must also be considered in relationship with other acts and other persons. Right or wrong can be used to designate the human act under this aspect. Thus an action may be wrong but not sinful. . . ." (*Themes in Fundamental Moral Theology,* p. 180). With this distinction in mind, Curran goes on to state, "There is no blanket gravity that can be assigned to every act of masturbation" (p. 181). And further,

> "The theology of sin in terms of fundamental option and modern psychological knowledge indicates that most often homosexual actions do not involve the person in grave or mortal sin. . . . (In) the cases in which modern medical science cannot help the homosexual . . . it seems to me that for such a person homosexual acts might not even be wrong." (p. 132)

And again:

> "I personally do see occasions where sexual intercourse outside marriage would not be wrong, but the exceptions are quite limited . . . In the theory of compromise one could imagine certain situations in which sexual relationships outside marriage would not be wrong." (p. 184)

Furthermore, Curran maintains that "at best the distinction between grave matter and light matter is a presumption. The presumption is that grave matter will usually call for an involvement of the core of the person whereas light matter tends to call for only a peripheral response. If grave and light matter are at best presumptive guidelines, then such axioms as *ex toto genere suo gravis* or *non datur parvitas materiae* lose much of their rigidity. However, my contention is that one cannot maintain the presumption that all complete sexual actuations outside marriage and all directly willed, imperfect sexual actuations outside marriage constitute grave matter. . . . If such complete sexual actuation outside marriage does not always involve grave matter, *a fortiori* directly willed, imperfect sexual actuation does not always involve grave matter." (*Contemporary Problems in Moral Tehology*, p. 167-8).

9) Finally, Father Curran openly declares his disagreement with Church teaching on contraception and sterilization.

> "*Humanae vitae* is important because for the first time it has been widely proposed and accepted that one can dissent from authoritative, noninfallible, hierarchical teaching and still be a loyal Roman Catholic. From the very first reaction to the encyclical, I was among those who insisted that the basic teaching condemning all artificial contraception for married couples was wrong and that a Roman Catholic could dissent in theory and practice from such a teaching."

> ("Ten Years Later," in *Commonweal*,
> 7 July 1978, p. 425)

> "I do not think that contraception violates an ideal; nor does it involve premoral or ontic evil. In my judgment both of these approaches still give too much importance to the physical aspects of the act and see the physical as normative. From the ecclesiological perspective we must face the more radical question of the existence of papal error and of the possibility of dissent. Even from a pragmatic and practical viewpoint, the contemporary church must address the question of dissent. There are some significant moral truths in *Humanae vitae*. Likewise, there has been some development in the teaching of the Catholic Church on procreation and marital relations. But the condemnation of artificial contraception found in *Humanae vitae* is wrong."

> (*Ibid.*, p. 427)

> "On the question of artificial contraception, the pope and bishops must be willing to publicly admit that the previous teaching is wrong. At the very least they need to acknowledge publicly the legitimacy of dissent on the question and the ramification of dissent in the entire life of the church." (*Ibid.*, 430)

With regard to sterilization, Curran's statement

"I disagree with the past teaching on sterilization and maintain that in practice Catholics can dissent from the authoritative teaching condemning direct sterilization" (*New Perspectives,* 203),

has been developed in this article and subsequently sustained in others (cf., for example, "The Catholic Hospital and the Ethical and Religious Directives for Catholic Health Facilities," in *Linacre Quarterly,* Feb. 1977). Hence Curran maintains,

"In my judgment sterilization involves basically the same moral issues as contraception. Whoever dissents from the teaching on contraception logically must also dissent from the prohibition of direct sterilization. The only difference is that sterilization tends to be permanent, and there should be a more permanent or serious reason to justify it. Consequently, sterilization if permitted cannot be restricted to just medical reasons, but any truly human reason which is of proportionate seriousness suffices — sociological, psychological, economic or other.

"The recent letter of Archbishop Bernardin and the document from the Doctrinal Congregation do not take away the legitimacy of dissent for a Roman Catholic. One must be open to the teaching of these documents, but the documents themselves claim only to be repeating the traditional teaching as already enunciated. If, after prayerful and thoughtful consideration, one has already dissented from such teaching, such dissent can continue to be a legitimate option for the loyal Roman Catholic" (*Issues in Sexual and Medical Ethics,* pp. 153-4).

Franjo Cardinal Seper, Prefect

SACRA CONGREGATIO
PRO DOCTRINA FIDEI
00193 Romae
Piazza del S. Uffizio, 11

Prot. N. 48/66

August 28, 1979

Dear Father Curran,

The Apostolic Delegate, Archbishop Jean Jadot, has notified us of the death of your father earlier this month. On behalf of Cardinal Seper, Prefect of the Congregation, and on my own behalf, I want to extend to you our sincere sympathy and prayers.

Naturally it will be entirely understandable for you to delay the reply requested of you in Cardinal Seper's letter of July 13 due to these circumstances.

Sincerely yours in Christ,
Fr. Jerome Hamer, O.P.


THE
CATHOLIC UNIVERSITY
OF AMERICA
Washington, D.C. 20064

August 29, 1979

His Eminence
Franjo Cardinal Seper
Praefectus, Sacra Congregatio pro Doctrina Fidei
Piazza del S. Uffizio, 11
00193 Rome

Dear Cardinal Seper,

I am responding to your letter of July 13, 1979, with the protocol number 48/66.

I received this letter from Cardinal William Baum on August 2, 1979. My primary purpose in writing at this time is to avail myself of the opportunity mentioned in paragraph three of your letter to take more time in responding than "a working month." A number of factors have made me most grateful for the possibility of a longer time to respond. As any other productive scholar I have a number of long standing commitments that must be honored both in terms of articles and in terms of lectures. In addition, in the last few months I have been quite occupied by the terminal illness and death of my eighty year old father and making plans for my mother. My father died from cancer on August 9th. As the executor of his will, it is my responsibility to take care of all legal matters and to make plans for the future for my seventy-nine year old mother. As a result of these factors, it has been impossible for me even to think about a detailed response to your letter at this time.

After prayer, reflection and taking counsel with a number of different people in the academic, theological and ecclesiastical worlds, I have decided that I will respond to the observations you sent me. However, in all honesty, I must admit that a number of circumstances almost convinced me that your request was seriously flawed, and that fundamental aspects of justice had been violated, so that the whole procedure was vitiated.

Above all, in my judgment, your Sacred Congregation has already violated its own principles by publicly condemning me. As a result, any fair minded person could readily conclude that I cannot receive a fair hearing from the same congregation. I refer specifically to the letter of J. Hamer (copy enclosed) to Bishop Joseph V. Sullivan of Baton Rouge, dated April 24, 1979, and with the same protocol number as the letter you sent to me. This letter was published in two national Catholic newspapers as well as in others, and copies of it were sent to some priests in the United States.

If we are both to undertake this discussion in the proper spirit, I think it is absolutely necessary that you be familiar with all my writings. According to your letter, "several" of my articles and books have been called to your attention. For example, nowhere in the sixteen pages of "Observations," which refer to my position on the hierarchical magisterium as the fundamental flaw, is mention made of *Dissent In and For the Church* a collegially written book, in which my colleagues and I justified our dissent from the condemnation of artificial contraception. I am enclosing a list of all the books I have published. If you do not have copies of them, I will be most happy to forward them to you. Please indicate to me which of these titles you need.

In addition, I would be willing to meet in a proper dialogical situation to discuss these writings with a representative of the Congregation in a personal meeting. If you believe this would be helpful, please notify me so that the necessary arrangements can be made.

Sincerely yours in Christ,
Charles E. Curran

CEC/pw
encs.
cc: William Cardinal Baum

## Books by Charles E. Curran

*Christian Morality Today* (Notre Dame, Ind.: Fides Publishers, 1966)

*A New Look at Christian Morality* (Notre Dame, Ind.: Fides Publishers, 1968)

*Contemporary Problems in Moral Theology* (Notre Dame, Ind.: Fides Publishers, 1970)

*Catholic Moral Theology in Dialogue* (Notre Dame, Ind.: Fides Publishers, 1972) — paperback edition: University of Notre Dame Press, 1976

*Crisis in Priestly Ministry* (Notre Dame, Ind.: Fides Publishers, 1972)

*Politics, Medicine and Christian Ethics: A Dialogue with Paul Ramsey* (Philadelphia: Fortress, 1973)

*New Perspectives in Moral Theology* (Notre Dame, Ind.: Fides Publishers, 1974) — paperback edition: University of Notre Dame Press, 1976

*Ongoing Revision: Studies in Moral Theology* (Notre Dame, Ind.: Fides Publishers, 1976)

*Themes in Fundamental Moral Theology* (Notre Dame, Ind.: University of Notre Dame Press, 1977)

*Issues in Sexual and Medical Ethics* (Notre Dame, Ind.: University of Notre Dame Press, 1978)

*Transition and Tradition in Moral Theology* (Notre Dame, Ind.: University of Notre Dame Press, 1979)

Charles E. Curran, Robert E. Hunt, *et. al., Dissent in and for the Church* (New York: Sheed and Ward, 1969)

John F. Hunt and Terrence R. Connelly with Charles E. Curran, Robert E. Hunt and Robert K. Webb, *The Responsibility of Dissent: The Church and Academic Freedom* (New York: Sheed and Ward, 1969)

*Editor:*

*Absolutes in Moral Theology?* (Washington: Corpus Books, 1968)
*Contraception: Authority and Dissent* (New York: Herder and Herder, 1969)
*Shared Responsibility in the Local Church,* ed. Charles E. Curran and George J. Dyer (Chicago: Catholic Theological Society of America, 1970)
*Readings in Moral Theology No. 1: Moral Norms and Catholic Tradition,* ed. Charles E. Curran and Richard A. McCormick (New York: Paulist Press, 1979).

SACRA CONGREGATIO
PRO DOCTRINA FIDEI
00193 Romae
Piazza del S. Uffizio, 11

Prot. N. 48/66

April 24, 1979

The Most Reverend Joseph V. Sullivan
Bishop of Baton Rouge

Your Excellency,

Your recent pastoral decision to refuse the use of diocesan facilities for a talk by Rev. Charles Curran at the University of Louisiana in Baton Rouge, together with your public statement explaining your reasons for this decision, have both been brought to the attention of this Congregation.

Please accept my personal thanks for providing public clarification of some of the ambiguous and erroneous teachings of Father Curran.

With cordial best wishes for Your Excellency, I am

Sincerely yours in Christ,
Fr. Jerome Hamer

SACRA CONGREGATIO
PRO DOCTRINA FIDEI
00193 Romae
Piazza del S. Uffizio, 11

Prot. N. 48/66

October 4, 1979

Dear Father Curran,

   With this reply I want to acknowledge receipt of your letter of
August 29, which undoubtedly crossed my letter of August 28 in
the mail. As I had indicated in my letter of that date, the Congregation had anticipated that you would need an extended period to
prepare your response to our letter of July 13 due to the circumstances which have arisen in connection with the death of your
father.

   The Congregation has at its disposition the books you included
on your publications list. Nevertheless, I would be pleased to accept your offer to send us a copy of *Dissent In and For the Church.*

   With kind regards, I remain

Sincerely yours in Christ,
J. Hamer


The
CATHOLIC UNIVERSITY
of America
Washington, D.C. 20064

October 26, 1979

His Eminence
Franjo Cardinal Seper
Praefectus, Sacra Congregatio pro Doctrina Fidei
Piazza del S. Uffizio, 11
00193 Rome

Dear Cardinal Seper,

   Enclosed you will find my response to the "Observations" which
were sent to me. Despite very significant deficiencies in the sub-

stance and style of the "Observations" from the viewpoint of theological discussion and the protection of human rights, I have expended much time and effort in trying to respond. The response concentrates on the "fundamental observation" about my "misconception of the specific competence of the authentic magisterium of the Church in matters *de fide et moribus.*"

I also want to acknowledge the letters of August 28 and October 4 sent to me by Archbishop Hamer. I am most grateful for your sympathy and prayers on the occasion of my father's death. In response to your request, I am sending a copy of *Dissent In and For the Church.*

In the light of my August 29 letter to you, I expected your letter of October 4 would have responded to other things I mentioned.

Sincerely yours in Christ,
Charles E. Curran

Re: Prot. No. 48/66

## RESPONSE

To the "Observations" of the
Sacred Congregation for the Doctrine of the Faith
on Some Writings of Father Charles E. Curran
(Prot. N. 48/66)

My response to the "Observations" will comprise four parts:

I. Some Preliminary Remarks
II. Five Questions
III. Response to the Citations on pages 2-4
IV. Concluding Remarks

### I. *Preliminary Remarks*

First, I must publicly state that the procedures of the Sacred Congregation for the Doctrine of the Faith as found in "Nova Agendi Ratio in Doctrinarum Examine" (*A.A.S.*, 63, 1971, pp. 234-236) are seriously flawed in terms of their protection of the rights of the individual involved. They fail to incorporate the elementary principles of due process which are accepted in contemporary legal structures. One has basic rights to know who are the accusers, what precisely are the charges and to have representation by an advocate of one's own choosing. In addition, as noted in my earlier letter, I have been publicly judged and condemned in the letter of J. Hamer to Bishop Joseph V. Sullivan dated April 24, 1979, and published in several national Catholic newspapers.

Second, as mentioned in my letter of August 28, the "Observations" are based on "several" of my articles and books and "some" of my writings. You maintain that "the fundamental observation to be made regarding the writings of Father Charles Curran focuses upon his misconception of the specific competence of the authentic magisterium of the Church in matters *de fide et moribus.*" I was dismayed that nowhere in the "Observations" is there a reference to my most systematic treatment of the question, *Dissent In and For the Church,* (New York: Sheed and Ward, 1969), a book collegially written with my colleagues in defending the right of public dissent to the encyclical *Humanae vitae.* Here the position is developed in a systematic monograph carefully developing all the aspects which enter into this complex picture. The chapter titles indicate the flow of the argument: (1) The Historical Context, (2) Preliminary Consideration Concerning the Nature of Theology and the Role of Theologians, (3) Preliminary Consideration Concerning the Nature and Function of the Magisterium, (4) Contemporary Ecclesiological Awareness of Catholic Theologians, (5) Public Dissent in and for the Church, (6) The Reasonableness of Responsible Dissent from One Particular Ethical Teaching of the Encyclical, (7) The Dissent from *Humanae vitae:* Onset and Aftermath, (8) *Epilogue:* Conclusions of the Catholic University Faculty Board of Inquiry. Anyone expressing disagreement with my position on the ordinary authentic hierarchical magisterium should deal precisely with the most systematic and extended treatment of it.

Third, the "Observations" are virtually all in the form of citations taken from my own works. This format of long selective quotations is not the most promising for discerning what, if any points, are held in disagreement. On the one hand, the citations occasionally leave out important parts of what I said. One of the generic observations on page one of the "Observations" accuses me of denying or not recognizing the assistance of the Holy Spirit given to the hierarchical magisterium. In your very first citation from my book, *Ongoing Revision in Moral Theology,* pp. 64-65 (Notre Dame, Indiana: Fides Publishers, 1975), the citation shows an ellipsis and leaves out a very significant paragraph in which the assistance of the Holy Spirit is explicitly mentioned (p. 64).

Also, random citations do not make for a good procedure for arriving at the real points in dispute. I could very easily respond to the "Observations" by citing other passages from my writings which contain the aspects which the "Observations" assert are not found in my writings. The "Observations" state on page 1: "Father Curran minimizes or even denies the specific value of the noninfallible magisterium which enjoys the presumption of truth grounded in the above mentioned assistance of the Holy Spirit (*Ongoing Revision*, p. 65). Also I have clearly spoken about the presumption of truth in such teachings:

> In fact, the assent "required" by the very nature of *Humanae vitae* was, or should have been, known as a matter of condition or qualification regarding a teaching that is *presumptively,* but only presumptively, true. In the final analysis the presumption can be weakened or effectively rebutted by serious reasons to the contrary.
>
> Assent to *Humanae vitae* can be suspended only because serious, personally convincing reasons lead a person to believe that the general presumption is not verified in this instance. (*Dissent In and For the Church,* p. 125)

Fourth, there is no clear detailing of the erroneous and ambiguous positions which I am said to maintain. The cover letter mentions the "principle errors and ambiguities" found in my writings. However, the "Observations" do not draw up a list of these clearly labeling what is erroneous and what is ambiguous. The "Observations" are deficient not only from the viewpoint of true theological dialogue but also from the perspective of legal due process. Charges as serious as these being made against me should be detailed and precise.

As a result of these significant deficiencies which can only raise serious questions in my mind, I am faced wih the added burden of trying to formulate the issues in a way in which intelligent theological discussions can take place. To facilitate such a discussion I will now procede in terms of a set of questions to determine just what are the differences that might exist.

## II. *Five Questions*

QUESTION ONE. Does the teaching of the ordinary noninfallible authoritative hierarchical magisterium constitute the only factor or the always decisive factor in the total magisterial activity of the Church? In other words is the theologian ever justified in going against such a teaching? (In the future this response will only deal with the ordinary magisterium in terms of the ordinary, authoritative or authentic, noninfallible hierarchical magisterium.) This question is posed because the "Observations" on page 1 deny the right of public dissent since it would in effect constitute an alternative magisterium. However, the "Observations" do acknowledge the possibility that an individual theologian could suspend or refuse assent. This question attempts to deal with the relationship of the hierarchical magisterium to the role and function of the theologian.

My negative response to this question has been developed at great length in chapters 2, 3, and 4 of *Dissent In and For the Church*. Of special importance is chapter 3: "Preliminary Consideration Concerning the Nature and Function of the Magisterium." There is no need for me to develop again what has been developed in these chapters.

The question is phrased in this way to avoid the problem of speaking about plural magisteria in the Church. In general I have tried in proposing my own position to avoid the terminology of two magisteria in the Church or a number of magisteria in the Church because I believe it can be somewhat misleading. There is a difference between the teaching of the hierarchical magisterium and the teaching of theologians. See, for example, my response to Dubay's critique that a right to dissent postulates two magisteria in the Church in *Ongoing Revision in Moral Theology*, pp. 44-48. In subsequent writings, especially in *Transition and Tradition in Moral Theology*, I have only used the term many magisteria in the Church in relating the positions proposed by Maguire and Congar (p. 48). (This is the same as my article "Ten Years Later," *Commonweal*, July, 1978, p. 427.)

Since the systematic treatment proposed by me in *Dissent In and For the Church,* some bishops and other theologians have dealt with the question and have denied that the teaching of the hierarchical magisterium constitutes the only factor or the always decisive factor in the magisterial activity of the Church. Yves Congar concludes a significant treatise on the forms of the "magisterium" and of its relations to the theologian by indicating that the function of the theologian cannot be totally defined in terms of dependence on the magisterium:

> If we may conclude a historical article with a theological perspective, we will say: the relationship between doctors and the magisterium calls for reconsideration. This supposes that we will first define the status of the "magisterium" in the Church, that it will not be isolated from the living reality of the Church. It will be necessary to recognize the fundamental character of the charisma and service of theologians, the necessary specificity of their work within the faith of the Church, to define the conditions for a healthy exercise of their service: an awareness of responsibility, of communion with the concrete life of the faithful, the doxological context and celebration of mysteries, a mutual criticism actively performed. We cannot define the dependent condition of theologians only with reference to the "magisterium," even while this retains its truth. In this area as in that of obedience we must not think of the issue just in two terms: authority, theologians. We must think in three terms; above, the truth, the transmitted apostolic faith, confessed, preached and celebrated. Beneath this, at its service, the "magisterium" of the apostolic ministry and the work or the teaching of theologians, as well as the faith of the faithful. It is a differentiated service, articulated organically, like all the life of the *ecclesia*. (Yves Congar, "Bref historique des formes du 'magistère' et des relations avec les docteurs," *Revue des sciences philosophiques et théologiques* 60, 1976, p. 112.)

Bishop Christopher Butler is very clear on this point:

> Despite a modern unfortunate use of the word *magis-*

*terium* to designate the bishops, the college of bishops, and the Pope, magisterial authority is not confined in the Church to official magisterial authority. It cannot reasonably be maintained, in the face of Vatican II, that the Church is divided into an *ecclesia docens* consisting of the Pope and the bishops and an *ecclesia discens* embracing all other baptized persons. On the contrary, everyone in the Church, from the Pope downwards, belongs to the "learning Chruch" and has to receive information from his fellow-believers; and everyone in the Church who has reached maturity has, at sometime or another, to play the role of the teacher, the magister, the *ecclesia docens*. (p. 422)

In the first place, then, the divine guarantee of doctrine appertains, in its fullest sense, only to those doctrines and dogmas to which the Church has fully committed herself, whether by the common consent of her believers (the *sensus fidelium*) or by the decisions of official authority. The claim of these doctrines on the adhesion of the believer is identical with the claim of the divine revelation itself. To require the same adhesion for the doctrines that are indeed taught by officials with authority but to which the Church has not irrevocably committed herself is to abuse authority; and if this requirement is accompanied by threatened sanctions it is also to abuse the power of constraint. It would seem that, in order to preserve clearly the distinction between irrevocable and provisional doctrinal decisions, the word "assent" should be confined to the type of adhesion properly required for irrevocable doctrinal decisions. (p. 424) (Bishop Christopher Butler, O.S.B. "Authority and the Christian Conscience," *The American Benedictine Review* XXV:4, December 1974, pp. 411-426.)

Some of the same points are made by Archbishop Robert Coffy. He maintains "it is necessary to avoid saying that theology is at the service of the magisterium. It is better to say that the magisterium and theology are both at the service of the Word of God." (Robert Coffy, "Magistère et theologie," *Bulletin du secrétariat de la conférence épiscopale française,* no. 18, novembre 1975, p. 9.)

Joseph A. Komonchak calls for an organical and not hierarchical relationship among the different bearers of authority in the Church:

> This shift in paradigms entails a shift also in the manner of conceiving the relationship between the magisterium and the other "bearers" of revelation and grace. On the classical model, these are all filtered through the magisterium, which is conceived as the *regula veritatis proxima et universalis* in distinction from the Scriptures and tradition, which are the "remote" rule of faith because they need authoritative interpretation by the "living magisterium." In *Humani generis* Pius XII gave a particularly clear expression of this view. The magisterium is "the proximate and universal norm of truth because to it Christ the Lord has entrusted the whole deposit of faith — the Scriptures and divine 'tradition' — for safeguarding, defense, and interpretation." Theologians are strongly urged to go to the inexhaustible sources of revelation; "For it is their role to point out how what the living magisterium teaches is found explicitly or implicitly, in the Scriptures and in the divine 'tradition.' " But, since it is the unique task of the magisterium "to illumine and enucleate what is contained in the deposit of faith only obscurely and implicitly," it would be a false method to attempt "to explain what is clear by what is obscure." Instead, "the noblest task of theology is to show how a doctrine defined by the Church is contained in the sources . . . in that very sense in which it has been defined by the Church."

As Bernard Sesboüe has pointed out, this theological method is a one-way street, from the magisterium to the "sources" of revelation but not back again. The magisterium illumines the Scriptures and tradition, but the obscure cannot throw light on the clear. When, in the extreme, the magisterium is thought to be *sibi fons veritatis,* the constitutive authority of the Scriptures and tradition is threatened, and the regulative function of the apostolic faith is in danger of being absorbed into or overshadowed by that of the bearers of the apostolic office.

The ecumenical sterility of his view hardly needs to
be pointed out, but this view does not even adequately
describe the concrete manner in which the Christian
message is borne from one generation to another. For,
in fact, this is accomplished through the interworking
of a whole complex of "bearers" of authority: the Scriptures, the tradition, the magisterium, the *sensus fidei,*
holy living, the liturgy, theological scholarship, etc. All
of these are community realities, and it is only within
the community of faith which they all mediate and
realize that any one of them — including both the Scriptures and the magisterium — works effectively or is accepted as an authority. They are interrelated organi-
cally and not hierarchically, and the Church's ever-
growing apprehension of the meaning of Christ's revelation derives from the distinctive and cooperative contributions of them all. No one of them is more "remote"
or more "proximate" than the others; they "mediate" one
another, in the sense that they all provide the intelligi-
ble and vital context outside of which no single one of
them can exist or function properly. None of the great
exclusive claims, then, adequately describes the concrete functioning of "authority" in the Church: not the
*sola Scriptura,* not the *soli magisterio,* not the *lex
orandi,* not the *sensus fidelium.* Authority in the
Church, like the community of faith itself, is *cir-
cumamicta    varietate.* (Joseph    A.    Komonchak,
"Humanae Vitae and Its Reception: Ecclesiological Reflections," *Theological Studies* 39, June 1978, pp. 229-
230.)

Richard A. McCormick recognizes that the important theory is
not the verbal acceptance of two magisteria in the Church, but
rather the independent competency of theology:

What theologians (and other scholars) have been
searching for is a formula which would incorporate two
things: (1) the practical admission of an independent
competence for theology and other disciplines; (2) the
admission of the indispensability of this competence for
the formation, defense, and critique of magisterial
statements. They are not interested in arrogating the

kerygmatic function of the Holy Father and the bishops. By "independent" I do not mean "in isolation from" the body of believers or the hierarchy. Theologians are first and foremost believers, members of the faithful. By "independent" competence is meant one with its own proper purpose, tools, and training. The word "practical" is used because most people would admit this in theory.

In practice, however, this is not always the case. This practical problem can manifest itself in three ways. First, theologians are selected according to a predetermined position to be proposed, what Sanks calls "co-optation." Second, moral positions are formulated against a significant theological opinion or consensus in the Church. Such opinion should lead us to conclude that the matter has not matured sufficiently to be stated by the authentic magisterium. Third, when theologians sometimes critique official formulations, that is viewed as out of order, arrogating the teaching role of the hierarchy, disloyalty, etc. Actually, it is performing one of theology's tasks. All three of these manifestations are practical denials of the independent competence of theology.

As for the third manifestation mentioned above, it ought to be said that when a particular critique becomes one shared by many competent and demonstrably loyal scholars, it is part of the public opinion in the Church, a source of new knowledge and reflection. Surely this source of new knowledge and reflection cannot be excluded from those sources we draw upon to enlighten and form our consciences; for conscience is formed *within the Church*.

An unsolicited suggestion might not be irrelevant here. Bishops should be conservative, in the best sense of that word. They should not endorse every fad, or even every theological theory. They should "conserve"; but to do so in a way that fosters faith, they must be vulnerably open and deeply involved in a process of creative and critical absorption. In some, perhaps increasingly

many, instances, they must take risks, the risks of being
tentative or even quite uncertain, and, above all, reliant
on others in a complex world. Such a process of clarification and settling takes time, patience, and courage. Its
greatest enemy is ideology, the comfort of being clear,
and, above all, the posture of pure defense of received
formulations. (Richard A. McCormick, "Notes on Moral
Theology: 1978," *Theological Studies* 40, 1979, pp. 96-
97.)

The question posed here is a very basic one. My position is clear
and supported by statements of bishops and other theologians in
the Church.

QUESTION TWO: Does there exist the possibility and even the
right of public dissent from authoritative noninfallible hierarchical teaching when a theologian is convinced there are serious
reasons to overcome the presumption of truth in favor of the teaching and judges that such an expression of public dissent will be for
the ultimate good of the Church?

The "Observations" seem to deny such a right of public dissent:
"But this suspension of assent does not provide grounds for a so-
called right of public dissent, for such public dissent would in effect
constitute an alternative magisterium contrary to the mandate of
Christ given to the Apostles and constantly exercised through the
hierarchical magisterium of the Church" (p.1).

I have explained my positions and reasons supporting the possibility and right of public dissent in chapter 5, "Public Dissent in
and for the Church," in *Dissent In and For the Church*. In the years
since that chapter was written, some Roman Catholic bishops and
other theologians have also recognized the right to public dissent
under the conditions mentioned in the phrasing of the question
and developed at further length in chapter 5.

In their collective pastoral letter of November 15, 1968, "Human
Life in Our Day," the American bishops recognized the right of public dissent and gave generic guidelines, while recognizing that
dialogue on how dissent should be expressed should be the object
of fruitful dialogue between bishops and theologians. "The expression of theological dissent from the magisterium is in order only if
the reasons are serious and well-founded, if the manner of the dis-

sent does not question or impugn the teaching authority of the Church and is such as not to give scandal." (p. 18 in the version of this letter published by the United States Catholic Conference).

Avery Dulles in commenting upon such public dissent maintains that, although the Council in its formal teaching did not advance the discussion of dissent beyond where it had been in the previous generation, Vatican II reversed the earlier positions of the Roman magisterium on a number of important issues. By its actual practice of revision, the Council implicitly taught the legitimacy and even the value of dissent. In effect the Council said that the ordinary magisterium of the Roman pontiff had fallen into error and had unjustly harmed the careers of loyal and able scholars. Some of the thinkers who had resisted official teaching in the preconciliar period were among the principal precursors and architects of Vatican II" (*The Resilient Church,* New York: Doubleday, 1976, p. 110).

To achieve the good which is involved in dissent and to avoid possible harms, Dulles gives six recommendations. The sixth one reads:

> Provided that they speak with evident loyalty and respect for authority, dissenters should not be silenced. As already noted, experience has shown that in many cases those who dissent from Church teaching in one generation are preparing the official teachings of the Church in the future. Vatican II owes many of its successes to the very theologians who were under a cloud in the pontificate of Pius XII. The Church, like civil society, should cherish its "loyal opposition" as a precious asset. (*The Resilient Church,* pp. 111-112)

*Dissent In and For the Church* lists the many individuals and groups who publicly dissented from aspects of the moral teachings of the encyclical *Humanae vitae* (pp. 202-203). William Shannon in *The Lively Debate* (New York: Sheed and Ward, 1969) devotes a chapter to "The Theologians and the Encyclical." In the period since the encyclical, many theologians have publicly dissented from some aspects of *Humanae vitae.* See Joseph A. Selling, "The Reaction to *Humanae vitae:* A Study in Special and Fundamental Theology," (STD Dissertation, Catholic University of Louvain,

1977). All three of these sources also cite numerous statements of bishops who acknowledge the possibility and right of public dissent.

In the years since the publication of *Dissent In and For the Church,* there have been many instances of moral theologians who have dissented in one way or another from the authoritative noninfallible teaching of the hierarchical magisterium; e.g., public dissent from various aspects of "Persona Humana" released by the Sacred Congregation for the Doctrine of the Faith on January 15, 1976, as illustrated in Alfons Auer *et. al.,* "Zweierlei Sexualethik," *Theologische Quartalschrift* 156 (1976), 148-158; "Document sur l'éthique sexuelle: Réactions réservées," *Informations catholiques internationales,* February 15, 1976, pp. 10-12.

Thus it seems that a vast number of contemporary Catholic theologians and bishops recognize the right of public dissent from authoritative noninfallible ordinary hierarchical teaching when there are sufficient reasons for so doing and the good of the Church demands it. A recent article summarizes much of the theory that has been proposed in the last decade or so to support that position. See Richard M. Gulla, S.S., "The Right to Private and Public Dissent from Specific Pronouncements of the Ordinary Magisterium," *Église et Theologie* 9 (1978), 319-343.

QUESTION THREE: Is *silentium obsequiosum* the only legitimate response for a theologian who is convinced that there are serious reasons which overturn the presumption in favor of the teaching of the authoritative noninfallible hierarchical magisterium? The question is quite similar to the previous one, but must be raised to see if there is any possibility other than the two alternatives mentioned in the "Observations" — the suspension of assent which is acceptable and "the so-called right of public dissent . . (which) would in effect constitute an alternative magisterium contrary to the mandate of Christ given to the Apostles and constantly exercised through the hierarchical magisterium in the Church" (p. 1). Again, this specific question is treated at length in chapter 5, "Public Dissent in and for the Church" in *Dissent In and For the Church.* It is recognized there that the manualists generally allowed *silentium obsequiosum* but nothing else. However, in the light of developments and better understandings in theology and in society in general, the right of public dissent is defended. In addition other authors are quoted in chapter 4 (pp. 116-131) in favor of the right of public dissent under the conditions mentioned earlier — S. Donlon, "Freedom of Speech," *New Catholic Encyclopedia* 6, p. 123; B. Schuller, "Bemerkunger zut authentischen Verkundigung des kirchlichen Lehramtes," *Theologie und Philosphie* 42 (1967), 534; K. Rahner, "Demokratie in der Kirche," *Stimmen der Zeit* 182 (July 1968), 1-15. Since I acknowledge the right of public dissent, *silentium obsequiosum* is not the only legitimate response for a theologian who is convinced that serious reasons exist to overturn the presumption of truth and that public dissent in this case is for the good of the Church.

Karl Rahner has addressed this specific question and concluded that *silentium obsequiosum* is not the only possible or even rightful response:

> Formerly anyone entertaining such doubts on a doctrinal decision of this kind was advised to keep silent about them even though they were, in the nature of the case, authorized. He was advised simply to be patient, and in the meantime to observe a *silentium obsequiosum*. One point to be made about this is that in contemporary society the constantly increasing communication of everyone with everyone else, reaching down into the most private spheres of human life, makes any such *silentium obsequiosum* quite impossible to maintain any longer. But quite apart from this the situation today is such that time is running out too quickly for us to be able to wait patiently in evey case until the mental attitudes of the official teachers who set the standards has changed spontaneously and without conscious thought in such a way that they themselves, without noticing it, have, of their own volition, undertaken to bring about this change of views or feel that such a change as put forward by others no longer in any sense constitutes a deviation from earlier doctrines. ("The Dispute Concerning the Church's Teaching Office," *Theological Investigations* 14, New York: The Seabury Press, 1976 p. 94.)

This third question has been treated briefly because anyone who accepts what is contained in the second question would also logically accept this. However, the question is raised to see if the "Observations" would allow only a *silentium obsequiosum* and nothing else.

QUESTION FOUR: Can the ordinary faithful prudently make a decision to act against the teaching of the ordinary authentic noninfallible hierarchical magisterium? The "Observations" on page 1 seem to say no: "The ordinary member of the faithful, lacking expertise in a particular question, could not prudently trust himself to human wisdom or theological opinion in making a decision in the face of the authentic teaching of those who 'by divine institution . . . have succeeded to the place of the Apostles as shepherds of the Church,' so 'that he who hears them hears Christ, while he who rejects them, rejects Christ and Him who sent Christ (cf. Luke 10:16)' (*Lumen gentium,* 20)." However, despite such a statement, the "Observations" still might allow the ordinary faithful the right to make such a decision if after prayer and study one is no longer lacking expertise on the particular subject and if the human wisdom and theological thought can be interpreted as mediations of the truth and of the Spirit. What is the position of the "Observations"?

*Dissent In and For the Church* clearly recognizes the right of the individual faithful after prayer and study to make a decision against the teaching of the authoritative noninfallible hierarchical magisterium when in conscience one is convinced there are serious reasons to overthrow the presumption of truth given to the official teaching. This position is buttressed in the book by citations from a number of different conferences of bishops showing that the faithful may so act. Statements are cited from the Dutch, Belgian, German, Austrian, Canadian, Swiss and Scandinavian hierarchies.

Not mentioned in the book but quite relevant is the 1967 statement of the German bishops on the Church which acknowledges the possibility of error in noninfallible Church teachings. Karl Rahner's commentary on the document is quite clear:

> Obviously, we should not overlook the point that "the conscience of the Christian needs to be guided by Christ and so by that which the Lord has entrusted with his mission." But is not this point constantly being

reitereated throughout the whole of the bishops' document itself? And is this statement of the necessity of this guidance gainsaid when the document draws the distinction it does, and points out that in particular cases the guidance, is after all, precisely a provisional one and *therefore* gives the one so guided, under certain circumstances a right and a duty, as a matter of concrete practice and not merely of abstract theory, to take such guidance for what it is and for what it is intended to be and nothing more, namely as provisional? (Karl Rahner, "The Dispute Concerning the Church's Teaching Office," *Theological Investigations* 14, pp. 95-96)

A task force of the Catholic Theological Society of America clearly recognizes the right of the ordinary faithful to make such a decision against an authoritative hierarchical teaching when the conditions mentioned above have been fulfilled:

Following these developments within the Church, it may safely be stated that moral decision makers affected by the new U.S. *Directives* — principally patients and physicians, but not excluding administrative and medical staff, as well as ethical advisors of the foregoing (clergy and chaplains, for example) — may, in individual cases and on moral grounds, licitly act contrary to the concrete (and hence non-infallible) ethical directives, provided: a) the decision is seriously arrived at in good conscience after careful reflection; b) respectful and openminded attention is paid to the authoritative teaching of the hierarchy, as well as other sources of moral wisdom, in the light of the Gospel; c) no undue harm is done to the life, well-being or rights of a third party; and d) scandal is avoided. This last condition means that precautions must be taken to prevent this exception from causing more harm than good, so as not to significantly and unnecessarily hinder the community role of the Catholic health facility and the moral welfare of others. ("Catholic Hospital Ethics: The Report of the Commission on Ethical and Religious Directives for Catholic Hospitals Commissioned by the Board of Directors of The Catholic Theological Society of

America," *Proceedings of the Twenty-Seventh Annual
Convention of the Catholic Theological Society of
America,* 1972, p. 266)

Consequently my position and that of some bishops and other
theologians clearly recognizes that an ordinary member of the
faithful can at times under the conditions mentioned prudently
make a decision against the presumed truth of the ordinary teaching of the magisterium. Again, it is not clear what is the position
taken in the "Observations."

QUESTION FIVE. In the course of history have there been errors in the teaching of the ordinary noninfallible magisterium
which have been subsequently corrected, often because of the dissent of theologians? An affirmative response is given and illustrated in *Dissent In and For the Church,* pp. 66-87. The same point
has been made by most of the authors who have been mentioned
thus far in this response.

It was necessary to pose these five questions because of the lack
of precision on the first page of the "Observations" sent to me. I believe that my answers to these questions are totally in accord with
Catholic faith and Catholic theology as expressed also by many
other contemporaries. My writings on the ordinary noninfallible
hierarchical magisterium are not contrary to the teaching of the
Church. In fact, I was commissioned by the editors to write the article on "The Theology of Dissent" for *The New Catholic Encyclopedia: Supplement 1967-1974,* 16, 127-129.

What my answers to these five questions have in common is a
contemporary and at the same time traditional understanding of
the ordinary noninfallible magisterium. The bishops and the
theologians cited previously (e.g. Coffy, Butler, Congar, Dulles,
Komonchak, McCormick, Rahner, Schüller) recognize that there
has been a shift in our understanding of the ordinary hierarchical
magisterium away from the Roman school of the nineteenth century with its neoscholastic categories, its juridical perspective, and
its insistence on the total subordination of theology to the hierarchical magisterium. With these and other authors my position recognizes the existence of many different ways of mediating Church
teaching throughout history and incorporates many of the theological positions proposed in the Second Vatican Council. According

to Congar, these newer approaches recognize the onesidedness in the historical development from the nineteenth century, reaching its zenith under Pius XII, according to which the *quo* (the formal pastoral authority) took absolute precedence over the *quod* (the Word of God itself).

### III. *Response to the Citations on Pages 2-4*

In the light of these five questions and my answers to them, it is now possible to respond more briefly to the citations taken from my writings and to the understanding of them proposed in the "Observations."

The first citation on page 2 of the "Observations" is taken from *Ongoing Revision in Moral Theology* pp. 64-65, and is interpreted to mean that there "can be no secure teaching of morality by the authentic magisterium." In reality this citation is dealing with the authoritative noninfallible hierarchical magisterium on specific issues, and says nothing more or less than what was said by the German bishops in 1967:

> The Church too in her doctrine and practice cannot always and in every case allow herself to be caught in the dilemma of either arriving at a doctrinal decision which is ultimately binding or simply being silent and leaving everything to the free opinion of the individual. In order to maintain the true and ultimate substance of faith she must, even at the risk of error in points of detail, give expression to doctrinal directives which have a certain degree of binding force and yet, since they are not *de fide* definitions, involve a certain element of the provisional even to the point of being capable of including error. (This statement is quoted by Rahner, *Theological Investigations* 14, p. 86.)

The second citation, taken from "Ten Years Later," *Commonweal*, July 1978, p. 427, is understood to move "immediately from the *possibility* of error by the noninfallible magisterium to the justification of his theory of dissent and of a plurality of (supposedly equivalent) magisteria." Note that the citation leaves out a very important sentence attributing the last sentence in your citation not to me but to Daniel Maguire. In the same way the follow-

ing sentences cite Yves Congar as their source. As mentioned in response to Question One, I have generally avoided the terminology
of two or more magisteria, even though outstanding theologians
such as Maguire, Dulles, and McCormick use the term. In the citation given I am performing the theological task of seeking intelligi-
bility. I am starting out with the fact of the possibility of error in
such teachings and trying to find the ultimate reason for such a
fact. The reason is found, to use the words of Question One above,
in the fact that the teaching of the ordinary noninfallible magisterium does not constitute the only factor or the always decisive
factor in the total magisterial activity of the Church. Statements
from both bishops and theologians support both the possibility of
error and the reasons given to explain it.

According to your understanding of the third citation on page 2
of "Observations" taken from *Ongoing Revision* page 47: "with regard to the prophetic office in the Church, Curran fails to recognize
the decisive role of the bishops in discerning the truth of Catholic
doctrine." The quotation here must be understood in relation to
Question One and Question Five. As mentioned in response to the
previous citation, we are not dealing with questions of *de fide* definitions but questions dealing with the ordinary noninfallible
magisterium. Such a magisterium does not constitute the only factor or the always decisive factor in the total magisterial activity of
the Church.

In Question Five I proposed and defended the thesis that statements of the ordinary magisterium have been wrong and have
been later corrected at least in part because of public dissent by
theologians. Note again that while admitting this, I also constantly
insist on the need to give due weight to the teaching of the hierarchical magisterium.

The first half of page 3 of the "Observations" claims that Curran
"appeals to a mistaken concept of pluralism in Catholic theology
and practice to justify dissent, not only private but even public." In
the context of all my writings, I have justified the possibility of dissent and public dissent for the reasons developed in the five questions above. It is a misunderstanding of my position to say that "he
fails to recognize that pluralism in moral theology classically involved disputes among theologians and not between the theologian
and the magisterium."

First, in the citations given in the "Observations," I am responding to a critic who claimed that contradictory pluralism harms the Church because it diminishes the support of a secular observer who will not pay attention to a group who cannot speak out authoritatively and with one voice on important matters. My point is that on many important matters (e.g. the approach to the social order as seen in the differences between a Dorothy Day and a William Buckley or between a Generalissimo Franco and a President Julius Nyererre) the Church does not and cannot speak with one voice. Second, I am here trying to explain why the teachings of the ordinary noninfallible hierarchical magisterium, in the words of the German bishops, "involve a certain amount of the provisional even to the point of being capable of including error." As a theologian seeking the reason for this, I find a partial explanation in terms of an epistemology (which is also the epistemology of Thomas Aquinas) which recognizes that on specific complex issues one cannot attain the degree of certitude that excludes all possibility of error.

The final citations on pages 3 and 4 do not "promote" public dissent but justify the right which has been discussed under Question Two.

## IV. *Concluding Remarks*

I have devoted much time and effort to this response because of the importance I attached to it. I must repeat that the format employed in the "Observations" together with the ambiguous nature of the remarks has not produced a good environment for theological discussion. However, on the basis of the five questions or theses which I have proposed and defended there is ground for a better type of discussion which will avoid the dangers of merely hurling citations at one another. According to the "Observations," the question of the hierarchical magisterium is the "fundamental observation" and the "fundamental flaw." I have thus concentrated my efforts on responding to this question. After we have been able to come to an understanding on this, then the other problems should fall into place. I have tried to show from my own writings and those of some bishops and of other theologians that my position on the hierarchical magisterium is truly Catholic and contains nothing opposed to Catholic faith.

The necessary emphasis in this response has been to defend the right of dissent and of public dissent. However, to speak only about this would distort my position. Invariably in discussing these questions, I point out the opposite danger of a false subjectivism and the omnipresent problem of self-deception. Anyone writing in the area of moral theology today must be aware of the false individualism that too easily pervades not only what is done in our society but also what is thought. Over ten years ago, I insisted, in talking about dissent, that "nowhere in these pages is an appeal made to an argument based on the general principle of the freedom of conscience" (*Contraception: Authority and Dissent,* New York: Herder and Herder, 1969, p. 11).

In my latest, most systematic treatment of conscience, I emphasize the need for authentic subjectivity and point out the abuses that have been committed in the name of conscience. Specifically the danger of abuse comes from a twofold source — our finitude and our sinfulness. One needs to be aware of these dangers and try to avoid them. The community of the Church, even from a purely ethical viewpoint prescinding from the God-given teaching function of the Church, has a very important role because the Church is able to strive to overcome the two-fold danger of finitude and sinfulness through its extension in time and space and through the presence of the Spirit. Thus even a purely ethical analysis insists on the importance of the teaching function of the Church as a help against a false individualism and selfishness which ultimately have their roots in human finitude and sinfulness. (*Themes in Fundamental Moral Theology,* pp. 220-226)

Throughout my writings I have pointed out the importance of avoiding oversimplistic solutions.

> Such dissent does not merely reduce the role of the papal teaching office to that of another theologian in the Church. Such dissent does not involve disrespect for the papal teaching office. No Catholic faithful or theologian can lightly dismiss the authoritative teaching of the papal or hierarchical teaching office in the Church. Great respect is due to such teaching. However, this does not mean that the teaching itself is always correct. The papal and hierarchical teaching offices must be seen in the whole context of a theology of the Church. A

good theological analysis will avoid the two simplistic extremes: either saying that a loyal Catholic can never dissent from the authoritative, noninfallible magisterium or maintaining that the Pope is just another theologian in the Church. (*Contraception: Authority and Dissent,* pp. 9-10)

Both in the words themselves and in the nuances employed, my writings have always showed a respect for the ordinary hierarchical teaching office in the Church. Frequently there are many comments, as indicated even in some of the citations in the "Observations," which refer to the "God-given role of the hierarchical teaching office" and the "due weight" which must be given to such teaching.

The very title of the major systematic work — *Dissent In and For the Church* — underscores that in my judgment the fact of public dissent is in no way a rebellion against Church teaching but rather is a form of critical loyalty. As a result of such an understanding of the role of dissent in the Roman Catholic Church, the teaching authority of the hierarchical magisterium will become more credible to believers in our modern world.

# II
# INTERVENING
# CORRESPONDENCE
# (March 1980-March 1982)

March 20, 1980.    Seper to Curran responding to some questions raised by Curran in his reply of October 26, 1979.

February 21, 1981.  Cover letter of James A. Hickey, Archbishop of Washington and Chancellor of the Catholic University of America, to Curran, sending the Seper letter.

February 9, 1981.   Seper informs Curran that after an examination of *Dissent in and for the Church* the "Observations" remain pertinent and asks for the response to the rest of the "Observavations."

May 21, 1981.     Curran to Seper expressing puzzlement over the fact that the congregation took fifteen months to reply and never entered into dialogue with Curran's first response.

June 9, 1981.     Seper responds to Curran and asks for the response to the second part of the "Observations."

January 8, 1982.   Hickey to Curran relaying Seper's request for the rest of Curran's response.

March 3, 1982.    Curran responds to Hickey expressing his difficulties with the congregation's procedures including its very long delay.

SACRA CONGREGATIO
PRO DOCTRINA FIDEI
Roma,
Piazza del S. Uffizio, 11
March 20, 1980
Prot. N. 48/66

Dear Father Curran,

With this letter I want to give a preliminary reply to your letter of October 26, 1979, with which you enclosed your Response to the Observations previously sent to you by this Congregation. This Response is under study at the present time.

1) In your preliminary remarks in this Response, you criticize the procedures of this Congregation as found in the "Nova agendi Ratio in Doctrinarum Examine" (AAS 63, 1971, pp. 234-236) as being "seriously flawed in terms of their protection of the rights of the individual involved" insofar as they "fail to incorporate the elementary principles of due process which are accepted in contemporary legal structures." Your objection seems to presuppose the model of a court trial when you suggest that "one has basic rights to know who are the accusers, what precisely are the charges, and to have representation by an advocate of one's own choosing."

The Congregation's "Ratio agendi" is not a trial but rather a procedure designed to guarantee a careful and accurate examination of the content of published writings by an author. Should this examination indicate the presence of opinions which seem to be in conflict with Church teaching, the author himself is contacted in order to give him an opportunity to explain how he sees his opinion(s) to be in accord with the teaching of the Church, in the hope that a satisfactory explanation may be forthcoming or, failing that, that appropriate correction may be made. There are hence no "accusers," only public writings; no "charges," only the results of a careful examination which are offered with a request for clarification or correction; the "representation" is furnished by the author himself, in writing and/or in person, and privately as a protection for the reputation of the person involved.

2) In your letter of August 29, and again in your formal Response of October 26, you objected to the April 24, 1979, letter of Arch-

bishop Hamer to Bishop Joseph Sullivan of Baton Rouge, in which you consider yourself "publicly judged and condemned." This letter to Bishop Sullivan, written to thank him for his clear explanation of his reasons for taking a pastoral decision in your regard, may be considered a normal adminstrative procedure. It was not given any publicity by this office, and does not affect the procedures being applied in accord with the "Ratio agendi."

3) In your formal Response you posed five questions which focus on the "fundamental observation" about your "misconception of the specific competence of the authentic magisterium of the Church in matters *de fide et moribus*." In your discussion of these questions you frequently cite the position developed in *Dissent in and for the Church,* a book written by you in collaboration with Robert Hunt and others.

Because of its joint authorship, the Congregation had not made this book the object of its examination. At your suggestion, this examination is now under way. The time required for this process will help to explain the necessary delay in providing you with our further reply to your Response.

Finally, please be assured that the Apostolic Delegation has informed this Congregation of the circumstances which prompted you to make a public statement in order to clarify press reports containing misinformation about your contacts with this Congregation.

Sincerely yours in Christ,
Franjo Cardinal Seper, Prefect


ARCHDIOCESE OF WASHINGTON
1721 Rhode Island Avenue, N.W.
Washington, D.C. 20036

OFFICE OF THE
ARCHBISHOP
February 21, 1981

Rev. Charles Curran
The Catholic University of America
Washington, D.C.

Dear Father Curran,

Cardinal Seper asked that the enclosed letter be forwarded to you through me; at the same time he asked me to review its contents.

You can readily understand that I am not party to prior discussion of this matter. But I really want to be of help, — to yourself and to the Holy See in clarifying and resolving the discussion.

While the letter of February 9th evidently calls for a response, or more precisely the completion of your previous response, and that directly to His Eminence, be assured that I am open to offering whatever assistance I can.

Assuring you of my prayers for you and asking yours for me, I am

In Christ,
James A. Hickey
Archbishop of Washington


SACRA CONGREGATIO
PRO DOCTRINA FIDEI
Roma,
Piazza del S. Uffizio, 11
Prot. N. 48/66

February 9, 1981

Dear Father Curran,

In its letter of March 20, 1980, the Congregation sent you a preliminary reply to your "Response" to the "Observations" previously forwarded to you, in accord with the procedure "Nova agendi ratio in doctrinarum examine." As noted in this letter, the Congregation had not included the book *Dissent in and for the Church* among the writings examined because of its joint authorship. Because you appealed to the arguments contained in this book in your "Response" to the first major consideration contained in the "Observations," you were informed that the Congregation was proceeding with an examination of this book.

It is now my duty to communicate the following points in regard to the examination of your theological writings:

1) after studying the book *Dissent in and for the Church,* the Congregation does not find in it new elements previously not considered which would serve to modify the doctrinal character of the "Observations";

2) hence the "Observations" remain pertinent, as formulated and with the significance attached to each point therein;

3) you are therefore cordially invited to complete your "Response," addressing each of the points of the "Observations" in turn, and giving careful attention to the precise meaning of and particular aspects treated in the "Observations" previously sent to you. This complete "Response" is required in order to permit the Congregation to arrive at a comprehensive vision of your actual theological opinions in the matters under examination.

Sincerely yours in Christ,
Franjo Cardinal Seper, Prefect

The
CATHOLIC UNIVERSITY
of America
Washington, D.C. 20064

May 21, 1981

His Eminence
Franjo Cardinal Seper
Praefectus, Sacra Congregatio pro Doctrina Fidei
Piazza del S. Uffizio, 11
00193 Rome

Dear Cardinal Seper,

I am responding to your letter dated February 9, 1981, with the protocol number 48/66.

Now that our semester has ended, I want to share with you my first reaction to your letter. My primary reaction is puzzlement.

First, I am puzzled because of the fifteen month delay in your responding to me. I never claimed that the positions taken in the book *Dissent In and For the Church* were different from those positions in my other writings. I only pointed out the incongruity and poor methodology in judging someone's writings without going to the place in which they were most systematically developed. My response itself indicated that I saw no substantial differences between that book and my other writings.

Second, I am puzzled by the fact that you have not responded to my response. I was quite serious in mentioning that your "Observations" as sent to me were insufficient in terms of dialogue and unjust in terms of not being specific. Consequently, I took upon myself the burden of focusing the dialogue so that it would be both more effective and more just. However, you apparently have paid no attention to this.

Third, I am puzzled by your apparent unwillingness to recognize the fact that the positions that I have taken on these questions have been proposed and maintained by many other moral theologians throughout the world.

Thank you for your kind consideration.

Sincerely yours in Christ,
Charles E. Curran

SACRA CONGREGATIO
PRO DOCTRINA FIDEI
Roma,
Piazza del S. Uffizio, 11
Prot. N. 48/66

June 9, 1981

Dear Father Curran,

The Congregation for the Doctrine of the Faith has received your letter of May 21, and has noted your initial reaction of puzzlement which you wanted to share with us. Such a reaction on your part was neither intended nor foreseen by the Congregation.

For this reason, I want to give you a further explanation of our letter of February 9, which I hope will be helpful in clarifying the puzzlement you have experienced. In July of 1979, the Congregation sent you detailed "Observations" with ample citations from your own writings by way of illustration of positions you have espoused which cause difficulty, and invited your response (cfr. n. 13 of our procedure "Ratio agendi. . .").

In October of the same year you forwarded a detailed response, discussing and defending your position on the question of the specific competence of the authentic magisterium of the Church in matters *de fide vel moribus*. It is clear that, as you informed us, you spent much time and effort in preparing this response. The response you sent has by no means been ignored or discounted; it does remain incomplete from the procedural point of view, however.

We have noted your opinion that, "after we have been able to come to an understanding on this (fundamental observation about the authentic magisterium), then the other problems should fall into place." Our procedure, however, requires an examination of and judgment upon the author's complete response to the points indicated to him (cfr. n. 15 sq. of "Ratio agendi"). For this reason, we asked you to complete your response, addressing each of the points of the "Observations" in turn, and giving careful attention to the precise meaning of and particular aspects treated in the "Observations" previously sent to you.

On the other hand, your perception that the "Observations" were "insufficient in terms of dialogue and unjust in terms of not being specific" is not one with which the Congregation can agree. It is our perception that the "Observations" provide sufficient elements of a specific nature about the theological opinions which you have publicly espoused to permit you to prepare a suitable response to them.

With cordial regards, I am

Sincerely yours in Christ,
Franjo Cardinal Seper, Prefect

ARCHDIOCESE OF WASHINGTON
1721 Rhode Island Avenue, N.W.
Washington, D.C. 20036

OFFICE OF THE
ARCHBISHOP

48/66

January 8, 1982

Rev. Charles Curran, S.T.D.
The Catholic University of America
Washington, D.C.

Dear Father Curran,

Recently I have beeen requested by the Sacred Congregation for the Doctrine of the Faith to inquire when it may expect your response to their last letter (of June 9th) and by reason of its content, your further response to their inquiry of February 9th, 1981.

As I understand it, the Congregation is anxious to have a response to all the points mentioned in its "observationes," i.e., over and above your response to the question treating the specific competence of the authentic magisterium of the Church in matters *de fide vel moribus.*

I urge you to answer their request at the earliest opportunity so that the dialogue between yourself and the Sacred Congregation my continue. I realize that such dialogue, especially when it is conducted in writing, takes much time. It will be well worth the effort involved if the several points under discussion can be resolved to the mutual satisfaction of the Holy See and of yourself. Please let me know if I can be of assistance.

Be assured of my prayers for you in this New Year of 1982.

Sincerely in Christ,
James A. Hickey
Archbishop of Washington

The
CATHOLIC UNIVERSITY
of America
Washington, D.C. 20064


March 3, 1982


The Most Reverend James A. Hickey, D.D.
Archbishop of Washington
1721 Rhode Island Avenue, N.W.
Washington, D.C. 20036


Dear Archbishop Hickey:

I apologize for not having responded earlier to your letter of January 8. I have delayed in the hope that I could give you and the Congregation for the Doctrine of the Faith a definite date to expect my response to their letter of February 9, 1981. Unfortunately, this has been a very busy semester for me with my duties here at the University and my research and writing commitments. The University of Notre Dame Press is scheduled to publish two of my books this spring. The first is on schedule and set for publication at the end of the month. The galley proofs for the second were due over a month ago, but have not arrived. When they come, I will have to work on the corrections and the index. In the light of these and other uncertainties, I cannot give you a definite date at this time.

Let me be very frank. I have many problems and difficulties with the way in which this whole matter has been conducted. I have expressed my opinion many times to the Congregation that their whole process is basically unfair. Many authors have made the same point in their public writings. In addition, a letter from the Congregation made public in this country did great injustice to me. I have been advised by Roman canonists that on the basis of that letter I should appeal the whole procedure to the Apostolic Signatura. However, I do not intend to do so at this time. As I tried to demonstrate in my first response, my positions on these questions are not all that different from the positions being maintained by many other moral theologians throughout the world. The Congregation itself must be aware of that fact.

On October 26, 1979, I sent a detailed well-researched, twenty-one page response concentrating on what the Congregation termed "the fundamental observation" in the observations that were sent to me.

I received a reply from them almost sixteen months later. The gist of the reply was that I should now respond to the other points that were made in the observations. There was no mention made of their reaction to the work that I had prepared and sent them. I was appalled by this procedure. It took them sixteen months to write back to tell me that I now have to finish the response. They could have written that same thing sixteen months before. What is any fair-minded person to conclude from this way of operating?

However, I am a person of my word. Despite all the difficulties I have with this procedure, I have promised to reply. I will reply. However, I also have to fulfill my other duties and responsibilities.

I trust that you will send a copy of this letter to the Congregation.

Sincerely yours,
Charles E. Curran

# III
# CURRAN'S RESPONSE TO
# THE SPECIFIC ISSUES
# (1982)

June 21, 1982.  Curran responds with 23 pages to the specific issues in the "Observations."

July 16, 1982.  Hamer acknowledges receipt of Curran's reply.

The
CATHOLIC UNIVERSITY
of America
Washington, D.C. 20064

June 21, 1982

His Eminence
Joseph Cardinal Ratzinger
Praefectus, Sacra Congregatio pro Doctrina Fidei
Piazza del S. Uffizio, 11
00193 Rome

Dear Cardinal Ratzinger:

Enclosed you will find my second response to the "Observations" that were sent to me. In my latest communication I informed you that I would respond when the school year ended and when I had finished the preparations for the publication of two new books from the University of Notre Dame Press. Fortunately, I have been able to devote the last month to the final preparation of this response.

Sincerely yours in Christ,
Charles E. Curran

CEC:bp
Re: Prot. No. 48/66

## SECOND RESPONSE

To the "Observations" of the
Sacred Congregation for the Doctrine of the Faith
on Some Writings of Father Charles E. Curran
(Prot. N. 48/66)

This response will address in order the list of "the more important errors and ambiguities found in these writings of Father Curran" ("Observations," pp. 4f.). My response will be in the context of the "Preliminary Remarks" and the substance of my response of October 26, 1979, to what was described as "the fundamental flaw" in my writing.

The first observation (p. 4) concerns the presentation of the theory of fundamental option. I am accused of giving "an ambiguous presentation of the notion of fundamental option emphasizing that a single, personal act will not normally be able to be called a mortal sin." Does Curran "affirm the Catholic tradition that permits a judgment about whether or not a particular act has been mortally sinful"?

The two citations quoted in the "Observations" are not taken from the place in which I have most fully developed my position — chapter six of *Themes in Fundamental Moral Theology*. I stand by the quotations given, but any attempt to study my position on the question must deal with my most systematic and in depth development of the matter.

The judgment made in the first comment about my writings is not accurate. Nowhere do you cite my saying that a "single, *personal* act will not normally be able to be called a mortal sin" (emphasis added). I am careful to use the word *external* act and not *personal* act. The external act is distinguished from a core, or fully, personal act.

My position on fundamental option is basically in agreement with the positions proposed by many contemporary Roman Catholic moral theologians. By definition a mortal sin involves a fundamental option. In the citation given on page five of the "Observations," I expressly reject the position that says mortal sin consists only in a formal refusal directly opposed to God's call and not in particular human acts. There can be no fundamental option apart from individual, particular acts. However, on the basis of the external act alone, one cannot know whether or not a fundamental option or mortal sin is involved. Those who propose the theory of fundamental option are also quick to point out that mortal sin in this understanding will be a less frequent occurrence than in the older manualistic approach.

Joseph Fuchs distinguishes between the level of basic freedom and the level of categorical freedom — a distinction which is derived from the difference between the transcendental and the categorical aspects of the act, between what is core and what is peripheral to the human person.

> The love that commits a person as a whole is not a specific act of love distinct from other specific moral acts, but a transcendental self-commitment in basic freedom that is realized and demonstrated in particular, specific acts of free choice.

> Obviously there exists in moral life an interdependence between basic freedom and freedom of choice. Above all, morality in the true and full sense only exists, as we have said, where our freedom, as basic freedom and freedom of choice, simultaneously determines our action. The basic freedom of personal self-commitment in basic freedom are not moral in a real and full sense, but only by analogy. For not every act of free choice necessarily corresponds to the self-commitment of the person — even when the moral quality of the act is recognized and its commission freely willed. A lie, recognized in its sinfulness, considered and freely willed, does not usually determine a self-commitment of opposition to God in basic freedom; for the intrinsic opposition to God of the lie, the No before God, which is always grave in itself, is in practice usually not sufficiently evaluated and is therefore not personally realized as such. An exceedingly large gift of alms by a sinner, made in full knowledge and freedom will very often express the beginning of change in him, often too, but by no means necessarily and always, true conversion in basic freedom from sinner to lover. Thus both the materially costly act of alms given and the materially light act of lying remain, seen in personal terms, "light," "superficial" acts, moral acts only by analogy because the self-commitment of the person in basic freedom does not enter into them. Many of our daily good or bad deeds do not involve the self-commitment of the person as a whole in basic freedom and are therefore — as acts only of free choice — merely "light" moral acts, acts peformed at the surface level of the person, moral acts by analogy (Joseph Fuchs, *Human Values and Christian Morality,* Dublin: Gill & Macmillan, 1970, pp. 100-103).

Bernard Häring makes the same general point about mortal sin as involving a fundamental option which is not necessarily present in every human act.

> Not every human act and action expresses the person in his totality. Mortal sin is a fundamental option that happens only where a sinful decision arises from the depth of consciousness and freedom or reaches into that depth and thus reveals the person's fully accountable misuse of the liberty. In the fundamental option, a person expresses and determines himself in his basic existence.

> This approach in no way negates the importance of the object of the act or the gravity of the matter; but gravity or relevance assumes moral meaning only in proportion to the actual development of a person's knowledge and freedom, and to the extent that the deep self-determination that we call fundamental option can be evoked (Bernard Häring, *Free and Faithful in Christ: Moral Theology for Clergy and Laity,* Vol. I, New York: The Seabury Press, 1978, p. 212).

Häring also recognizes that the reality of mortal sin is ordinarily the culmination of a process involving many imperfect actions.

> Such a reversal of the basic commitment from God to idols, from genuine love to an inverted self-love, is a weighty act. Normally, the way is prepared by many imperfections and venial sins, acts that do not fully respond to God's grace and failures to do the good that is within one's reach. Venial sins, which can be less or more grave, may first weaken some of the important virtues or fundamental attitudes, but they also indirectly weaken the rootedness of the fundamental option. (Häring, p. 213)

Sean Fagan also recognizes the difficulty of making a judgment as to whether or not a fundamental option has occurred.

> Christian realism demands that we accept this uncertainty and learn to live with it. This applies not only to

our basic option, but even to individual sin-actions. Such is the basic imperfection of our human nature, the influence of sub-consciousness factors, the weight of external pressures from the sinful world around us, and the gradual and groping development of our freedom and moral insight, that we can seldom be sure that a particular action is central, that it flows from the core of our personality and the depth of our conscience. (Sean Fagan, *Has Sin Changed?* Wilmington, DE: Michael Glazer, Inc., 1977, pp. 76-77).

The citation quoted from me on page five of the "Observations" explicitly says that "the external act involves mortal sin only if it signifies and expresses the breaking of the fundamental relationship of love with God." Also, "one can never know just from the external act alone whether or not mortal sin is present." All would have to admit that this is totally in keeping with the Catholic theological tradition. The manuals of theology, as well as the catechism, constantly emphasize the fact that three conditions are necessary for mortal sin — grave matter, full consent and full knowledge. Consequently, even in the light of the traditional Catholic teaching, one can never know just from the external act alone whether or not mortal sin is present. I have made this point very explicitly in *Themes in Fundamental Moral Theology* on page 154. In the light of this, I do not know what "Catholic tradition" is being referred to in the comment on the top of page five of the "observations" as being in opposition with what I say about the judgment of the external act.

In my systematic presentation of sin in the light of the theory of the fundamental option, I have been very conscious that "In the newer perspective there is the danger of not giving enough importance to the external act itself." I go on to say that, "Catholic theology in the last decade has embraced the more personalist categories of thought, but there is an inherent danger that such thought patterns will not pay enough attention to the social, political and cosmic aspects of reality" (*Themes in Fundamental Moral Theology,* p. 156). This latter warning is consistent with my fear that some transcendental approaches do not give enough importance to the social and political aspects of morality (*Themes in Fundamental Moral Theology,* p. 216). Thus I go out of my way to point out the danger in some approaches of not giving enough importance to external actions. It is for this reason that I emphasize the relationality model and the need to see all morality, including sin, in terms of the multiple relationships that the individual Christian has with God, neighbor, self and world.

In addition, in my systematic development of sin and mortal sin in the light of the theory of fundamental option, I also point out that "the contemporay Catholic is at times tempted to forget the whole concept of sin. . . . The perennial danger is to be lulled into forgetting the existence of sin. Then one's whole life and one's Christianity can become very comfortable. Is this not the problem with much of what passes for Christianity today?" *(Themes in Fundamental Moral Theology,* p. 160). This emphasis on sin is connected with the stance which I have proposed for moral theology which specifically includes the reality of sin *(New Perspectives in Moral Theology,* pp. 65-75).

Observation two maintains that through "Curran's theory of compromise the objective moral order is so affected by sin that the Christian is no longer held to its full observance."

The major problem centers on what is the objective moral order. This is the precise problem which is debated at length in many recent contributions to moral theology in the light of the theory of ethical compromise (Ferdinando Citterio, "La revisione critica dei tradizionali principi morali alla luce della teoria del'compromesso ethico," *La Scuola Cattolica,* 110, 1982, 29-64). The author is opposed to these revisions, but this survey indicates the great number of contemporary moral theologians who hold positions on the objective moral order that are similar to my own and differ from what is found in the manuals of theology.

My own theology of compromise is much narrower than many of those proposed under this same rubric by Citterio. I limit the theory of compromise to those situations in which the reality of sin enters into the objective order. This position is consistent both with my stance for moral theology and with my insistence on the presence of sin.

The first logical consideration in moral theology is the question of stance, posture, or horizon. In my judgment this stance or horizon is the way in which the Christian experiences the world in terms of the fivefold Christian mysteries of creation, sin, incarnation, redemption, and resurrection destiny. This experience, based on objective reality, is falsified if one or more elements are missing. Theories in moral theology are deficient if they fail to incorporate all these aspects. I have pointed out the failure in both some Protestant and Catholic understandings to give enough importance to the reality of sin (*New Perspectives in Moral Theology,* pp. 47-86).

In later writings I have attempted to show that the theology of compromise is in keeping with Catholic theological tradition — sin affects objective reality and because of sin certain actions are justified which would not be justified without the presence of sin. The Fathers of the Church recognized a relativity about natural law, for the material demands of natural law differ in the various situations in the history of salvation. Secondary natural law comes about because of the transforming significance of the invasion of sin into human history.

> Examples of secondary, relative natural law abound. Human society, family, marriage, and the state all belong to the absolute natural law. They are part of human existence as such. However, there are certain characteristics of these realities which exist only in the history of salvation after sin. The state in the present condition involves coercion, but this does not belong to the absolute natural law, for sin makes it necessary. Killing in self-defense, just war, capital punishment, revolution and the toleration of evil in society are all examples of relative natural law recognizing the presence of sin. Specific institutions such as slavery and private property are thus called into existence because of the situation of sin in the world. Before the fall there would have been no place for slavery or for private property. The historical situation after the fall brought about certain applications of the absolute natural law in the light of the presence of sin in the world. Fuchs reminded Catholic theology about this approach in its own tradition (*Transition and Tradition in Moral Theology,* pp. 74-75).

My theology of compromise is grounded on this understanding accepted by the Fathers of the Church and on the contemporary emphasis on the sin of the world. I build on the patristic theory by recognizing that sin can be present in particular situations and affect the objective moral order in those situations. My first discussion of the theology of compromise used the illustration of sin-filled situations which Christians experience in connection with war, concentration camps, and resistance movements (*A New Look at Christian Morality*, p. 171). My position thus maintains that sin is present in our world and affects the objective moral order. Certain actions can be justified in the presence of sin which are not justified without the presence of sin. In these conditions, God's will is not the same as it is when sin is not present.

Such a position not only has roots in the Catholic tradition but also a neo-Thomist philosopher such as Jacques Maritain has recognized its basic reality.

> The answer obliges us to face a most difficult problem in moral life and that sad law, which I previously pointed out, according to which the application of moral rules immutable in themselves takes lower and lower forms as the social environment declines. The moral law must never be given up, we must fasten on to it all the more as the social and political environment becomes more perverted or criminal. But the moral nature of specification, the moral object of the same physical acts, changes when the situation to which they pertain becomes so different that the inner relation of the will to the thing done becomes itself typically different. In our civilized societies it is not a murder, it is a meritorious deed for a fighting man to kill an enemy soldier in a just war. In utterly barbarized societies like a concentration camp, or even in quite particular conditions like those of clandestine resistance in an occupied country, many things which were, as to their moral nature, objectively flawed or murder or perfidy in ordinary civilized life cease, now, to come under the same definition and become, as to their moral nature, objectively permissible or ethical things (Jacques Maritain, *Man and the State*, Chicago: The University of Chicago Press, 1956, p. 73).

The third observation maintains that Curran mistakenly accuses St. Thomas Aquinas and the Catholic moral teaching of physicalism. Such an approach denies the existence of moral absolutes and appeals to personalism to justify a departure from objective moral truth.

I do employ the term physicalism to describe some of the Thomistic and manualistic teaching. The problem is whether or not such a position is mistaken. My appeal to personalism does not justify a departure from objective moral truth but is an attempt to understand what is objective moral truth. Note that whereas the observation broadly accuses me of denying "that one can arrive at a clear understanding of absolutes," my own position, even as found in the citation given on page seven of the "Observations," is much more nuanced — I "deny the existence of negative moral absolutes; that is, actions described solely in terms of the physical structure of the act."

I believe my arguments on the existence of physicalism are convincing, but there is no sense of repeating them again. Here I will only point out that many other other contemporary Catholic moral theologians accept my description of physicalism or what I sometimes have called biologism.

Ronald Modras interprets Karol Wojtyla as making a similar theoretical judgment by calling for a more personalist approach and criticizing the understanding of the person as a biological organism.

> In looking to the ultimate aim of human behavior and taking nature as a point of departure, Thomism viewed the human person along the lines of a biological organism in which everything is explained in terms of "maturing," achieving one's goal. Such a view "is not enough for us anymore," maintains Wojtyla. Moral theology needs to assume a personalist character and seek to establish the basis for moral norms (Ronald Modaras, "The Thomistic Personalism of Pope John Paul II, *The Modern Schoolman* 59, 1982, 126).

In reaction to *Humanae vitae* many Catholic theologians also objected to the physicalism and biologism found in the reasoning of the encyclical. Bernard Häring strongly criticizes the encyclical's insistence on the observation of biological and physical laws.

*Humanae vitae* confines the procreative meaning of the
marital act to the faithful observance of biological laws
and rhythms. It implied therein that God's wise and divine plan is revealed to the spouses through these absolutely sacred physiological laws. This is undoubtedly
the philosophy underpinning the argumentation of the
whole encyclical. It goes so far as to declare biological
laws as absolutely binding on the conscience of men
(Bernard Häring, "The Inseparability of the Unitive-
Procreative Functions of the Marital Act," in *Contraception: Authority and Dissent,* ed. Charles E. Curran, New
York: Herder & Herder, 1969, p. 180).

Ph. Delhaye points out significant differences between the approach of *Gaudium et spes* to marriage and the approach taken in
*Humanae vitae.* Delhaye maintains that the teaching of *Humane
vitae* employs the criterion of nature understood in a biological
sense as opposed to a personalist criterion of intersubjectivity (Ph.
Delhaye "L'encyclique Humane Vitae et l'enseignement de Vatican II sur le Mariage et la Famille, *Gaudium et spes," Bijdragen*
29, 1968, 364). For other views on the relationship between the
methodology employed in the two documents see Marcelino Zalba,
"Ex personae eiusdemque actuum natura," *Perodica de re morali,
canonica, liturgica* 68 (1979), 201-232; Joseph A. Selling, "A Closer
Look at the Text of *Gaudium et spes* on Marriage and the Family,"
*Bijdragen* 43 (1982, 30-48).

Delhaye also maintains that the concept of natural law found in
*Humanae vitae* is based on Ulpian's understanding of natural law
as the primitive moral instinct common to human beings and ani-
mals especially in the domain of sexuality and of procreation. He
distinguishes such an understanding of the natural law from that
of Gaius and some scholastics who opposed animal nature and
human reason (p. 262). This is the same criticism that I have given
of the natural law theory behind the condemnation of artificial contraception.

In a recently published volume, originally a doctoral disserta-
tion done at St. Michael's College of the University of Toronto,
David F. Kelly studies Roman Catholic medical ethics in North
America — *The Emergence of Roman Catholic Medical Ethics in
North America: A Historical-Methodological-Bibliographical*

*Study* (New York: Edwin Mellen Press, 1979). Kelly entitles the long fourth chapter of his book, "Early Works (1897-1940): The Development of Physicalism." Kelly concludes this chapter in the following manner: "By 1940 the physicalist modality is largely fixed in application to medical ethical issues. It continues to be of great operational significance in the second period of our discipline" (p. 310).

Without doubt, the most significant debate in contemporary Catholic moral theology concerns the existence and grounding of moral norms. What might be called the revisionist approach, which often goes under the name of commensurate reason or proportionalism, has been proposed by many theologians from all parts of the world — Knauer, Janssens, Fuchs, Schüller, Böckle, McCormick, Chiavacci, etc. With some modifications I have expressed general agreement with the direction of this movement. The whole movement shares a common recognition of the problem of physicalism which was present in the older Catholic moral theology. This approach distinguishes between moral evil and physical evil (Knauer); moral evil and ontic evil (Janssens); moral evil and premoral evil (Fuchs). The basis for such distinctions, which are at the heart of the theories, is the unwillingness to identify the physical aspect of the act with the moral aspect of the act. Thus all these authors recognize the problem of physicalism in the moral theology of the manuals. Many of the significant articles both pro and con in this contemporary debate have been collected in English and published in *Readings in Moral Theology No. 1: Moral Norms and Catholic Tradition,* ed. Charles E. Curran and Richard A. McCormick (New York: Paulist Press, 1979).

This same body of literature also bears out the truth of the citation from my writings found on pages seven and eight of the "Observations"; namely, the disputed question in contemporary moral theology. The principal areas of debate are: "medical ethics, particularly in the area of reproduction;" conflict situations solved by the principle of the indirect voluntary, especially conflict situations involving life and death, e.g., killing, abortion; sexuality; euthanasia; and divorce."

The final comment on page nine of the "Observations" is not *ad rem*. I appeal to the changed teaching on religious liberty to point out an example of a greater emphasis given to the subject. The comments made here have already been discussed in my response to the role of the hierarchical teaching office in the Church.

The charges made in the observation that I wrongfully accuse Aquinas and the Catholic tradition of physicalism and appeal to personalism to justify a departure from objective moral truth are reminiscent of the judgment made by Marcelino Zalba that I am guilty of a grave injustice in accusing the ecclesiastical magisterium of physicalism and am mistaken in erroneously appealing to personalism (Zalba, p. 232). I obviously disagree with Zalba's judgment, but the important point is that Zalba's article mentions not only myself as guilty of accusing the hierarchical magisterium of physicalism but also Häring, Delhaye, Hortelano, and Janssens.

In commenting on this article by Zalba, André Guindon maintains that instead of anathematizing Curran and proposing a very doubtful hermeneutic of the conciliar text, Zalba would have been better advised to explain to Curran and the many theologians who agree with him how one is able to affirm, without giving a normative character to the biological processes, that each coital act ought to be open to the transmission of life. According to Guindon, to his knowledge no one has truly responded to this fundamental objection against the argumentation proposed in *Humanae vitae* (André Guindon, "Pour une fécondité sexuelle humaine," *Science et Esprit* 33, 1981, 33-34, fn. 16). This remark by Guindon is echoed by Franz Böckle, who maintains there is no successful proof that demands the connection between the expression of love and fruitfulness in every sexual act (Franz Böckle, "Biotechnik und Menschenwurde," *Die neue Ordnung* 33, 1979, 357).

Richard A. McCormick has also commented on my study indicting *Persona humana* for physicalism — the same study mentioned on page six of the "Observations." McCormick refers to this particular article as "a careful and balanced study." McCormick notes my negative judgment on the physicalism and the methodology of the document which is limited to an analysis apart from the person. According to McCormick, "this latter point is important and is certainly what distinguishes, and unfortunately divides, most contemporary theologians from those writing for the Congregation" (Richard A. McCormick, "Notes on Moral Theology," *Theological Studies* 38, 1977, 110).

The fourth observation refers to the use of the Scripture in general and the scriptural teaching on the indissolubility of marriage in particular. There are obvious errors in the statement of this observation — probably due to translation difficulties. The observation reads: "Father Curran's use of Scripture as containing ethical teachings which represent an ideal or goal of the quest for Christian perfection, rather than a concrete obligation for moral living, even in those cases in which Church tradition has given a definitive interpretation about the presence of such an obligation, gives evidence of a faulty methodology in the understanding and use of Scripture in moral theology." No one should deny that the Scriptures contain ethical teachings which represent an ideal or goal of the quest for Christian perfection. The Catholic tradition has long recognized such ideals or goals as found in the Scripture in terms of voluntary poverty, celibacy, and peace and nonviolence to mention just a few. The second error concerns the statement that the Church has given a "definitive interpretation" about the presence of such an obligation in this particular case of the indissolubility of marriage. There has never been a definitive interpretation given by the Church affirming the existence of a specific, concrete, and universal moral norm as found in the Scriptures.

My scriptural interpretation recognizes the existence of ideals and goals in the Scripture based on the call to be perfect even as the heavenly Father is perfect (Matthew 5:48). The eschatological coloring of the Sermon on the Mount supports this interpretation. My position that the Scriptures contain some goals or ideals is intimately connected with two other aspects of my theology — the stance and the call for continual conversion or growth in the Christian life. "Redemption and resurrection destiny thus serve to create the proper tension by which the Christian is constantly reminded of the need for change and growth in his individual life and in the life of society, but at the same time realizes that the fullness of growth and progress will only come at the end of time and in some discontinuity with the present" (*New Perspectives in Moral Theology,* p. 85).

I do look upon the indissolubility of marriage "as a radical demand of the Gospel that is seen as a goal but not as an absolute norm" (*New Perspectives in Moral Theology,* p. 272). I do not contrast normative and ideal, for I see a normative character to the ideal. "Indissolubility of marriage in such a perspective can only be the goal which is imperative for all and which the couple promises to each other in hope; but which, without their own fault, might at times be unobtainable" (*Ongoing Revision in Moral Theology,* p. 105).

When discussing these scriptural teachings on indissolubility I have been careful to quote the opinions of Scripture scholars who make the same point. I am consequently dependent on them and their interpretation of the scriptural data. The first discussion of the matter in my writings refers to the teachings of Bruce Vawter, Dominic Crossan, and others such as Thomas L. Thompson and Myles M. Bourke (*New Perspectives in Moral Theology,* pp. 253-257). In addition other authorities could also be cited as holding the same position; e.g., W.J. O'Shea, "Marriage and Divorce: The Biblical Evidence," *Australasian Catholic Record* 47 (1970), 89-109; Joseph A. Grispino, *The Bible Now* (Notre Dame, IN: Fides Publishers, 1971), 95-107; Gregorio Ruiz, "Indisolubilidad del matrimonio en la Biblia: Afirmación de un principio-ideal que admite interpretaciones," *Sal Terare* 62 (1974), 779-789.

George W. MacRae is representative of some scholars who are reluctant to describe indissolubility as "merely an ideal." Note that in my opinion the word ideal is not used in the sense of "mere ideal" or "an impossible ideal" but rather as a normative ideal of the Christian life. However, at the same time MacRae cannot accept the New Testament teaching as an absolute universal prohibition of all divorce in all circumstances. The early Church made some adaptations in the eschatological teaching of Jesus — the exception clauses in Matthew and the practice of Paul in I Corinthians 7. MacRae concludes that an ever growing number of theologians and Christian social scientists believe there are grounds for the discernment of new situations in the life of the modern Christian which require new interpretations and new adaptations of the New Testament teaching on divorce (George W. MacRae, "New Testament Perspectives on Marriage and Divorce," in *Divorce and Remarriage in the Catholic Church,* ed. Lawrence G. Wrenn, New York: Newman Press, 1973, pp. 1-15). My scriptural interpretation basically rests on the fact that the early Church made some adaptations in the radical teaching of Jesus on divorce in the light of the needs of the Church, and in different times and circumstances the Church can make other adaptations in the light of the signs of the times (*Ongoing Revision in Moral Theology,* p. 91).

Observation five deals with cooperation. "Curran contradicts Catholic moral teaching on cooperation when he suggests that the person cooperating is not responsible for a personal moral judgment, but can rely on the intention of the principal agent ("Observations," p. 9). This charge is both misleading and erroneous.

There is no doubt that my position on cooperation is different from the traditionally accepted position in Catholic moral theology. I take great pains to explain what the traditional approach is and give reasons for the revision I propose. This is the responsible way for anyone to proceed in proposing revisions of any tradition. I am not trying to hide my differences with the tradition, but I am trying to show how one can make tradition into a living tradition. I indicate that the new thrust which now must be incorporated into the consideration of cooperation in a pluralistic society is the "subjectivity and rights of conscience of the person who is acting." My revised notion of cooperation sees it not primarily as cooperating in an act which is wrong but cooperating with a person. I am the one who has carefully tried to point out exactly how my position attempts to revise the older position in the light of emphases which have now been accepted in a somewhat analogous subject matter — religious liberty (*Ongoing Revision in Moral Theology*, pp. 210-228). Thus it certainly is misleading merely to assert the fact that I contradict Catholic moral teaching on cooperation.

The observation is simply erroneous in saying that I suggest that the person cooperating is not responsible for a personal moral judgment, but can rely on the intention of the principal agent. The citations which are quoted on page ten of the "Observations" actually disprove the above assertion. In making the judgment about cooperation the second paragraph quoted from me maintains that the cooperation "must *also* (emphasis added) consider the right of the individual person to act in accord with one's own decision of conscience." Note the word also. There are other aspects that must be considered before the cooperator can make the judgment to cooperate. In applying the new concept of cooperation I spell out in the article cited on page ten of the "Observations" what are the other various elements that enter into the judgment of cooperation. "One should not cooperate with another if this harms the public order — the rights of other innocent person, the peace, and common morality of society. Thus one could not immediately cooperate in lying or stealing which are opposed to justice and to the common morality necessary for public order" (*Ongoing Revision in Moral Theology,* page 222).

As a case in which the public order is not involved, I bring up the question of a doctor who in conscience is opposed to sterilization but has a patient who believes that sterilization is morally good and acceptable. In this case I recognize that the doctor can refuse to do the sterilization.

> In normal circumstances one can readily uphold the right of both persons to act in accord with their own consciences. The doctor in conscience can refuse to do what is personally believed to be wrong, and the patient can find another doctor to perform the operation. Obviously, society profits very much if we respect the freedom of individuals in these matters. Moral integrity certainly calls for people to act in accord with their consciences and the neutral outsider can applaud the actions of both (*Ongoing Revision in Moral Theology,* p. 221).

But I go on to say that the doctor could (note the word) come to a different conclusion with the reason being "that the patient has the right to obtain the medical care that one needs and wants" (*Ongoing Revision in Moral Theology,* p. 222). Thus my position is not accurately described by saying that one "can rely on the intention of the principal agent."

Observation six maintains that my "position on Christian marriage — its indissolubility and the pastoral practice resulting from this — contradicts the teaching and practice of the Church." Once again I object to the erroneous statement of my position and the selective citations which accompany it.

There is no doubt that I have clearly called for a change in the Church's teaching on divorce and have tried to give my reasons for such a position. However, in my major discussion of the marriage tribunal and pastoral practice I have explicitly pointed out at the very beginning of the study:

> For the sake of discussion in this study the consideration of the first two questions of the legal provisions and pastoral solutions for those who are divorced and remar-

ried will generally accept the present teaching of the Church. The third section will develop my reasons for changing the teaching and practice of the Church on indissolubility; but by prescinding from this position in the first two questions the conclusions reached about legal provisions and pastoral solutions will be able to stand even if one does not accept the more radical conclusions proposed in the third section (*New Perspectives in Moral Theology,* p. 213).

In the first citation taken from my writings on page eleven of the "Observations" the text explicitly says: "My personal conviction that the Church should change its teachings and practice on the indissolubility of Christian marriage obviously influences such a negative judgment on the tribunal system, but the arguments against the existence of the tribunal system still have validity apart from the contention that the Church should change its basic teaching." Thus from the very beginning of my discussion of the topic and even on the basis of the citation given in the "Observations," it is evident that my entire discussion wants to avoid the problem that my recommendation for pastoral practice results only from my asking for a change in the teaching on indissolubility. It is erroneous to say without any qualification that my proposals for pastoral practice result from my teaching on indissolubility.

In the discussion of pastoral practice and internal forum solutions I distinguish four different types of cases, thereby trying to be clearer than those who discussed the question earlier and often failed to recognize the different aspects of the question. In one of the four cases I recognize the difficulty of proposing a pastoral solution without changing the teaching on indissolubility. Page eleven of the "Observations" cites my mentioning that there is no difficulty in this one type of pastoral case if (note the if) one accepts the need to change the teaching on indissolubility. However, the "Observations" fail to cite what is found in the following paragraph where I mention it might be possible to accept such a pastoral practice without changing the teaching on divorce. "I grant that the argument has its weaknesses, but it appears to be the best argument that can be made for justifying such a second marriage without disagreeing with the Catholic teaching on the indissolubility of consummated sacramental marriages" (*New Perspectives in Moral Theology,* pp. 247-248).

It is true that I constantly emphasize I do not think the change in pastoral practice is enough. Such a change should lead to a change in the theoretical teaching. However, I have been very careful to show that the proposed pastoral practices can stand on their own and do not necessarily entail a change in the teaching on indissolubility. In the four types of pastoral cases I have considered, other authors who maintain the same pastoral practices are cited. Thus in the area of pastoral practice what I have espoused can stand apart from my proposal on indissolubility and is in agreement with the position of many other theologians.

Once again, it is I who have pointed out repeatedly, and hopefully responsibly, that my proposal on indissolubility differs from the existing Roman Catholic teaching. I have already mentioned the scriptural aspect of the teaching in these pages. Elsewhere I have cited articles and books in all languages which propose similar positions (*Ongoing Revision in Moral Theology,* pp. 66ff). Since that time on the American scene many others have called for a change in the teaching on divorce, e.g., Stephen J. Kelleher, *Divorce and Remarriage for Catholics?* (Garden City, New York: Doubleday and Co., 1973); Dennis J. Doherty, *Divorce and Remarriage: Resolving a Catholic Dilemma* (Saint Meinrad, Indiana: Abbey Press, 1974); Bernard Häring, *Free and Faithful in Christ,* Vol. II, pp. 538-543; James Gaffney, "Marriage and Divorce," *New Catholic World* 222 (Jan.-Feb. 1979), 20-23.

However, even in proposing the need for some change in the Church's teaching on indissolubility, I have been very careful to point out that the most important thing is for the Church to help Christian people live up to the radical call of the Gospel. James P. Hanigan has recognized this concern in my work.

> But is it, and why is it always morally wrong to attempt a second marriage after a divorce? This is the question that is debated along with the concern that a change in the Church's teaching would further weaken the ideal of indissolubility and the stability of marriage. Such a concern is clearly evident, for example, in Charles Curran's carefully nuanced argument for a change in the teaching on indissolubility. Even while advocating the change, Curran urges that the real task is to "expend every effort possible to strengthen the loving marriage

> commitment of spouses, even if the eschatological ideal cannot always be fulfilled in our present and limited world" (James P. Hanigan, *What are They Saying About Sexual Morality?*, New York: Paulist Press, 1982, p. 115).

I have devoted one essay to the question of indissolubility with a primary emphasis on this need to create the conditions so that Christians can live up to their commitment.

> Reasons were briefly recalled for justifying the need for divorce and remarriage, but the major thrust of the paper was to show that there are also many elements in the contemporary culture which stand in opposition to the Christian understanding of marriage. In the light of this situation the Church must extend its pastoral efforts to create an ethos somewhat opposed to the prevailing cultural ethos so that the ideal of Christian marriage remains a possibility. Yes, Christian theory and practice must accept the possibility of divorce, but an even greater source of challenge focuses on the need to create an atmosphere in which Christian marriage may be both understood in theory and lived in practice (*Issues in Sexual and Medical Ethics*, pp. 26-27).

Observations seven, eight, and nine maintain that Curran advances positions contrary to or in partial conflict with "the Church's magisterium" on issues such as abortion, euthanasia, sexual morality, sterilization, and contraception. These observations thus all are reduced to the "fundamental observation" of my conception of the role and function of the hierarchical magisterium. Since I have already responded at length to this fundamental observation, there is no need to discuss this point again. In all the cases mentioned in the final three observations, it should be noted that I have accurately and fairly described the teaching of the hierarchical magisterium and tried to reasonably propose my own position. In all these cases it is common knowledge that many contemporary Catholic moral theologians hold similar positions.

SACRA CONGREGATIO
PRO DOCTRINA FIDEI
00193 Romae,
Piazza del S. Uffizio, 11

July 16, 1982

Prot. N. 48/66

Dear Father Curran,

Your letter of June 21, together with your second response to the "Observations" that were sent to you has arrived at this Congregation.

Thanks very much for this letter and for your response. In due course your document will be examined by the Congregation and we shall send you any comments that may be considered necessary.

With kindest regards and every best wish,

Sincerely yours in Christ,
Jerome Hamer, O.P.

# IV
# A SECOND SET
# OF OBSERVATIONS
# FROM THE CONGREGATION
# (February-June 1982)

February 10, 1983.   Cardinal Ratzinger, now the Prefect of the Congregation, informs Curran that his responses are not satisfactory. Fuller statement to follow.

May 22, 1983.   Hickey's cover letter sending Ratzinger's letter.

May 10, 1983.   Ratzinger to Curran with 8 pages of "Observations" and letter asking if Curran wishes to revise his dissenting positions and asking for responses to Part Three of enclosed "Observations."

May 24, 1983   Curran to Hickey acknowledging receipt of Ratzinger materials.

June 23, 1983.   Curran to Ratzinger about his response.

June 23, 1983.   Cover letter from Curran to Hickey.

SACRA CONGREGATIO
PRO DOCTRINA FIDEI
00193 Romae
Piazza del S. Uffizio, 11

Prot. N. 48/66

February 10, 1983

Dear Father Curran,

   Since our last letter of July 16, 1982, when we acknowledged receipt of your second response to the observations sent to you by this Congregation, we have studied and evaluated both of your responses in light of the questions we posed. We are now in a position to conclude that your responses on the whole have not proven satisfactory.

   We shall shortly forward to you a fuller statement of our position.

Sincerely yours in Christ,
Joseph Cardinal Ratzinger


Archdiocese of Washington
5001 Eastern Avenue
Post Office Box 29260
Washington, D.C. 20017

Office of the Archbishop

May 22, 1983
48/66i

Rev. Charles Curran, S.T.D.
Department of Theology
School of Religious Studies
Catholic University of America
Washington, D.C.


Dear Father Curran,

   On May 20th I received the enclosed letter and Observations addressed to you by the Sacred Congregation for the Doctrine of the

Faith. Since I shall be out of the city for a few days I hasten to transmit these materials to you, by messenger, so that you may give them your immediate attention. I shall return to Washington in the afternoon of May 25th and can be contacted here at the Pastoral Center — 853-4540.

I note that the Holy See requests a response, if possible, within one working month. Please feel free to make use of my office in transmitting your reply or, if you prefer, to write directly to the Holy See through the assistance of the Apostolic Delegation.

It is my understanding that this procedure is a confidential one. If there is some way that I can be of help in furthering dialogue and clarification between yourself and the Holy See, please let me know.

Praying that the Holy Spirit guide and assist us all in our service of the Church, I am

Sincerely in Christ,
James A. Hickey
Archbishop of Washington
Chancellor, Catholic University of America


SACRA CONGREGATIO
PRO DOCTRINA FIDEI
00193 Romae
Piazza del S. Uffizio, 11

Prot. N. 48/66i

May 10, 1983
                           Confidential
Dear Father Curran,

In our letter of February 10, 1983, we communicated to you that your second response to this Congregation's Observations was not satisfactory. We are now in a position to indicate those areas where we found your response inadequate and we have enclosed a second set of Observations. You will note that they are divided into three sections, the first on the notion of public dissent itself, the second on areas where you have clearly and publicly dissented from the Church's Magisterium, and the third on issues which still remain unclear.

We would now like to invite you to indicate in writing to this Congregation whether or not you would like to revise those positions in clear public dissent from the Magisterium. We would also like you to respond to the questions raised in Part Three. We would further appreciate it if you would respond within one working month (cf. Art. 13, *Ratio Agendi*). If you should foresee some difficulty with this, please contact us as soon as possible.

We are grateful for your cooperation with this process in the past, and rely on your assistance now.

Sincerely yours in Christ,
Joseph Cardinal Ratzinger

w. enclosure

May 24, 1983

Most Reverend James A. Hickey
Archbishop of Washington
5001 Eastern Avenue
P.O. Box 29260
Washington, DC 20017

Dear Archbishop Hickey,

I am writing to inform you that I did receive the hand delivered envelope which you sent to me on the twenty-third of May. I am most appreciative of your courtesy and kindness in sending this to me in the quickest way possible.

I am now dictating this letter on the evening of the twenty-third of May since I have to leave early tomorrow morning. My schedule does not call for me to return to Washington until the fifth or sixth of June. I have a four day institute to give in Florida, a major paper at the College Theology Society, and a paper to give at a Roman Catholic-Jewish colloquium at Notre Dame.

My primary purpose for writing you this hurried note is just to assure you that I have received the envelope. When I return I will write a more formal letter to you and the Congregation.

However, I must point out even now that I have a number of commitments that have already been made including a commitment on a book manuscript. I will have to honor these commitments and at the same time try to respond to the Congregation. Above all others, the Congregation itself should be aware of the difficulty and impossibility of responding within such a time frame.

Sincerely yours in Christ,
Charles E. Curran

(Dictated by Charles E. Curran
and signed in his absence by
Cynthia Vian, Secretary)


cec/cv

# OBSERVATIONS OF THE SACRED CONGREGATION FOR THE DOCTRINE OF THE FAITH REGARDING THE REVEREND CHARLES E. CURRAN

## April, 1983

### Summary of points

1. *Dissent*

a. With a defense of personal or private dissent from the "authoritative, non-infallible hierarchical Magisterium", Fr. Curran justifies public dissent.

b. While in theory and in print, Fr. Curran acknowledges the authoritative role of the Magisterium, in practice he rarely, if ever, cites the Magisterium's position except to criticize it, and effectively treats it as one might treat the opinion of any single theologian.

2. *Issues where there is clear dissent*

a. artificial contraception

b. indissolubility of marriage

c. abortion and euthanasia

d. masturbation, pre-marital intercourse, homosexual acts, direct sterilization, artificial insemination

3. *Issues which remain unclear*

a. Is Fr. Curran certain that the Magisterium is wrong on those issues about which he dissents?

b. Theory of Compromise

c. New Testament "ideals"

d. Frequency of dissent a cause to change the Magisterium's position?

e. physicalism, biologism

# Part One: Dissent in General

The issue of whether a person who privately dissents from the ordinary Magisterium of the Church has the consequent right to

dissent publicly is at the basis of the SCDF's difficulties with
Father Curran. To dissent even privately requires a personal certitude that the teaching of the Church is incorrect.

To further dissent publicly and to encourage dissent in others
runs the risk of causing scandal to the faithful and to assume a certain responsibiltiy for the confusion caused by setting up one's own
theological opinion in contradiction to the position taken by the
Church.

The Congregation contends that Fr. Curran confuses the fact of
personal dissent with a right to public dissent from the ordinary
magisterium of the Church.

In *Lumen gentium* 25, the Fathers of the Vatican Council II
taught, "Religious submission of the will and the intellect must be
given, in a special way, to the authentic teaching authority of the
Roman Pontiff, even when he does not speak *ex cathedra*, in such a
way that his supreme teaching authority be acknowledged with respect, and sincere assent be given to decisions made by him, according to his manifest mind and intention, which is made known
either by the character of the documents in question, or by the frequency with which a certain doctrine is proposed, or by the manner
in which the doctrine is formulated."

On p. 14 of his first response (R.1) to the Observations of the
SCDF first sent to him in 1979, Fr. Curran "clearly recognizes the
right of the individual after prayer and study to make a decision
against the teaching of the authoritative non-infallible hierarchical magisterium when in conscience one is convinced there are
serious reasons to overthrow the presumption of truth given to the
official teaching."

On p. 15 of R.1, he states, ". . . my position . . . clearly recognizes that an ordinary member of the faithful can at times under
certain conditions mentioned, prudently make a decision against
the presumed truth of the ordinary teaching of the magisterium."

Regarding theologians specifically, Fr. Curran poses the issue of
dissent in question form. "Does the teaching of the ordinary non-infallible authoritative hierarchical magisterium constitute the only
factor or the always decisive factor in the total magisterial activity
of the Church? In other words, is the theologian ever justified in

going against such a teaching?" (p.4, R.1) Referring probably to the first formulation of his question, Fr. Curran says, "My negative response to this question has been developed at great length in chapters 2, 3, and 4 of *Dissent in and for the Church.*"

The SCDF's Observations held that "this suspension of (private) assent does not provide grounds for a so-called right of public dissent, for such a public dissent would in effect constitute an alternative magisterium. . . ."

It is true that Fr. Curran has explicitly articulated and defended the role of the hierarchical magisterium as he notes on pp. 2 and 3 of R.1, but in his actual treatment of different issues, as will be seen below, he effectively treats the position of the Magisterium as he would the opinion of an ordinary theologian. In fact, on the contested issues, Fr. Curran does not cite the Magisterium's position at all, except to criticize it and set it aside. This practice is hardly reconcilable with his avowed acceptance of the Magisterium as authoritative and as assisted by the Holy Spirit.

It should be noted as well that Fr. Curran is not alone in holding many of the positions he does. He appeals to the fact that several theologians have held similar views without criticism from the Church, and implicitly therefore, he construes any eventual action taken against him to be inequitable.

It is not just Fr. Curran who cites other theologians in disagreement with the Church, but they in turn also cite him. This circular method of contestation cannot enjoy immunity from criticism by the Church, even though in singling out the tenets of a particular theologian, the Church may at first risk being perceived as unjust.

On the specific issues to follow, it is apparent that Fr. Curran has taken a position, publicly, in clear dissent from the position taken by the Magisterium. In this first section, however, it has simply been our purpose to point out that a fundamental disagreement between the SCDF and Fr. Curran on the issue of dissent in general, and of public dissent in particular, provides a kind of context against which the individual dissenting positions he has taken should be evaluated.

## Part Two: Issues Where There is Clear Dissent

*Artificial Contraception*

As is well known, in 1968 Paul VI published the encyclical, *Humanae vitae* (AAS 60 [1968] pp. 481-503), and in it taught that every marital act should remain open to the transmission of life.

As is also well known, Fr. Curran has not personally accepted this position, and has organized dissent from it. In *Moral Theology: A Continuing Journey,* p. 144, Fr. Curran states, "Human beings do have the power and responsibility to interfere with the sexual faculty and act. The official Catholic teaching is often accused of a physicalism or biologism because the biological or physical structure of the act is made normative and cannot be interfered with. I take this dissenting position."

## Indissolubility of Marriage

The teaching of the Council of Trent on the indissolubility of marriage (DS 1797) was clearly reiterated at the Vatican Council II in *Gaudium et spes,* 47-52, describing the nature of marriage as "an indissoluble bond between two people." Having seen the family and human society itself as grounded in the family, *Lumen gentium* 11 shows the proper Christian attitude toward marriage as well as all the Sacraments when it states, "Strengthened by so many and such great means of salvation, all the faithful, whatever their condition or state though each in his own way, are called by the Lord to that perfection of sanctity by which the Father Himself is perfect."

Fr. Curran opts "for the strenuous ethical teachings of Jesus in the Sermon on the Mount as a goal or an ideal."

He holds this idealist opinion even in those cases where the tradition of the Church has given a definitive interpretation about the presence of a concrete obligation in the teachings of Jesus.

But Fr. Curran goes on to say, "In light of these and other reasons, I propose that indissolubility remains a goal and ideal for Christian marriage; but Christians, sometimes without any personal fault, are not always able to live up to that ideal. Thus the Roman Catholic Church should change its teaching on divorce." *Issues in Sexual and Medical Ethics,* pp. 15-16.

## Abortion and Euthanasia

In *Gaudium et spes* 51, the Vatican Council II taught, "Life must be protected with the utmost care from the moment of conception. Abortion and infancticide are unspeakable crimes." Cf. GS27. Paul VI, in *Humanae vitae* 14, repeated the Council's condemnation of abortion. Even more recently, the SCDF expressed the Church's revulsion for abortion in its Declaration of 18 Nov. 1974 (AAS 66 [1974], pp. 730-747.)

On 5 May, 1980, the SCDF also issued a Declaration on Euthanasia (AAS 72 [1980], pp. 542-552.) which clearly stated "No one can make an attempt on the life of an innocent person without opposing God's love for that person, without violating a fundamental right, and therefore without committing a crime of the utmost gravity."

Fr. Curran, in *Ongoing Revision,* p. 157, says, "My own teaching constitutes a dissent from the authoritative Church teaching on the two questions of when does human life begin and how can one solve conflict situations, but my dissent is not all that great." p. 160, "What about euthanasia or the active and positive interference to bring about death? Traditionally Catholic teaching and the hierarchical teaching have opposed euthanasia. Two arguments are usually given." "These two arguments in my judgment are not absolutely convincing in all cases." In "The Catholic Hospital *Linacre Quarterly,* Feb. '77 Fr. Curran notes, "The reasons . . . mentioned justifying the possibility of dissent from . . . Church teaching are also present with regard to the possibility of dissent on abortion and euthanasia. Legitimate dissent in these areas remains a possibility because of the complexity and specificity of the material . . . and the fact that one cannot obtain the degree of certitude that excludes the possibility of error."

### *Masturbation, Pre-Marital Intercourse, Homosexual Acts*

Again, Vatican Council II taught in *Gaudium et spes* 51, ". . . it is not enough to take the good intention and the evaluation of motives into account; the objective criteria must be used, criteria drawn from the nature of the human person and human action, criteria which respect the total meaning of mutual self-giving, and human pro-creation in the context of true love; all this is possible only if the virtue of married chastity is seriously practiced."

In its 1975 *Declaration on Certain Questions Concerning Sexual Ethics,* (AAS 68 [1976]: pp. 77-96), the SCDF explicitly recalled the

Council's teaching when it noted, "It is respect for its finality that ensures the moral goodness of this (sexual) act." (par. 5) Par. 7 states that the opinion that pre-marital sex can be justified "is contrary to Christian doctrine." Par. 8 refers to those . . . who . . . judge indulgently or even . . . excuse completely homosexual relations between certain people." It continues, "This they do in opposition to the constant teaching of the Magisterium."

And "no pastoral method can be employed which would give moral justification to these acts on the grounds that they would be consonant with the condition of such people. For according to the objective moral order, homosexual relations are acts which lack an essential and indispensable finality."

Par. 9 refers to those who call into doubt or expressly deny the Catholic doctrine that masturbation is a grave moral disorder. To do so "is contradictory to the teaching and pastoral practice of the Catholic Church." "The Magisterium of the Church . . . (has) declared without hesitation that masturbation is an intrinsically and seriously disordered act."

In *Contemporary Problems in Moral Theology,* pp. 179-80, Fr. Curran notes, "I personally do see occasions where sexual intercourse outside marriage would not be wrong. . . ." et iterum. pp. 142-143, "I believe in all the areas mentioned above (contraception, direct sterilization, and masturbation) there are circumstances in which such actions would be morally permissible and even necessary."

In *Themes in Fundamental Moral Theology,* p. 182, "(In) the cases in which modern medical science cannot help the homosexual . . . it seems to me that for such a person, homosexual acts might not even be wrong."

## Part Three: Issues Which Remain Unclear

Perhaps the best format in this section is to phrase the issues which remain unclear to this Congregation in the form of questions.

Fr. Curran often cites the fact that many moral questions are quite complicated and then infers that the general position held by the Magisterium does not "absolutely" bind in "every case." Should

not this infinity of specific details, in a given instance of moral decision-making, likewise make certainty improbable on Fr. Curran's
part that the Magisterium is, in fact, wrong, so completely and so
often?

Regarding his "theory of compromise", Fr. Curran maintains
that a compromise is often "the best one can do" in an evil situation.
Is this theory of compromise likely to be helpful to most people in
most situations where the element of self-justification is likely to
enter into the moral decision-making process? Is not such a theory
effectively susceptible to more abuse than not? If a moral agent in
his decision-making process is successful at exonerating himself
via this theory of compromise, are not the real claims of justice
likely to be ignored since the compromise itself is the work of the
moral agent, from his personal and necessarily self-interested
viewpoint?

Regarding the interpretation of New Testament moral norms as
"ideals", is there a true opposition between "moral ideal" and
"moral norm"? What is Fr. Curran's notion of "moral norm"? Is it
not an oversimplification to see all New Testamental moral injunctions as pervaded by that particular type of eschatological expectation which viewed the end of the epoch as coinciding with the end
of the physical world and the Parousia itself? Are there not other
eschatological dimensions in the NT which would see the epoch as
coinciding with the life of the individual? In such a case, would not
Fr. Curran's "ideals" rather become every Christian's personal responsibiltiy to emulate? Is not the term "ideal", especially in English, an inept and infelicitous choice since it is commonly con-
strued as the opposite of real, no matter how particularly Fr. Curran might want to restrict its use?

When Fr. Curran cites, as in the case of divorce and remarriage,
or the use of artificial contraception, a frequency of inattention to
the position taken by the Magisterium, what precise weight does
he claim for that frequency, from a theological methodological
viewpoint? If the Church should change her position on indissolubility in light of the large numbers of Catholics who ignore the
Magisterium on this point, would the results of a similar poll on
the question of, say, dishonesty imply that the Magisterium should
now hold that dishonesty is somehow now good, or at least not bad?
Is not the argument for a change of principle from frequency of

abuse actually and profoundly legalistic? Is Christian marriage indissoluble because the Church *says* it is, or does the Church say Christian marriage is indissoluble because it is?

Granting that physicalism or biologism used as an *exclusive* source of moral argument would be untenable, is that what *Humane vitae* has in fact done? Is that what Fr. Curran says *Humanae vitae* has done? Does Fr. Curran see any part for the physical dimension to play in the moral decision-making process? Could not a *non*-physicalist argument, on an issue of such obviously physical import as that of artificial contraception, be actually accused of angelism, unrealism and irrelevancy?

In light of the Apostolic Constitution *Familiaris Consortio* of John Paul II, has Fr. Curran given any thought to reconsidering his positions on contraception, divorce, and giving communion to the divorced and remarried? Does *Familiaris Consortio* appear to him to be an instance of the ordinary Magisterium of the Church in the sense intended by *Lumen gentium* 25?


The
CATHOLIC UNIVERSITY
of America

Washington, D.C. 20064

June 23, 1983

His Eminence
Joseph Cardinal Ratzinger
Praefectus, Sacra Congregatio pro Doctrina Fidei
Piazza del S. Uffizio, 11
00193 Rome

Dear Cardinal Ratzinger,

I want to acknowledge receipt of your letter and observations of May 10, 1983, in response to my letter and response of July 16, 1982.

Enclosed you will find a copy of the letter I sent to Archbishop Hickey on the occasion of receiving your May 10 letter and observations. This letter explains why I cannot respond immediately. However, as you note in your letter, I have cooperated in the past; and I will continue to cooperate.

My first reaction, especially to Part One, is dismay. I am quite disappointed by the quality of the dialogue and the failure to engage the substantive questions framed in my response of October 26, 1979. For these reasons I intend to respond as soon as I can to that section. However, in the meantime I must fulfill previous teaching and writing commitments which I have accepted.

Sincerely yours in Christ,
Charles E. Curran

CEC/cv

Re: Prot. No. 48/66

June 23, 1983

Most Reverend James E. Hickey
Archbishop of Washington
5001 Eastern Avenue
Post Office Box 29260
Washington, D.C. 20017

Dear Archbishop Hickey,

Enclosed you will find my letter to Cardinal Ratzinger.

To facilitate the delivery of the letter, I will take it directly to the Apostolic Delegation this afternoon (Thursday) so that it can be sent out in the diplomatic pouch on Friday. However, I want to make sure you receive a copy of it. You will notice my disappointment over the quality of the dialogue.

Best regards for a good summer.

Sincerely yours in Christ,
Charles E. Curran

cec/cv

# V
# CURRAN'S
# FINAL RESPONSES
# (August 1983-October 1984)

| | |
|---|---|
| August 10, 1983. | Curran to Ratzinger enclosing a 16 page response on the noninfallible hierarchical magisterium. |
| August 10, 1983. | Curran to Hickey sending a copy of the above response. |
| January 3, 1984. | Hickey to Curran enclosing a letter from Ratzinger. |
| December 2, 1983. | Ratzinger to Curran asking for a complete response. |
| February 28, 1984. | Curran to Hickey expressing frustration about the whole process and suggesting Hickey send this to the congregation. |
| May 7, 1984. | Handwritten cover letter of Hickey to Curran enclosing Ratzinger letter. |
| April 13, 1984. | Ratzinger to Curran claiming that the congregation's position on public dissent is clear and setting September 1 as the final deadline for Curran's response. |
| August 24, 1984. | Curran to Ratzinger enclosing 24 page response including Curran's problems with the congregation's process. |
| October 26, 1984. | Ratzinger to Curran acknowledging receipt of final response. |

The
CATHOLIC UNIVERSITY
of America

August 10, 1983

His Eminence
Joseph Cardinal Ratzinger
Praefectus, Sacra Congregatio pro Doctrina Fidei
Piazza del S. Uffizio, 11
00193 Rome

Dear Cardinal Ratzinger,

Enclosed you will find my response to the "Observations" sent to me with your covering letter of May 10, 1983 which was received by me on May 23.

As I mentioned in my letter to you of June 23, 1983 I would respond as quickly as I could in the light of my other commitments and responsibilities. This response attempts to spell out in greater detail what I mentioned in the last paragraph of that letter.

Sincerely yours in Christ,
Charles E. Curran

Re: Prot. No. 48/66

### RESPONSE

to the
"Observations of the
Sacred Congregation for the Doctrine of the Faith
Regarding the Reverend Charles E. Curran"

(Prot. N. 48/66)

August 10, 1983

In the course of our correspondence I have constantly reiterated that the quality of the dialogue is poor. Perhaps I have not taken the time or the effort to make my point clear. In this response I will concentrate on this aspect first in a somewhat general way and then in a specific point by point reaction to the "Observations" dated April 1983 and received by me on May 23, 1983. I will concentrate on the understanding of noninfallible hierarchical magisterium which the "Observations" of July 1979 called "the fundamental observation to be made regarding the writings of Father Charles Curran" and the "fundamental flaw" in my writings. Throughout this response all references to teaching authority will refer to the authoritative or authentic noninfallible hierarchical magisterium.

My first response of October 1979 attempted to focus the dialogue in such a way that the areas of agreement and disagreement could be readily discovered. In my judgment, Catholic moral theory has always operated by establishing the principles, the norms, or the criteria that govern human actions and then relating these to specific and particular cases. In my writing and in the writings of most Catholic ethicists, situation ethics has often been criticized for a methodology that attempts to go from a very broad general assertion to a very specific conclusion. I have referred to this approach as theological actualism. In contrast to this methodology, the Catholic approach has insisted that reasoning go from the more general to the more specific. Such a methodology does not necessarily have to be deductive nor is it necessarily limited to the Catholic ethical tradition. Most ethical approaches do attempt to spell out principles, norms, or criteria for guidance in particular moral decision making. Witness, for example, the emphasis in some Protestant writings on the importance of middle axioms.

In their pastoral letter of November 15, 1968 (*Human Life in Our Day* [Washington, DC: United States Catholic Conference, 1968]), the American bishops recognize the need for such an approach with regard to the specific issue of theological dissent in the church. This pastoral letter proposes general guidelines for theological dissent, but also recognizes in today's changed circumstances the need for further refinement and specification of these norms through dialogue between bishops and theologians (pp. 18, 19).

The expression of theological dissent from the magisterium is in order only if the reasons are serious and well-founded, if the manner of dissent does not question or impugn the teaching authority of the Church and is such as not to give scandal.

Since our age is characterized by popular interest in theological debate and given the realities of modern mass media, the ways in which theological dissent may be effectively expressed, in a manner consistent with pastoral solicitude, should become the object of fruitful dialogue between bishops and theologians. These have their distinct ministries in the Church, their distinct responsibilities to the faith, and their respective charisms.

My first response of October 1979 was framed in the light of this background. It is imperative first of all to establish the guidelines or the criteria that govern dissent and then relate these guidelines to the particular case. Hopefully, in general, bishops and theologians could agree on the guidelines and then relate them to the particular circumstances. If there were disagreement on guidelines, or on the more specific aspects of the guidelines, then at least the area of differences would be known. Efforts have continued in the United States to work in this direction. See for example, *Cooperation Between Theologians and the Ecclesiastical Magisterium: A Report of the Joint Committee of the Canon Law Society of America and the Catholic Theological Society of America.* ed. Leo J. O'Donovan, S.J. (Washington: Canon Law Society of America, 1982).

The five questions proposed in my October 1979 response to the Congregation attempted to enter into dialogue on the nature of the norms or guidelines governing dissent. These questions raised the most fundamental issues before going into more concrete determination about how dissent should take place. There was a very logical progression to the questions. From the "Observations" sent me it seems clear that the Congregation recognizes the legitimacy of theological dissent under certain circumstances.

The second question went one step further and raised the issue of public dissent — the possibility and even the right of public dissent by the theologian. I am still not clear what is the position of the Congregation with regard to this. The April 1983 "Observations" refer to public dissent as "the basis of the SCDF's difficulty

with Father Curran." The question is: unlike the American
Bishops, does the Congregation deny all possibility and right of
public dissent? Since your position was not entirely clear in the
first "Observations," although there were some indications that
the "Observations" do deny the possibility and right of any public
dissent, I then raised a third question: "Is *silentium obsequiosum*
the only legitimate response for a theologian who is convinced that
there are serious reasons which overturn the presumption in favor
of the teaching of the authoritative noninfallible hierarchical
magisterium?" If this is the criterion proposed and accepted by the
Congregation, then it does provide a very clear norm which would
obviously preclude any public dissent.

The fourth question referred to the right of dissent on the part of
the individual faithful. This question is important because it im-
pinges on the corresponding obligations and responsibilities of
theologians in the Church. If the legitimate possibility of dissent
exists for the faithful, then they do have a right to be informed on
these questions. In this context, the possible problem of scandal is
quite mitigated. If the faithful cannot legitimately dissent from authoritative noninfallible hierarchical teaching, then the role of the
theologian vis-à-vis the faithful would be somewhat changed. This
question was never addressed in the 1979 "Observations," but the
1983 "Observations" could possibly be interpreted as denying the
legitimacy of such dissent because they juxtapose a citation from
*Lumen gentium* 25 with a citation of my affirmative position.

The fifth question inquired if the Congregation recognizes that
there have been errors in the teaching of the ordinary noninfallible
magisterium in the past which have been subsequently corrected
often because of the dissent of theologians. The purpose of this
question is to ascertain the role of theological dissent in the
Church. In my judgment, all in the Catholic Church must answer
yes to the above question. Such an affirmative answer recognizes
that there is an important role to be played by theological dissent
in the life of the Church. The question is then how is this role to be
exercised. We once again then return to questions two and three as
attempts to discover the more general norms governing such dissent.

The entire logic of the five questions is to seek out the most general norms governing theological dissent. True and fruitful
dialogue requires that both parties be willing to express what the

norms are that they are following and how these norms are to be applied. First the more general norms should be discovered and then the more specific. As yet, our dialogue has been unable to agree even on the more general norms governing dissent.

I have tried to raise objective questions in the hope of being able then to formulate the norms governing dissent. Perhaps the Congregation feels that the questions I have posed are not the most helpful or fruitful for arriving at the very general norms governing theological dissent. If the congregation is not willing to respond to the questions, is the Congregation willing to accept the norms proposed by the American bishops who recognize the possibility of public dissent and propose three general norms to govern the expression of such dissent — if the reasons are serious and well founded, if the manner of dissent does not question or impugn the teaching authority of the Church, and is such as not to give scandal?

I do not think that true dialogue can continue unless the Congregation will clearly state whether or not it accepts any possibility of legitimate public theological dissent in the Church. If not, at least there exists a clear criterion for judgment (even though I would obviously disagree with such a criterion). If yes, then there is the need to elucidate further what the conditions are.

## Specific Comments

The second section of this response will now deal more specifically with the April 1983 "Observations."

The "Observations" begin with a summary of points which mentions two points under dissent. The entire first point reads ("a") "With a defense of personal or private dissent from the 'authoritative noninfallible hierarchical magisterium,' Father Curran justifies public dissent."

This statement is false.

I have consistently recognized that the legitimacy of personal or private dissent does not of itself justify public dissent. My response of October 1979 specifically begins by raising two different questions — the first dealing with theological dissent in general and the second dealing with public dissent. Here I properly separate the two questions to show that they are distinct and different. It is obvious there is a logical connection between the two. If dissent in general or private dissent is not acceptable, neither is public dissent. The posing of the second question recognizes that a positive response to the first question is a necessary but not a sufficient condition for a positive response to the second question.

My separating and clearly distinguishing the two issues of theological dissent in general and public dissent is not only obvious from the two different questions posed in my response to the Congregation, but also from the way in which public dissent was discussed in the 1969 book *Dissent In and For the Church*. The logical progression of that book deals in order with preliminary considerations on the nature of theology and the role of theologians, preliminary considerations on the nature and function of the magisterium, and the contemporary ecclesiological awareness of Catholic theologians. In the light of this background in which the legitimate possibility of dissent from authoritative noninfallible hierarchical teaching is proven, the entire chapter five is then devoted to "Public Dissent In and For the Church." The opening paragraph explains the relationship of this chapter to what went before and clearly indicates why the question must be treated in itself in an in-depth manner (p. 133):

> In chapter two, theologians representative of the manualist tradition were cited as clearly teaching the possibility of dissent from authoritative noninfallible teaching of the hierarchical magisterium. One or another of them imply that this 'possibility' may become an obligation for someone who perceives such cogent contrary reasons that to maintain assent would be a perversion of his rational faculties. On the question of *public* dissent or disagreement, however, most of the manualists maintain that one who suspends his internal assent still must keep a *silentium obsequiosum* and present his difficulties privately to the hierarchical authority itself. It has already been noted that some contemporary Catholic theologians, such as Schueller, K. Rahner, and Donlon, writing before the issuance of *Humanae vitae,* explicitly recognized the limited horizon of the manualists' restriction and openly taught that *public* dissent might be called for in some instances.

In the teaching of the manualists there are, nonetheless, elements which definitely argue for further development of the question; in fact, a contemporary rationale for 'external' dissent seems quite continuous with some of the underlying principles and values which can be gleaned from the manualists themselves.

This chapter recognizes the need to treat the question of public dissent in the light of the Church's contemporary teaching on the right to know, the duty to inform, the right to free self-expression, the role of public opinion in the church, and the use of modern means of communication. In this context the chapter spells out the responsibility of theologians to the different people they serve. The discussion recognizes that responsible theological interpretation, even when it takes the form of dissent, must always show respect for the hierarchical teaching authority in the Church.

Public dissent requires a balance of values and ultimately is a function of prudence or practical judgment. The chapter recognizes there conceivably can be some harm involved in public dissent and requires that the good of the Church and its public image must outweigh possible harm that might result. Thus the book clearly recognizes that public theological dissent is a distinct issue from dissent in general or private dissent, proves its legitimacy, and proposes more concrete norms which should govern its expression.

The second summary point under dissent ("b") of the April 1983 "Observations" reads in its entirety: "While in theory and in print Fr. Curran acknowledges the authoritative role of the magisterium, in practice he rarely, if ever, cites the magisterium's position except to criticize it, and effectively treats it as one might treat the opinion of any single theologian."

The sentence as it stands is false.

It is true that in the limited number of cases cited in the "Observations" I do cite the position of the magisterium and then criticize it. However, this is not true of the entire corpus of my writings. For example, the *Journal of Religious Ethics* has recently accepted for publication my article "Roman Catholic Teaching on Peace and War Within a Broader Theological Context." This article begins with a section summarizing the official hierarchical Church teaching on peace and war. The following three sections show the connection and the relationship of this teaching to the areas of general theory, eschatology, and ecclesiology. This scholarly paper is based on the presentation I was asked to give to the National Conference of Catholic Bishops' Committee on War and Peace, as they were preparing the Pastoral Letter which was finally issued in May 1983.

As another example, I have accepted the invitation to write the article "Papal Social Encyclicals" for the forthcoming new edition of the *Dictionary of Christian Ethics*. I assume I was asked to contribute this article on the basis of my previous writings on the subject. In one particular article ("The Changing Anthropological Bases of Catholic Social Teaching," *The Thomist* 45 [1981], 284-378), I traced the developments in the area of anthropology as found in the teaching of the official hierarchical magisterium from Leo XIII to the present.

The entire corpus of my writings thus illustrates the role of the theologian which was spelled out in *Dissent In and For the Church*. The function of the theologian in relation to the authoritative noninfallible Church teaching is best described in terms of interpretation. Precisely because I am a Catholic theologian I must give importance to the official Church teaching and interpret that teaching. At times that interpretation might take the form of dissent. However, in many articles and books, as illustrated by the examples given above, this interpretation does not take the form of dissent. It is false, misleading, and a travesty of justice and true dialogue to assert, " . . . In practice he rarely, if ever, cites the magisterium's position except to criticize it."

The summary point of the April 1983 "Observations" goes on to claim that "Curran effectively treats it [the authoritative noninfallible hierarchical magisterium] as one might treat the opinion of any single theologian."

This part of the statement is likewise false. The very number of times I have cited the teaching of the hierarchical magisterium in my writings proves that I do not treat it like the opinion of any single theologian. As a Catholic theologian I must interpret this teaching on the many issues where it comes into play. I have never given such an importance or prominence to the work of any one theologian.

Page two of the "Observations" gives a more accurate (but in the end a contradictory) statement by saying, "In fact, in the contested issues, Father Curran does not cite the magisterium's position at all, except to criticize it and set it aside." This statement is true because it is limited to the contested issues. However, it fails to take into consideration the entire corpus of my writings and the many places I cite, explain, and agree with the teaching of the authoritative hierarchical magisterium. In addition, this statement contradicts what the "Observations" say elsewhere. The very first page of the July 1979 "Observations" states that the theologian must have "reasons which appear to be clearly valid to him" in order to suspend or refuse assent. Thus in order to dissent, a theologian must explain the teaching and give the reasons and arguments which the theologian believes are clearly valid to justify the dissent. To follow any other procedure in "contested" cases would be irresponsible. I cannot be criticized for doing what the "Observations" say should be done in such circumstances.

Since I have already pointed out the falsity of the two summary statements of my positions on dissent, I will now address the other points made on pages one and two of the April 1983 "Observations."

I have already responded to the first and third paragraphs of page one which maintain that the right to public dissent is at the heart of the SCDF's difficulties with Father Curran and that he "confuses the fact of personal dissent with the right to public dissent."

The second paragraph claims, "To further dissent publicly and to encourage dissent in others runs the risk of causing scandal to the faithful and to assume a certain responsibility for the confusion caused by setting up one's own theological opinion in contradiction to the position taken by the Church."

The statement is carefully nuanced with the words "runs the risk." Does this mean that if there is no risk, or if the risk is compensated for by other goods, then the Congregation recognizes the legitimacy of public dissent? This again points out the need for the Congregation to clearly express its position on the norms governing public dissent.

My own writings have dealt with the issue of the risk of scandal in the context of commenting on the third norm governing public dissent proposed by the American bishops — "the expression of theological dissent . . . must be such as not to give scandal." *Dissent In and For the Church* (pp. 213ff) distinguishes between scandal in the strict sense and scandal in the lesser or nontechnical sense which is often what is meant in this context. Again the book calls attention to the need for prudence and practical judgment. In complex human affairs it is impossible to avoid all negative effects coming from one's actions. Prudence in the matter of public dissent requires that whatever bad effects there are be outweighed by the good effects. In the academic hearings held at Catholic University after the dissent from *Humanae vitae,* expert witnesses testified (and later the faculty hearing committee agreed with their testimony) that much greater harm could have resulted if the theologians had not made their dissent public. I have constantly maintained that the prudential judgment about public theological dissent must take cognizance of the risk of scandal, try to mitigate as much as possible any negative effects, and can be justified only if the good achieved outweighs the evil.

Although the risk of scandal must always be taken account of in public dissent, there are important aspects other than scandal that must also be considered. In the course of my writings I have tried to point out those aspects and I framed my original questions in my first response with these other considerations in mind. A primary consideration here is that of truth itself. If one admits that individual Catholic faithful can possibly legitimately dissent in theory and in practice in their lives, then the theologian has an obligation to these people. Chapter five of *Dissent In and For the Church* develops the various publics who have a right to know theological scholarship including the interpretation of dissent. In this light one can rightly conclude that at times it would be a scandal if theologians did not dissent publicly. Many other writers have pointed out that too often the Church has been worried about the scandal of the weak but not that of the strong. If, as many maintain, there is a right to dissent in the Church for theologians and ordinary faithful as well, and if there is a right for theologians to dissent publicly, then under the proper conditions there is no real scandal.

The long fourth paragraph of page one cites *Lumen gentium* no. 25 (a paragraph I too have often cited as I tried to interpret it) and then merely cites my questions saying that an individual Catholic can at times under certain conditions prudently make a decision against the presumed truth of the hierarchical teaching. Does the juxtaposition of these two quotations mean that the Congregation denies any possibility of legitimate dissent for the faithful? If so, how does the Congregation relate to the fact, that according to the report of Archbishop Quinn in the International Synod of Bishops, over 70% of American Catholic women use a form of birth control which is condemned by the encyclical *Humanae vitae*? At the very minimum, anyone familiar with the contemporary debate in Catholic theology about dissent cannot accept as a legitimate theological argument against dissent by the faithful the mere citation of *Lumen gentium* 25 without any further explanation or elucidation. Some statements of National Bishops' Conferences have recognized the possibility of such dissent.

The last two paragraphs of page one merely cite my first question about whether the teaching of the ordinary noninfallible hierarchical magisterium constitutes the only factor or the always decisive factor in the total magisterial activity of the Church. Then the "Observations" quote the 1979 "Observations" that "the suspension of (private) assent does not provide grounds for a so-called right of public dissent. . . ." Again, these paragraphs falsify my position by failing to recognize that the issue of public dissent was raised by me as a separate question which could not be justified merely by the existence of a right to dissent in general or by a right to private dissent.

In my discussion of the summary points of the April 1983 "Observations," I have already discussed the matter contained in the first paragraph on page two of these same "Observations."

The next two paragraphs note my assertion that there are many other theologians who also hold similar positions. "It is not just Fr. Curran who cites other theologians in disagreement with the Church, but they in turn also cite him. This circular method of contestation cannot enjoy immunity from criticism by the Church, even though in singling out the tenets of a particular theologian, the Church may at first risk being perceived as unjust." Note that the "Observations" make this comment in the context of dissent.

That some theologians who have justified dissent in the Church cite me is true. That all or even the majority of those who have justified dissent cite me is not true. The inference behind this statement that I am the source and cause of most of the dissent in the Church is ludicrous.

Recall that the American bishops themselves have recognized the legitimacy of public dissent in the Church under certain circumstances. Not only the American bishops and some other bishops but the vast majority of Catholic theologians writing today affirm the legitimacy of public dissent under certain circumstances. In this context, see the aforementioned study by the joint committee of the Canon Law Society of America and the Catholic Theological Society of America.

The majority of the theologians I cited in my first response of October 1979 in support of the legitimacy of the theological dissent including public dissent do not cite me. This includes bishops such as Butler and Coffy and theologians such as Congar and Rahner. To infer that those who justify some dissent in the Church are merely a small group who cite one another and that I have a major role in that group is patently false.

In conclusion, in this response I have tried to develop at length the statement in my June 23, 1983 letter to the effect that I am quite disappoinated and dismayed by the quality of the dialogue and the failure of the Congregation to engage the substantive questions found in my response of October 26, 1979. These questions were framed in such a way as to discern and determine what are the general norms governing dissent in the Church. In any number of places I have proposed such norms. There can be no true dialogue on this matter unless the Congregation itself is willing to say what are the norms that should govern dissent in the Church. I do not think that my request for clarification of this central issue can be looked upon as unreasonable.

The
CATHOLIC UNIVERSITY
of America

August 10, 1983

Most Reverend James A. Hickey, D.D.
Archbishop of Washington
5001 Eastern Avenue
P.O. Box 29260
Washington, D.C. 20017

Dear Archbishop Hickey,

Enclosed you will find my response to the "Observations" from the Congregation for the Doctrine of the Faith which you forwarded to me on May 23.

To expedite matters I will send the response directly to Cardinal Ratzinger through the diplomatice pouch of the Apostolic Delegation.

I am sorry to hear that you have been ill. I hope and pray that you are feeling better.

Sincerely yours in Christ,
Charles E. Curran


ARCHDIOCESE OF WASHINGTON
5001 Eastern Avenue
Post Office Box 29260
Washington, D.C. 20017

Office of the Archbishop

January 3, 1984

Rev. Charles Curran
The Catholic University
Washington, D.C. 20064

Dear Father Curran,

I regret my delay in transmitting to you this important letter from the Sacred Congregation for the Doctrine of the Faith. Cardinal Ratzinger gave it to me during my *ad limina* visit and, inexplicably, it was mislaid in my papers. I pass it on to you now, and I shall also inform the Holy See of the reason that you received it late.

The Cardinal explained to me that he is anxious to receive a reply to all the observations presented to you. Your response of August tenth responded to some but not all of the concerns raised by the Holy See.

As usual, please address your reply to the Holy See through the Apostolic Delegate; if you choose to share a copy with me, it will be much appreciated.

May this New Year help us all to see Christ more clearly and love Him with greater strength in all we do in the service of our University and of the Church.

Sincerely in Christ,
James A. Hickey
Archbishop of Washington


SACRA CONGREGATIO
PRO DOCTRINA FIDEI
00193 Romae,
Piazza del S. Uffizio, 11
Prot. N. 48/66
December 2, 1983

                                  Confidential

Dear Father Curran,

On May 10, 1983, this Congregation wrote to you asking that you reply to a second set of Observations which were forwarded to you at that time. In accord with the Ratio Agendi, Art. 13, we asked you to send us your reply within one working month.

On August 10, 1983, you sent a reply to the first of the three sections of the Observations, for which we are very grateful.

We would like to remind you that we still await your complete reply.

Sincerely yours in Christ,
Joseph Cardinal Ratzinger

The
CATHOLIC
 UNIVERSITY of
 AMERICA
Washington D.C. 20064

February 28, 1984

The Most Reverend James A. Hickey
Archbishop of Washington
5001 Eastern Ave.
P.O. Box 29260
Washington, D.C. 20017

Dear Archbishop Hickey:

I want to respond to your letter of January 3, 1984 which was here at the University when I returned after the semester break. In the last few weeks I have been in contact and correspondence with a number of theologians and others in this country and abroad seeking their advice and counsel. I wanted to check my own reactions with those of others before I responded to your letter.

My reaction is one of growing frustration. I mentioned this to you in earlier correspondence and have said the same in my most recent detailed response to the Congregation itself.

From my very first response in October 1979 I have tried to determine as exactly as possible the differences between the Congregation and myself on the question of dissent. I formulated five questions at that time, but the Congregation has been unwilling to respond to them. I ended my response of August 1983 with the request that the Congregation state what are the norms that should govern dissent. Only if we have criteria can judgments be made about particular cases. The elemental principles of logic say that one cannot go on to questions 2 and 3 in the letter to me of May 1983 (areas in which I clearly dissent and those areas in which they are not sure if I dissent or not) unless one first gives the norms to govern dissent. Why has the Congregation been unwilling to answer that question? Why are they stalling?

My frustration is increased by the fact that in view of many others my positions are not that different from those proposed by Catholic moral theologians throughout the world. Again, no satisfactory response has been given to me on this issue. Some have suggested to me that it is this fact which also helps respond to the question I raised in the last paragraph.

As you know, I spent an entire academic year (1968-1969) defending my position on dissent. I have written extensively precisely to explain and defend my approach. I feel that the Congregation has been unwilling to engage me in a true dialogue on this subject. Why?

I am now in the midst of the second semester with the usual teaching and writing commitments. However, I want to share this preliminary reaction with you now. It might be helpful if you send a copy of it to the Congregation.

Sincerely yours,
Charles E. Curran

CEC/mzh


From the desk of:
ARCHBISHOP JAMES A. HICKEY

May 7, 1984

Dear Father Curran,

I received this letter toward the end of last week, and hasten to forward it to you in accordance with the request of Cardinal Ratzinger.

Godfrey tells me that it was convenient for you to visit me here at the Pastoral Center on Saturday, May 12th.

As indicated in the Congregation's letter, the time for your complete reply has been extended to Sept. 1st, 1984. I have been advised, however, that the date set is not subject to further extension.

Please lay aside the time needed to comply with the directive of the Congregation. It means much to yourself and to the University.

Looking forward to seeing you in a few days. I am

Sincerely in Christ,
James A. Hickey

SACRA CONGREGATIO
PRO DOCTRINA FIDEI
00193 Romae,
Piazza del S. Uffizio, 11
Prot. N. 48/66

April 13, 1984

Dear Father Curran,

You will recall that on May 10, 1983, this Congregation wrote to
you asking you to reply to a second set of Observations which we
sent to you at that time. Those second Observations, revised in
light of a lengthy intermediate correspondence, were intended to
continue and to focus the inquiry which the Congregation began
when the first Observations were sent to you in 1979.

On August 10, 1983, you sent a partial reply, responding only to
the first of the Observations' three parts. On December 2, 1983,
seven months after you received our request for a full response, we
again asked for your cooperation. We understand that that letter
reached you after your semester break when, on February 28,
1984, you wrote to Archbishop Hickey, suggesting to him that he
copy the letter to this Congregation, in which you accuse the Congregation of "stalling" and insist that the Congregation clarify its
understanding of dissent.

The Congregation has made clear its position regarding public
dissent in its explicit citation in the Observations of *Lumen gentium* n. 25, in which religious assent is required of all the faithful
for the authentic teaching of the Pope, even if that teaching is not
"ex cathedra." The Observations state, moreover, that "to dissent
even privately requires personal certitude that the teaching of the
Church is incorrect," and notes its concern that "To further dissent
publicly and to encourage dissent in others runs the risk of causing
scandal to the faithful, and to assume a certain responsibility for
the confusion caused by setting up one's own theological opinion in
contradiction to the position taken by the Church."

Archbishop Hickey has asked that you be given an extended
period of time in which to answer the Congregation's Observations
and suggests the date of September 1, 1984. I would like to advise
you that the Congregation is willing to grant this extension and

that your complete reply to the Observations is urgently requested by that date. You may forward your reply to Archbishop Hickey.

Failure to comply with the provisions of this arrangement will have to be interpreted according to the *Ratio Agendi,* n. 16: "Si autem auctor non responderit . . . Congregatio ordinaria opportuna consilia inibit."

Sincerely yours in Christ,
Joseph Cardinal Ratzinger

August 24, 1984

His Eminence
Joseph Cardinal Ratzinger
Praefectus, Sacra Congregatio pro Doctrina Fidei
Piazza del S. Uffizio, 11
00193 Rome

Dear Cardinal Ratzinger:

Enclosed you will find, in accord with the directions of your letter dated April 13, 1984, my Response to the Observations of the Congregation for the Doctrine of the Faith addressed to me.

At the end of this Response I note that I have answered, often in great detail, every question which has been asked of me. However, it seems that the process thus far has not achieved the goals of either truth or justice. I am prepared and willing to do whatever is helpful and necessary to achieve these goals.

Sincerely yours in Christ,
Charles E. Curran

CEC/mzh

RESPONSE

To the questions posed in the letter from
Cardinal Ratzinger dated April 13, 1984,
the letter from Cardinal Ratzinger dated May 10, 1983
and the Observations dated April 1983


Charles E. Curran
(Prot. N. 48/66)
August 24, 1984


This response is in reply to the letter of the Congregation for the Doctrine of the Faith to me dated April 13, 1984 and received by me on May 7, 1984. The letter notes my claim that the Congregation is stalling and my insistence that the Congregation clarify its understanding of dissent. Then in one paragraph the Congregation maintains it has made clear its position on dissent. The Congregation's letter points out that on August 10, 1983 I responded only partially to the May 10, 1983 Observations and in the last paragraph asks that my full response to the Observations of May 10, 1983 be made by September 1, 1984.

This response will be divided into three parts: 1) my claim that the Congregation is stalling; 2) my judgment that to this day the Congregation has not made clear its position regarding dissent; 3) the "full" response to the Observations of May 10, 1983.

I.

The claim of stalling is somewhat connected with but broader than my judgment that the Congregation has not made clear its position on dissent and especially public dissent. The historical record supports this contention.

I received the original letter from the Congregation on August 2, 1979. Shortly afterward my eighty-year-old father died, and I was executor of the will and had some shared responsibility to provide for my mother. On October 26, 1979 I sent a detailed twenty-one page response to the Congregation divided into four parts beginning with "Some Preliminary Remarks" and dealing with questions of dissent which the Congregation itself had described as the

"fundamental observation" and the "fundamental flaw" in my writings.

Under date of March 20, 1980 the Congregation gave a preliminary reply containing three points. The first two points responded
to two of my preliminary remarks. I did not necessarily agree with
the responses, but it was an effort to engage in true dialogue. The
third part mentioned the five questions I posed about the hierarchical magisterium but said that in this connection the Congregation was reviewing the book *Dissent In and For the Church* and
such a review "help(s) to explain the necessary delay in providing
you with our further reply to your Response."

As a result of this letter written March 20, 1980, or about five
months after my response, I assumed a response would be forthcoming. I heard nothing until I received a letter dated February 9,
1981, about eleven months later. Imagine my surprise when there
was no response to my questions but only an invitation to complete
my response. This answer could have been given long before. It
does not take over thirteen months to make that kind of response.

I replied in a mild letter of May 21, 1981 noting my puzzlement
that there was no response to my questions. The Congregation's
answer of June 9, 1981 noted my opinion "that 'after we have been
able to come to an understanding on this (fundamental observation about the authentic magisterium), then the other problems
should fall into place.' Our procedure, however, requires our
examination of and judgment upon the author's complete response
to the points indicated to him (cfr. n. 15 sq. of 'Ratio agendi')." Why
was this not said to me immediately after my original response of
October 26, 1979? Why did the Congregation on March 20, 1980
reply to the first part of my response of October 26, 1979? In addition, I did not read number 15 of the *Ratio agendi* in this way, since
this refers to what happens at the end of the total process and not
to what transpires within the process itself.

I was quite disappointed by these facts and decided that I would
take my norm of acting from that used by the Congregation especially in terms of the time-frame. On June 21, 1982 I responded
with a twenty-three page paper to the other questions proposed in
the original Observations. On February 10, 1983 I received a one
paragraph letter saying the response was unsatisfactory. A following letter of May 10 enclosed another set of Oberservations and

asked only two things of me — do I want to revise any of my positions and would I respond to the questions raised in part three of the new Observations described as "issues which remain unclear?"

When my civil lawyer read that letter his comment was that the Congregation was refusing any real discussion and had already made up its mind. (The exact quote was that the response was tantamount to saying, "when are you going to stop beating your spouse.")

Again I was upset that the Congregation had ignored the original questions which I had asked in an attempt to discover what precisely was the position of the Congregation with regard to dissent in the Church and expressed my dismay and frustration that there was still no response to my questions. On August 10, 1983 I sent a sixteen page response once again trying to settle the issue which had been described as the fundamental flaw — my position on the role of the hierarchical magisterium and the possibility of dissent. In an effort to go the extra mile I was willing to recognize that my questions might seem to be not objective to the Congregation. If the Congregation did not want to answer my questions, I asked if the Congregation would be willing to accept the norms of public dissent proposed by the American bishops in 1968. I specifically pointed out that it is "blatantly false to say that Curran with a defense of personal or private dissent . . . justifiies public dissent." This response on my part tried to develop in a very straightforward, strong, but respectful way the fact that I was disappointed with the quality of the discussion. The response ended with a request that the Congregation state what are the criteria or norms that should govern dissent in the Church.

## II.

In response to my request for the Congregation to state its position on the norms governing dissent, the letter of April 13, 1984 claims that the Congregation has made clear its position in the Observations and mentions three things — the citation of *Lumen gentium* n. 25, the fact that to dissent even privately requires personal certitude, the concern that to dissent publicly and to encourage dissent in others runs the risk of scandal and means one assumes responsibility for the confusion caused.

In my view any fair-minded observer in the light of all that has been written on the subject of dissent would not find in this very short paragraph a clear position at all. In reality only one of these three parts of the Congregation's response refers explicitly to public dissent. And here in the very words of the Congregation there is no categorical rejection of public dissent but the carefully nuanced phrasing that public dissent runs the risk of causing scandal and the one doing it assumes responsibility for the confusion involved. The logic of the argument thus seems to be that if there is no scandal present then public dissent is permitted. Is this the position of the Congregation? If this is the position, then the whole discussion for the last five years should have been on this issue of scandal. But that has not been the case.

In addition the letter of April 13, 1984 containing the short paragraph shows no recognition of the fact that I devoted two full pages of my August 10, 1983 response to this particular claim (pages 12-14). My first comment was that the carefully nuanced statement again points out the need for the Congregation to clarify and clearly express its position on the norms governing public dissent. Then my response indicated how my writings had dealt with the question of scandal but went on to recognize the need for prudential judgments which take account of many other aspects involved in the question such as the truth of the matter itself.

I can only once again plead that reason and justice demand that the Congregation spell out the norms governing dissent especially public dissent, show how I have violated these norms, and finally indicate how and why my declarations and positions differ from those of many other Catholic theologians.

Perhaps my dissatisfaction with the process and the failure of the Congregation to spell out the criteria governing dissent comes from the experience I have had with a previous inquiry to which I was subject here at The Catholic University of America in the 1968-1969 academic year. As a result of the dissent to *Humanae vitae* by twenty professors on the faculty of The Catholic University of America, the board of trustees of The University called for an inquiry through academic due process to determine if the professors who signed the recent statement of dissent had violated by their declarations or their actions their responsibility to the Catholic University. The due-process nature of the investigation, despite some procedural shortcomings which were pointed out at the time, permitted an inquiry in which both the claims of truth were able to be clearly discussed and the rights of all people involved were safeguarded. The issues were clearly focused and an opportunity was given to address them from both sides of the discussion. The faculty board of inquiry unanimously concluded, "The 30 July statement of the subject professors represents a responsible theological dissent from the teaching of the Encyclical *Humanae vitae* and this dissent is reasonably supported as a tenable scholarly position." The Inquiry Report further maintained "that the declarations and actions of the subject professors with regard to the papal encyclical *Humanae vitae* did not violate any of their obligations to Catholic University . . ., did not offend against responsible academic procedure and did not depart from the spirit of the University."

Having the experience of such a thorough hearing in which it was possible to pinpoint the specific issues and address them, my first reaction in my response of October 26, 1979 (p. 1) was to protest the procedures as found in the *ratio agendi*. In my judgment made at that time and still my contention today these procedures "fail to incorporate the elementary principles of due process which are accepted in contemporary legal structures." It seems that the Congregation agrees with my judgment. In the March 20, 1980 response it is pointed out that the *ratio agendi* is not a trial. The letter explicitly says there are no accusers and no charges. Apparently then the Congregation recognizes that it is not following accepted due process procedures.

However, even if the Congregation does not follow due process, it still claims to have a procedure whose purpose is "to guarantee a careful and accurate evaluation of the content of published writings by an author. Should this examination indicate the presence of opinions which seem to be in conflict with Church teaching, the author himself is contacted in order to give him an opportuniity to explain how he sees his opinion(s) to be in accord with the teaching of the Church. . . ." In order to fulfill its own mandate, it seems to me that the Congregation must state as clearly as possible what are the norms governing dissent in the Church. I have been trying to elicit such norms ever since this process began in 1979. I reiterate the last sentence of my response of August 10, 1983: "I do not think that my request for clarification of this central issue can be looked upon as unreasonable."

### III.

The Congregation's letter to me of April 13, 1984 asked me to send a complete reply by September 1, 1984 since I had only responded to the first of the three parts of the Observations sent under the cover letter dated May 10, 1983. My purpose in responding so quickly to the first part was once again to draw attention to the primary issue and to see if the Congregation would spell out precisely what the norms governing dissent in the Church are. However, in that covering letter of May 10, 1983 the Congregation did not ask for a response to the first or the second part of the Observations. I was asked to respond to only two questions. First, do I want to revise and change any positions in clear public dissent from the magisterium? Second, would I respond to the questions raised in part three which covered issues which were unclear? It was my judgment that the Congregation had already reached its own conclusion, but I was still totally dissatisfied with the basis on which this conclusion was made. Having made very forcefully but respectfully my position that the Congregation has not focused the inquiry and has not spelled out precisely what is its position with regard to the fundamental flaw of dissent in the Church, I will now respond to the two questions raised in that covering letter.

The first question asks if I want to revise the positions I have taken in clear dissent from the hierarchical magisterium. The last paragraph in the Observations asks if I have given any thought to reconsider my positions in the light of *Familiaris consortio*.

Very honestly I found this question insulting. I have dedicated my life as a Catholic theologian to the pursuit of truth. If I change my position on important issues, I believe there is a strong moral obligation to state that as clearly as I can in the same way and manner that I stated the contrary positions. In addition I have not taken these positions without a great deal of prayer, study, consultation, and discernment. Since *Familiaris consortio* is an apostolic constitution, any Catholic theologian recognizes that it does not claim the same importance as an encyclical. If one has in good Catholic conscience judged there were sufficient reasons to dissent from the teaching found in an encyclical, one would not expect a declaration from the Holy Office or an apostolic constitution to cause one to change the earlier position especially if no new reasons were given for the position in question.

Perhaps from a juridical viewpoint the question was posed to me so that I might be given a last chance to change, but I still find the question insulting to my integrity as a Catholic, a theologian, and a person.

I will now respond to the questions raised in part three. The first issue on page 7 talks about my insistence that in the midst of complexity and specificity one cannot have certitude or absolute binding force in every case. "Should not this infinity of specific details, in a given instance of moral decision-making, likewise make certainty improbable on Fr. Curran's part that the magisterium is, in fact, wrong, so completely and so often?"

In my writings I see the question of certitude as an epistemological question which recognizes that as one goes from the general to the specific the possibility of certitude or absolute application becomes less. Thus in *Ongoing Revision* (pp. 38-39) I wrote:

> In my judgment the ultimate reason is epistemological. On specific moral questions one cannot have a certitude which excludes the possibility of error. Such an epistemological approach distinguishes the degree of certitude which can be had depending on the degree of generality or specificity with which one is dealing. As one goes from the general to the more specific, the possibility of a certitude which excludes error is less. One can be quite certain, for example, that murder is always wrong, but the problem is to determine in practice what is murder.
>
> One can assert with great certitude that a Christian should be a loving, self-sacrificing person of hope and a sign of the fruits of the Spirit to the world, but one cannot know with great certitude how to solve conflict situations involving human lives. Roman Catholic theology in the past has solved the question of conflict situations which might involve killing or abortion on the basis of the understanding of the principle of double effect. Such a solution rests on a philosophical understanding of human actions in which the meaning of direct effect is defined in terms of the physical structure of the act itself. Such a solution is based on one philosophical un-

derstanding of the human act, but many people, including Roman Catholic theologians today, point out the inadequacy of that particular philosophical understanding as a solution to conflict situations.

The Catholic theological and ethical traditions following
Aquinas have insisted on an intrinsic and rational understanding
of morality. Something is commanded because it is good and not
the other way around. When the reality itself is so complex and
specific one cannot claim to have the certitude that excludes the
possibility of error. Thomas Aquinas himself recognized the same
basic understanding of moral reality (I-II, q. 94, a. 4). The consultation in Rome involving Vatican officials, representatives of European bishops' conferences, and the American bishops on peace and
disarmament recognizes different levels of generality and specificity calling for correspondingly different levels of certitude. "A
clear line must be drawn between the statement of principles and
practical choices based on prudential judgment" (*Origins* 12 [April
7, 1983], 693).

It might be objected to me that certitude excluding the possibility of error can exist on the level of principles but not on the level of
practical judgments, and that in the questions that are contended
between us one is really dealing with principles. In response it is
necessary to recognize that principles themselves have a wide
range going from the less specific to the more specific. There is a
difference between principles and concrete rules which by their
very nature are specific. The Congregation itself is not unaware of
the debate about exceptionless norms in moral theology and their
binding force since the Congregation itself has heard and partici-
pated in the debate (cf. *Sittliche Normen: Zum Problem ihrer
allgemeinen und unwandelharen Geltung,* ed. W. Kerber Düssel-
dorf: Patmos, 1982). Once again it is evident that many other Catholic moral theologians have made the same point that I have been
making. The epistemology and logic involved indicate that the very
specific and complex nature of the material being dealt with indicates that absolute certitude cannot be achieved on these matters.

In the light of all that I have written earlier, I object to the statement that Curran holds "that the Magisterium is, in fact, wrong so
completely. . . ." As pointed out above my theory has consistently
recognized that as one descends to specifics the possibility of cer-

titude decreases. However, there can and should be great certitude and agreement on the levels of the more general. I have never said that the hierarchical Magisterium is so completely wrong. The problem arises at the level of complexity and specificity. In commenting on *Humanae vitae* I have publicly recognized that "many positive values concerning marriage are expressed in Paul VI's encyclical." It is wrong to say that I so completely claim that the magisterium is wrong. My writings both in explaining epistemological theory in general and in dealing with specific questions indicate that the area of pluralism becomes greater when one descends to the area of the more complex and the more specific. I logically applied the same approach to the area of social ethics. In this context I have criticized a "theological actualism," which desires to have a greater certitude on complex specific questions than the complexity and specificity of the matter itself allow. "As one descends from the general to the specific there is bound to be a lesser possibility of certitude and the admission of a greater plurality of possible options and opinions" (*The Crisis in Priestly Ministry,* p. 136; see also *New Perspectives in Moral Theology,* pp. 132ff).

The second paragraph on page 7 deals with my "theory of compromise" and raises the same basic question in terms of abuse, the danger of self-justification, and the danger of forgetting claims of justice.

The Catholic tradition has always proposed a classical response to such an objection: *abusus non tollit usum.* Our tradition has always recognized the just war theory with its acceptance of the fact that not all wars are just. All would have to admit the fact that historically there have been many unjust wars and there is always a danger for nations and leaders to deceive themselves, to justify their wrong actions, and thereby to ignore the real claims of justice. However, despite the possibility of abuse, the Catholic tradition has maintained the just war theory.

However, in dealing with questions in which the possibility of abuse exists, it is true that ordinarily one should be expected to point out this fact and recognize some of the dangers involved. My position on compromise has tried to do that as is clear in the places in which I have developed the theory at great length (*Catholic Moral Theology in Dialogue,* pp. 184-219 and *Transition and Tradition in Moral Theology,* pp. 73-78).

The theory of compromise is basically grounded in my recognition of the presence of sin in the world affecting what might truly be called the objective moral order. I have concluded that the Catholic tradition has failed to give enough importance to the reality of sin and especially the sin of the world. On a number of occasions I have disagreed with and dissented from the methodology employed in some papal social encyclicals especially using *Pacem in terris* as an example. "*Pacem in terris* well illustrates the failure of papal social teaching to give enough importance to the reality of sin" (*Catholic Moral Theology in Dialogue*, pp. 122ff; see also *Politics, Medicine, and Christian Ethics: A Dialogue with Paul Ramsey,* pp. 36 and passim). Sin is incorporated in my theory into the fivefold stance of creation, sin, incarnation, redemption, and resurrection-destiny. Such a stance theoretically wants to recognize the role of sin but at the same time not to absolutize it.

In this light I have explicitly recognized the danger of misusing the theology of compromise by forgetting the fact that Christians are called to struggle against sin in all its forms including the sin of the world:

> One must never forget there is a twofold aspect about the sin of the world. On the one hand, the Christian is called to struggle against sin. The whole of the Christian message calls for the Christian in union with Jesus to strive through the power of love to overcome sin. The call to conversion reminds the individual of the need continually to change one's heart as well as struggle to change the conditions of the world in which we live. It seems at times that the theory of the fathers of the church failed to recognize this aspect of sin. They too readily justified and accepted the reality of slavery as being brought about by the evil of sin and did not struggle enough to do away with such an institution. On the other hand, one must admit that in our imperfect world, in which the fullness of grace is not yet here, there will always remain some aspects of the sin of the world in our life. This is the truth that was recognized in the early centuries of the Church (*Transition and Tradition in Moral Theology,* p. 76).

I have consistently pointed out that there are limits to the theory of compromise and insisted on the generic limits of the rights of other innocent persons and the rights of society (*Catholic Moral Theology in Dialogue*, p. 218). As applied to homosexuality I have also recognized the limits of compromise in this particular case. Compromise cannot justify any type of homosexual behavior but only within a loving relationship striving for permanency. In developing my understanding, I later pointed out that the theology of compromise needs further ethical mediating principles to avoid any danger of abuse (*Transition and Tradition in Moral Theology*, p. 77). Most recently I have discussed, criticized, and evaluated four other positions concerning homosexuality and once again tried to clarify my own mediating position by responding to some objections that had been raised against my position both by more conservative and by more liberal ethicists. Here again I stressed the limits and possible abuses of the theology of compromise in general and the existence of these dangers in its specific use in the area of homosexuality. In general, sometimes sin in the world cannot be overcome here and now, for God's grace will be fully present only at the end of time. On the particular question of homosexual activity, the limits are placed by the need for a loving, faithful relationship striving for permanency. Thus the fact of having a particular kind of orientation by that fact alone cannot justify the acts based on that orientation. There are limits to what can be accepted on the basis of a theology of compromise (*Critical Concerns in Moral Theology*, pp. 93-95).

The third issue mentioned is "New Testament ideals." First of all it is necessary to clear up some misinterpretation and/or error found in the Observations. The Observations ask: "is it not an oversimplification to see *all* (emphasis added) New Testamental moral injunctions as pervaded by that particular type of eschatological expectation which viewed the end of the epoch as coinciding with the end of the physical world and the Parousia itself?" Nowhere do the Observations give any evidence that I ever made such a statement. To my knowledge no such statement has ever been made by me. Such an understanding would go against the recognition of complexity which has characterized my entire moral methodology.

The two places in which I have dealt most extensively with ideals in the New Testament have been the radical ethical teaching of Jesus and the specific question of the indissolubility of marriage.

In both cases I was arguing that the ethical obligation could not be understood as absolute, exceptionless moral norms binding on all in all circumstances.

As my treatment of the radical ethics of Jesus indicates this has been a controversial and debated question almost from the very beginning of Christian theology. I do understand these radical teachings of Jesus as often found in the Sermon on the Mount in terms of the eschatological tension between the now and the fullness of the eschaton. Once again this also follows from the stance I have proposed as the first logical step for moral theology. In addition to the moral ideal I also frequently used the words "goal" "direction" and "thrust" to explain how this radical ethic is relevant to moral decision-making and action at the present time (*Themes in Moral Theology,* pp. 14-19). I know of no Catholic theologians or of any teaching of the Church which would understand the radical ethic of Jesus in terms of a norm as understood in my description above.

I have devoted three studies to the question of the indissolubility of marriage and divorce. I have argued that indissolubility should not be understood as a norm in the sense described above — that is, a norm which is always and everywhere obliging and the breaking of which always involves moral wrong on the part of the individual. In the process, I have noted that the official teaching and practice of the Catholic church does not understand indissolubility as an exceptionless norm, but in its own way has made an accommodation with the radical ethical teaching of Jesus. "The Church has so interpreted the teaching of Jesus throughout the years that now less than twenty percent of the marriages in the world are absolutely indissoluble" (*Ongoing Revision in Moral Theology,* p. 89).

The earlier response of June 21, 1982 deals with the specific question of indissolubility. Note briefly that I tried to show how even the early Church found it necessary to make accommodations and exceptions in the radical ethical demand of Jesus. In that response (pp. 15-17) I strongly objected to an interpretation of the term ideal as a "mere" ideal. The idea of indissolubility has a moral obligatory force, but such force is not the same as that of an absolute exceptionless norm. There might be other ways of expressing this obligatory force. Häring speaks of goal commandments. Childress and other Protestant authors speak of presumptions. I have gone out of my way to insist that ideal does have an obligatory character about it, but as a goal and not as an absolute norm binding on all to the extent that the breaking of this norm is always and everywhere morally wrong. I wrote one article precisely to emphasize the obligatory aspect of the call to indissolubility and the need in this regard for the Church and all concerned with indissolubility to struggle against a number of aspects in our present culture which militate against indissolubility (*Issues in Sexual and Medical Ethics*, pp. 3-29).

I could accept the fact of "every Christian's personal responsibility to emulate" this teaching but interpreted in the way explained above.

The fourth issue is phrased as "Frequency of dissent a cause to change the magisterium's position?" The longest question in this paragraph is phrased as follows: "If the Church should change her position on indissolubility in the light of the large numbers of Catholics who ignore the magisterium on this point, would the results of a similar poll on the question of, say, dishonesty imply that the magisterium should now hold that dishonesty is somehow now good, or at least not bad?"

Any fair observer familiar with my writings would judge the question to be both insulting and simplistic. In general I have insisted above all on the complexity of many different elements that go into the decision-making process. In addition, I have specifically responded to this very objection in my writings on the subject of indissolubility which is the subject matter mentioned in the question posed by the Congregation.

> However, in any evaluation of possible change one must learn from the history of Roman Catholicism that change often does follow this particular route. Contemporary Catholic moral theology realizes the importance of pastoral practice and the experience of Christian people. The whole Church can and often does learn through the experience of Christian people as a *locus theologicus,* but one can never determine morality merely from what people do. The discernment of the Spirit is not reducible to a Gallup Poll with moral truth decided by a majority vote. Our human experience is conditioned by the limitations and sinfulness which

form a necessary part of our existence. Experience then
cannot be absolutely accepted without a critical discernment. But when a large number of apparently good
Christian people are involved in a particular mode of
acting, at least the Church and the theologians must
take them seriously and be willing to reexamine the
teaching (*Ongoing Revision,* p. 81).

The above is not an isolated quotation as anyone familiar with
my work realizes. For example, in *Contemporary Problems in
Moral Theology,* (pp. 127-128) I pointed out, "Of course, just as
theological methodology can never become totally inductive (the
theologian always begins with the revelation of God in Christ), so
too experience can never become the only factor in the formation of
the Christian ethic. However, experience has a very important role
to play."

My calling the experience of Christian married people a *"locus
theologicus"* has been echoed at the 1980 Synod of Bishops in the
words of Cardinal Basil Hume. "This prophetic mission of the family, and so of husbands and wives, is based upon their experience
as married persons and on an understanding of the sacrament of
marriage of which they can speak with their own authority. This
experience and this understanding constitute, I would suggest, an
authentic *fons theologiae* from which we, the pastors, and indeed
the whole Church can draw" (*Origins* 10 [1980], 276).

The next question in this section states: "Is not the argument for
a change of principle from frequency of abuse actually and profoundly legalistic?" The question obviously begs the entire question for the matter under dispute is whether or not the experience
does constitute an abuse. Would the Congregation say that the
change in the teaching of the Church on religious liberty at the Second Vatican Council was based on an abuse? The Council document (n. 1) declares that this desire for the free exercise of religion
in society which had already been existing in the desires of human
beings is greatly in accord with truth and justice. When did the
teaching on religious liberty become true? Only when a document
was signed at the Second Vatican Council? The conciliar document
itself recognizes that the newer teaching was true before the official Church teaching changed.

As for the last question in this section I have maintained often and frequently (e.g., *Themes in Fundamental Moral Theology,* pp. 81ff) that moral obligation in the Catholic tradition is intrinsic and realistic. Something is commanded because it is good. Something is not good because it is commanded. However, your question again assumes as true what is the point of discussion and therefore does not truly attempt to arrive at the truth of the matter. The question reads: "Is Christian marriage indissoluble because the Church *says* it is or does the Church say Christian marriage is indissoluble because it is?"

However, your question logically accepts and ratifies the basic principle supporting my whole approach to dissent — namely, the hierarchical magisterium must conform itself to truth and is subject to this truth. As I have phrased it in *Critical Concerns in Moral Theology* (p. 247):

> In discussing the possibility of dissent, again it is important to understand the question properly and not merely in terms of opposition between the authoritative Church teaching and the conscience of the individual believer. Here too there is the all-important third term — the Christian moral truth to which both the hierarchical teaching role and the individual conscience are subordinated. However, such an understanding does not mean that the teaching of the hierarchical magisterium and the conscience of the individual believer are on exactly the same level. Traditionally Catholic theology has talked about a presumption in favor of the teaching of the hierarchical magisterium on noninfallible issues precisely because of the gift of the Spirit given to the hierarchical office of the Church. This presumption itself, however, always cedes to the truth.

The last issue brought up in the Observations concerns physicalism and biologism. Again the first questions merely point out the differences between the position I am maintaining and the one maintained by the Congregation. Is physicalism or biologism as an exclusive source what the encyclical *Humanae vitae* has done or is it only what Fr. Curran says it has done? In my judgment both questions are to be answered in the affirmative. I have explained

my reasons for this position many times and more specifically in
my response of June 21, 1982. Again it must be pointed out that my
position is supported by the majority of Roman Catholic moral
theologians writing today. All those who pose and accept theories
distinguishing between moral evil on the one hand and premoral,
nonmoral, ontic or physical evil on the other hand in principle accept my position. What does the Congregation answer to the four
pages (pp. 9-14) of my earlier response trying to prove my position
and quoting another author as saying that no one has truly responded to this fundamental objection made by Curran and many
others against the argumentation proposed in *Humanae vitae?*

The Observations then raise two questions — is there any place
for the physical dimension in the moral decision-making process
and what about the danger that a nonphysicalist argument is
guilty of angelism, realism, and irrelevancy?

Once again, anyone familiar with my writings knows I have not
only recognized the danger of not giving enough importance to the
physical but I have even highlighted this possible danger in my
writings. In an early dialogue with Joseph Fletcher, I criticized
Fletcher for not giving enough importance to the earthly realities
and to the physical dimension of things. I pointed out that although Catholic teaching has occasionally gone too far and
canonized physical acts and processes, the problem is not solved by
going to the opposite extreme as Fletcher does in giving no importance to the earthly and the physical (*A New Look at Christian
Morality,* pp. 166-167).

The last paragraph of my long discussion of natural law in *Contemporary Problems in Moral Theology* (p. 148) begins with the following caveat. "A word of caution is in order. It seems that some
proponents of situation ethics have not given enough importance
to the bodily, the material, the external, and the physical aspects
of reality." In *Transition and Tradition in Moral Theology* (pp. 32-
33) the discussion on physicalism begins with the very same
caveat.

> However, a word of caution is in order. The physical or
> biological structure of the act is not necessarily identical
> with the moral aspect, but sometimes the physical and
> the moral cannot be separated. The best example is the
> human person. The human person and the physical life

of the human person cannot be separated — at least in this world. There is no human person apart from the physical reality of the person. The test for the death of a human person, whether it is the lack of heartbeat, or breathing or brain waves, is based on physical criteria. In attacking the problem of physicalism one must avoid the extreme of giving no importance to the physical or denying that at times the physical and the moral are the same.

## Conclusion

Many times in past letters I have expressed my dissatisfaction with the process as a means of guaranteeing "a careful and accurate examination" of my writings. My pleas have apparently fallen on deaf ears. The tone and content of this response are purposely strong but always respectful in order to express once again the inadequacy of the process to achieve its goal. Any fair-minded person who reads this correspondence must come to the conclusion that the process thus far is severely wanting.

However, despite all these problems I have faithfully responded to every single question which has been raised to me. I would now hope that the opportunity is present to pursue this inquiry in a way that will enable the real differences to be specified and spelled out as specifically as possible. In order to achieve this purpose it is necessary for the Congregation to spell out what are the norms of dissent, to show how I have violated those norms, and to show how my position differs from that of many other Roman Catholic theologians. This response on my part fulfills the request that has been made of me but in my judgment it in no way ends the discussion. It is imperative for true dialogue to continue and I am prepared to cooperate in every way to achieve this purpose.

SACRA CONGREGATIO
PRO DOCTRINA FIDEI
00193 Romae
Piazza del S. Uffizio, 11

Prot. N. 48/66

October 26, 1984

Dear Father Curran,

I would like to acknowledge receipt of your letter of August 24, 1984, with its attached responses to this Congregation's Observations sent to you on April 13, 1984.

We are in the course of studying the theological content of the reply at the end of which we shall let you know the results of our examination and the remaining steps we consider necessary for a just settlement of this matter.

With my best wishes, I remain

Sincerely yours in Christ,
Joseph Cardinal Ratzinger

# VI
# FINAL DECISION
# (September 1985-
# September 1986)

September 17, 1985.   Ratzinger to Curran concluding the inquiry and asking for reply. One who holds such positions cannot be called a Catholic theologian and cannot teach in the name of the Church.

November 11, 1985.   Ratzinger to Hickey responding to Curran's oral query about the assent of faith.

December 9, 1985.   Curran to Hickey giving a preliminary response to the Ratzinger letter of September 17 and pursuing the matter of the assent of faith.

January 28, 1986.   Curran to Ratzinger requesting informal meeting.

February 8, 1986.   Ratzinger to Curran accepting the informal meeting and offering March dates.

February 13, 1986.   Curran to Ratzinger making final arrangements for March 8 informal meeting.

March 10, 1986.   Ratzinger to Hickey asking for Curran's definitive written response.

April 1, 1986.   Curran's final written reply to Ratzinger.

July 25, 1986.   Ratzinger to Curran informing him that he is no longer suitable nor eligible to exercise the function of a Professor of Catholic Theology.

August 27,1986   Curran to Ratzinger acknowledging receipt of above letter and sending his public remarks.

SACRA CONGREGATIO
PRO DOCTRINA FIDEI
00193 Romae
Piazza del S. Uffizio, 11

Prot. N. 48/66

September 17, 1985

Dear Father Curran,

In your letter of August 24, 1984, you forwarded your response
to this Congregation's critical "Observations" on your work which
we had sent to you with our letter of May 10, 1983. We would like
to assure you that your responses have been carefully studied and
to say that we are now, after a multiple exchange of correspondence, in a position to bring this inquiry to a conclusion. The results
of the Congregation's inquiry were presented to the Sovereign Pontiff in an audience granted to the undersigned Cardinal Prefect on
June 28, 1985, and were confirmed by him.

The results of this study make it essential to refer here, however
briefly, to some theological and juridical points which give definition to all theological teaching in the Catholic Church. Above all,
we must recall the clear doctrine of the Vatican Council II regarding the principles for the assent of faith (*Lumen gentium* 25). This
doctrine was incorporated in the revised Code of Canon Law which
in c. 752 sums up the thought of the Council on this point.

The Apostolic Constitution *Sapientia Christiana* makes specific
application of these principles to the particular requirements of
theological instruction and says that Catholic theologians, hence
those teaching in ecclesiastical faculties, do not teach on their own
authority but by virtue of the mission they have received from the
Church. (*Sap. Chris.* 27 par. 1; cf. 26 par. 2). In order to guarantee
this teaching, the Church claims the freedom to maintain her own
academic institutions in which her doctrine is reflected upon,
taught and interpreted in complete fidelity. This freedom of the
Church to teach her doctrine is in full accord with the students' corresponding right to know what that teaching is and have it properly explained to them. This freedom of the Church likewise implies the right to choose for her theological faculties those and only
those professors who, in complete intellectual honesty and integ-

rity, recognize themselves to be capable of meeting these requirements.

In the correspondence exchanged between yourself and this Congregation, you have clearly affirmed that the positions you have maintained on various important elements of moral doctrine are in open contrast with the teaching of the Magisterium, about which the above-mentioned official documents speak. In what follows, we would like to list briefly the points on which this dissent has been verified.

The first area of dissent is with regard to the principle of the Church's teaching according to which every marital act must remain open to the transmission of life, and therefore artificial contraception and direct sterilization are forbidden as intrinsically wrong. This is in perfect agreement with the living tradition of the Church, made evident in the teaching of recent Popes, the documents of the Vatican Council II, and explicitly affirmed by Pope Paul VI in *Humanae vitae*. Since that time, it has been confirmed in *Familiaris consortio* by Pope John Paul II, and steadily repeated by him on several occasions.

Likewise, regarding the issues of abortion and euthanasia, the teaching of the Church, from which you dissent, has been unequivocal, and, despite pressure to the contrary, the Magisterium has recently reaffirmed the sacred and inviolable character of human life from the moment of conception. Every true Catholic must hold that abortion and euthanasia are unspeakable crimes, that is to say, actions that cannot be approved of for any motive or in any circumstance. No one can take the life of an innocent human being whether a fetus or an embryo, child or adult, elderly, incurably ill or near death, without opposing God's love for them, without violating a fundamental right, and therefore without committing a crime of the utmost gravity. (*Gaudium et spes* 51; *CDF Decree on Abortion* 14; *CDF Decree on Euthanasia*, II.).

With respect to the third area noted in the "Observations", i.e., masturbation, pre-marital intercourse and homosexual acts, all the faithful are bound to follow the Magisterium according to which these acts are intrinsically immoral. On this point, the 1975 *Declaration on Certain Questions Concerning Sexual Ethics* is clear. Whatever the motive may be, the deliberate use of the sexual faculty, outside normal and legitimate conjugal relations, essentially contradicts its finality, the purpose intended by the Creator.

Finally, as was again pointed out in the "Observations", the teaching of the Council of Trent on the indissolubility of sacramental and consummated marriage was clearly taught by the Vatican Council II, which described marriage as an indissoluble bond between two persons. A Catholic cannot affirm the contrary. (cf. *Gaudium et spes* 48-51). This truth has likewise been incorporated in the revised Code's c. 1056.

In light of the indispensable requirements for authentic theological instruction, described by the Council and by the public law of the Catholic Church (cf. supra), the Congregation now invites you to reconsider and to retract those positions which violate the conditions necessary for a professor to be called a Catholic theologian. It must be recognized that the authorities of the Church cannot allow the present situation to continue in which the inherent contradiction is prolonged that one who is to teach in the name of the Church in fact denies her teaching.

The consignment of this letter to you by the competent authorities is meant to assure a just resolution of this case for yourself and for all the parties involved.

We would ask that you forward your reply to this letter to the Most Reverend Chancellor of the Catholic University as soon as possible in a time period not to exceed two months.

In your letter you indicated that you had not taken the positions you have, without "a great deal of prayer, study, consultation and discernment." This fact inspires us to hope that by further application of these means, you will come to that due adherence to the Church's doctrine which should characterize all the faithful.

Sincerely yours in Christ,
Joseph Cardinal Ratzinger

SACRA CONGREGATIO
PRO DOCTRINA FIDEI
00193 Romae
Piazza del S. Uffizio, 11

Prot. N. 48/66

November 11, 1985

Most Reverend James Hickey
Archbishop of Washington, D.C.
U.S.A.

Your Excellency,

I would like to acknowledge your letter of October 23, 1985 in which you reported some disagreement on the part of Fr. Charles Curran regarding a phrase in our letter to him of September 17, 1985. The issue is the *assensus fidei* as contrasted with the *obsequium religiosum*.

When canon 752 of the Revised Code was written, to which explicit reference was made in our letter, it rightly distinguished between the assent of faith and religious submission, in accord with the distinction made in *Lumen gentium* 25. The canon noted that even (quidem) when the assent of faith is *not* required, as in the case of some papal positions, the religious submission is still expected.

While I am not certain of what Fr. Curran precisely wished to contest, it may be that he feared the Congregation was implying that the *assensus fidei* was always required. Please assure him that such was not our intention, which is why c. 752 was cited explicitly.

With my sincere thanks for your invaluable collaboration in this entire matter, and with my best wishes, I am

Sincerely yours in Christ,
Joseph Cardinal Ratzinger

The
CATHOLIC
  UNIVERSITY of
    AMERICA

Washington, D.C. 20064


December 9, 1985

The Most Reverend James A. Hickey, D.D.
Archbishop of Washington
5001 Eastern Avenue
P.O. Box 29260
Washington, D.C. 20017

Dear Archbishop Hickey,

I am enclosing three different documents in this letter: a letter
addressed to you which incorporates my preliminary response to
the September 17 letter of the Congregation to me; another letter
to you which, in the light of Cardinal Ratzinger's letter to you of
November 11, tries to clarify my exact problem with what the September 17 letter to me said about the assent of faith; a memoran-
dum summarizing our recent meeting.

At our December 4 meeting in response to your question I said
that I would not be willing to accept a compromise whereby I teach
only doctoral level students. I have reflected on this in the meantime and still come to the same conclusion.

If there are any problems or questions which arise before you
leave for Rome, please feel free to contact me.

I am sending to Cardinal Bernardin by overnight express mail a
copy of all that I am giving you now.

Sincerely yours in Christ,
Charles E. Curran


CEC/ddk

December 9, 1985

The Most Reverend James A. Hickey, D.D.
Archbishop of Washington
5001 Eastern Avenue
P.O. Box 29260
Washington, D.C. 20017

Dear Archbishop Hickey,

In the light of the two meetings I have had with Cardinal Bernardin and yourself, I want to make a preliminary response to the letter of Cardinal Ratzinger to me under the date of September 17, which was officially handed over to me at our October 10 meeting. I emphasize that this is only a preliminary response with the very restricted focus of trying to pinpoint as accurately as possible the differences as I see them between the Congregation and myself. Many of the points have emerged in the course of our conversations, but in this letter I want to address three aspects in a somewhat systematic way.

The first aspect concerns a factual clarification. Cardinal Ratzinger's letter of September 17, 1985 emphasizes teaching and my role as a teacher. Our previous correspondence has not discussed my teaching and the particular courses that I teach. As a matter of fact, I have not taught the course in marriage and sexual ethics in our Department of Theology for at least the last ten years. I have no plans for teaching in this area in the foreseeable future.

The second aspect concerns the exact nature of the primary area of difference between the Congregation and myself. I was quite surprised and taken aback by the Congregation's assertion that the *assent of faith* is the theological point involved. (In a separate letter I will respond to what the September 17 letter said about the assent of faith in the light of Cardinal Ratzinger's November 11 letter to you which you so kindly forwarded to me). From my perspective I have constantly emphasized that my position on dissent in no way involves or contradicts Catholic faith and the assent of faith made by me as a Catholic believer and as a theologian. I do not now and never have challenged what belongs to Catholic faith as such. This point is absolutely crucial for me both as a Catholic believer and a Catholic theologian.

This letter of September 17 marks the first time the Congregation has ever described our differences in terms of the assent of faith. The very first paragraph of the first "Observations" sent to me by the Congregation in 1979 describes the issue as the assent due to noninfallible church teaching. According to the Congregation the "fundamental flaw" in my writings is my understanding of the "role of the Church's authentic magisterium." All the subsequent correspondence between the Congregation and myself has centered on the *obsequium religiosum* which is the response due to authoritative, authentic, noninfallible hierarchical teaching.

Although the previous correspondence between the Congregation and myself agreed that the question of the *obsequium religiosum* was the fundamental issue, there was disagreement between us on what this response requires and especially the possibility of dissent.

As I read the September 17 letter, it says that a Catholic theologian cannot dissent from authentic, noninfallible hierarchical teaching and still be considered a Catholic theologian. If this criterion were applied in the church today, a very large number of those who were actively engaged as Catholic theologians could not truly be considered to be Catholic theologians. In previous correspondence with the Congregation I cited a large number of bishops and theologians who would strongly disagree in theory and in practice with the criterion that dissent from such noninfallible teaching means that one is no longer a Catholic theologian. Those who disagree with the criterion proposed in the September 17 letter and who have affirmed the possibility and legitimacy of some dissent from noninfallible teaching include the bishops of the United States, the West German bishops, the Canadian bishops, and many other hierarchies as seen especially in their responses to *Humanae vitae* (see Joseph A. Selling, "The Reaction to *Humanae vitae:* A Study in Special and Fundamental Theology" [S.T.D. Dissertation, Catholic University of Louvain, 1977]); also individual bishops such as Coffy, Butler, and others. Theologians holding the same basic position include such well recognized international Catholic theologians as Rahner, Congar, and Häring; United States theologians such as McBrien, McCormick, Tracy, and a number of different committee reports issued by the Catholic Theological Society of America; Catholic University of America theologians such as Dulles and Komonchak. This is only a small sampling of those who hold such a position as distinguished from the position taken by the Congregation in this letter of September 17.

I still remain quite disappointed with the dialogue that has ensued between the Congregation and myself on this matter. Both good theology and justice demand that the Congregation explicitly state what are the norms governing the legitimacy or the possibility of dissent from such noninfallible teaching and then indicate how I have violated these norms. In 1979, I proposed five questions and my answers to these questions in an attempt to find out what might be the norms that the Congregation is proposing, but there has never been a response to these questions. Later I expressed my willingness to accept the criteria for dissent proposed by the United States bishops in 1968, but again the Congregation was unwilling to accept these norms. The September 17 letter apparently accepts the criterion that any theologian who dissents from noninfallible church teaching can no longer be considered a Catholic theologian. In my judgment such a criterion is theologically false and pastorally disastrous for the life of the church.

The third issue for clarification concerns the exact nature of the positions I take on the issues mentioned in the September 17 letter. It is true that I dissent on these issues, but my positions have always been carefully nuanced and they are often in basic agreement with the noninfallible hierarchical teaching. It is impossible to repeat here all that I have written on the subject, but I will attempt now to summarize as accurately and briefly as possible the positions I have taken so that the real differences between myself and the Congregation will be clear. These differences are much narrower than the September 17 letter implies.

The September 17 letter lists four areas of my dissent — contraception and sterilization; abortion and euthanasia; masturbation, premarital sexual acts, and homosexual acts; the indissolubility of marriage.

On the question of contraception and sterilization I have maintained that these actions are not intrinsically evil but can be good insofar as they are governed by the principles of responsible parenthood and stewardship. However, I have also pointed out the danger of abuse in connection with both contraception and sterilization. (See, among other sources, *New Perspectives in Moral Theology*, pp. 194-211; *Transition and Tradition in Moral Theology*, pp. 29-43; *Moral Theology: A Continuing Journey*, pp. 141-169.)

On the issues of abortion and euthanasia, I have in a number of places developed in an in-depth way my position on abortion; e.g., *New Perspectives in Moral Theology*, pp. 163-193; *Transition and Tradition in Moral Theology*, pp. 207-250. My position can be succinctly stated: truly individual human life begins at the time of individuation which occurs between the fourteenth and the twenty-first day after conception. One can be justified in taking the individual life only for the sake of the mother or for a value commensurate with life itself. In determining the time of individuation as the beginning of truly individual human life I have rejected positions proposed by other Catholic theologians for a later time. Recently two distinguished professors from Louvain University, J.-F. Malherbe and E. Boné, have proposed the same criterion for the beginning of truly individual human life (*Le Supplément*, No. 153, Juin 1985, 125-134). My position on the solution of conflict cases in abortion is consonant with that proposed by all those theologians who accept a theory of proportionate reason.

I have never done an in-depth study on euthanasia, but have occasionally referred to euthanasia as an illustration of other points I was making; e.g., *Ongoing Revision*, pp. 160-161; *Themes in Fundamental Moral Theology*, pp. 72-73; *Issues in Sexual and Medical Ethics*, pp. 154-155, 157-158. Here I tentatively proposed that when the dying process begins there seems to be no difference between the act of omission (not using extraordinary means) and the positive act of bringing about death. I point out that in practice this position would differ only slightly from the official hierarchical teaching and also recognize possible abuses which may be sufficient reason not to adopt this position in practice.

On the question of sexuality I have discussed at various times the question of masturbation; e.g., *A New Look at Christian Morality*, pp. 201-221; *Issues in Sexual and Medical Ethics*, pp. 49-50. Again, my position is quite nuanced. Masturbatory acts are ordinarily not very important or significant and usually do not involve grave matter. Such actions are generally symptomatic of other realities and should be treated as such. However, masturbation falls short of the full meaning of human sexuality and should not generally be seen as totally good or praiseworthy.

I have also devoted a number of studies to homosexuality; e.g., *Catholic Moral Theology in Dialogue,* pp. 184-219; *Critical Concerns in Moral Theology,* pp. 73-98. On the basis of a theology of compromise I propose that for an irreversible, constitutional, or genuine homosexual, homosexual acts in the context of a loving relationship striving for permanency can in a certain sense be objectively morally good. However, in accord with this theology of compromise, such acts are good for these persons because of their objective condition. In general, sexuality should be seen in terms of the female-male relationship so that homosexual relationships fall short of the full meaning of human sexuality. This position obviously does not accept or condone homosexual acts without personal commitment. In the second study, I situate my position as a mediating position between the official hierarchical teaching and the position held by a numbar of Catholic theologians and others according to which sexual morality is judged only on the basis of the quality of the relationship, whether it be heterosexual or homosexual relationships.

I have not devoted separate studies to premarital sexuality but have considered it within the broader context of sexuality in general; e.g., *Themes in Fundamental Moral Theology,* pp. 182-185; *Issues in Sexual and Medical Ethics,* pp. 46-48. I insist that the full meaning of human sexuality involves a permanent commitment of love between a woman and a man. Pastoral practice here requires prudence in dealing with people who do not accept such an understanding in practice. Only in very rare and comparatively few situations would I justify premarital sexuality on the basis of a theology of compromise.

I have dealt at length with the question of the indissolubility of marriage on a number of different occasions; e.g., *New Perspectives in Moral Theology,* pp. 212-276; *Ongoing Revision,* pp. 66-106; *Issues in Sexual and Medical Ethics,* pp. 3-29. I have argued that the Catholic Church should change its teaching on indissolubility and allow divorce in certain circumstances. The pastoral practice proposed by myself and many others for dealing with divorced and remarried Catholics at the present time does not necessarily depend upon this more theoretical position. It should also be noted that many other Catholic theologians have taken a similar position about changing the teaching on indissolubility. One Catholic commentator (James P. Hanigan, *What Are They Saying About Sexual Morality*, p. 115) has described my approach as follows:

> But is it, and why is it always wrong to attempt a second marriage after a divorce? This is the question that is debated, along with the concern that a change in the church's teaching would weaken the ideal of indissolubility and the stability of marriage. Such a concern is clearly evident, for example, in Charles Curran's carefully nuanced argument for a change in the teaching on indissolubility. Even while advocating the change, Curran urges that the real task is to "expend every effort possible to strengthen the loving marriage commitment of spouses, even if the eschatological ideal cannot always be fulfilled in our present and limited world."

In respect to this third area of clarification I have tried to indicate briefly and accurately the precise positions I have taken and how they relate to official, hierarchical, noninfallible church teachings. I have always presented the positions of the hierarchical magisterium clearly and with great respect. Very often my position is in substantial agreement with the hierarchical teaching. Even in my dissent on contraception and sterilization I appeal to the broader Catholic principles of stewardship and responsible parenthood. I have proposed my positions after much study, prayer, and reflection. I am convinced of the truthfulness of these positions at the present time, but I am always open to change these positions in the light of persuasive and convincing reasons. In the light of the preliminary nature of this response I have not tried to demonstrate that similar positions are held by many other Catholic moral theologians. In fact, the positions taken by other Catholic moral theologians are often in greater disagreement with official Catholic teaching than the positions I have taken.

In conclusion, this letter is a preliminary response to the September 17 letter of the Congregation to me. The primary purpose of this letter has been to indicate what in my judgment are the precise areas of difference between the Congregation and myself. I hope that this preliminary response will be helpful.

Sincerely yours in Christ,
Charles E. Curran

The
CATHOLIC
  UNIVERSITY of
    AMERICA

Washington, D.C. 20064

December 9, 1985

The Most Reverend James A. Hickey, D.D.
Archbishop of Washington
5001 Eastern Avenue
P.O. Box 29260
Washington, D.C. 20017

Dear Archbishop Hickey,

Thank you very much for sending me the letter from Cardinal Ratzinger to you of November 11, 1985. Cardinal Ratzinger in his letter referred to my problem with what his September 17 letter to me said about the assent of faith.

I will try to summarize what I have discussed with you in our previous meetings about this question. The second paragraph of the September 17 letter refers to "some theological teaching in the Catholic Church. Above all we must recall the clear doctrine of the Vatican Council II regarding the principles for the assent of faith (*Lumen gentium* 25). This doctrine was incorporated in the revised Code of Canon Law which in c. 752 sums up the thought of the Council on this point."

Note that the explicit theological reference in the Congregation's letter recalls the clear doctrine regarding the principles for the assent of faith. The next sentence states that this doctrine was incorporated in Canon 752 of the new Code.

As they stand, these two sentences are not saying the same thing. Canon 752 explicitly prescinds from the assent of faith and discusses the religious respect of intellect and will which is to be given to nondefinitively proclaimed teachings of the magisterium.

I concluded that it seems that the letter of the Congregation of September 17 understands the point of difference between us to concern both the assent of faith and the religious respect of intellect and will. The letter from Cardinal Ratzinger of November 11 gives the same interpretation.

However, my major problem is the assertion that the assent of faith is in any way involved in the differences between myself and the Congregation. I have always maintained that my positions in no way involve a denial of the assent of faith. I am dealing with noninfallible teachings which call for the *obsequium religiosum*. In its previous correspondence over the last six years the Congregation has agreed that the differences between us concern the area of noninfallible teaching and the *obsequium religiosum*.

In my longer letter to you incorporating my preliminary response to the Congregation's September 17 letter, I develop this point in greater detail.

In this present letter I have just tried to explain what is the exact problem I have with what the Congregation said about the assent of faith in its September 17 letter to me.

Sincerely yours in Christ,
Charles E. Curran

CEC/ddk

The
CATHOLIC
 UNIVERSITY of
 AMERICA

Washington, D.C. 20064

January 28, 1986

His Excellency Joseph Cardinal Ratzinger.
Sacra Congregatio Pro Doctrina Fidei
Piazza del S. Uffizio, 11
00193 Rome
ITALY

Dear Cardinal Ratzinger,

I have been informed by Archbishop Hickey that the Congregation would be willing to receive me to discuss the questions that have been raised about my writings in our correspondence and in particular the issues raised in your letter to me of September 17, 1985.

Since I want to leave no stone unturned in this whole matter, I hereby respectfully ask that I might have an opportunity to discuss these issues face to face with the Congregation. I am very willing to accept the other stipulation communicated to me by Archbishop Hickey — I agree to the joint press release that would be issued by the Congregation and myself after the conversation.

To avoid any unnecessary delays. I would suggest that a convenient time for me would be the week of February 16, probably closer to the end of the week such as Thursday. However, this is only a suggestion, and I am willing to meet at any time which is convenient for you.

In the interest of facilitating the meeting, it would be helpful to have some idea in advance of exactly how you think the meeting should be structured. Since this meeting is so important and has so many possible consequences for me personally, I trust that I will be able to bring to the meeting appropriate counsel.

Sincerely yours in Christ,
Charles E. Curran

CEC/ddk


SACRA CONGREGATIO
PRO DOCTRINA FIDEI
00193 Romae
Piazza del S. Uffizio, 11
Prot. N. 48/66

February 8, 1986

Dear Father Curran,

I would like to acknowledge your letter of January 28, 1986, in which you request a meeting here at the Congregation. May I assure you that the Congregation is willing to arrange this.

For such a meeting to be fruitful, of course, it is necessary that we have a shared understanding of its nature and purpose. As you are fully aware, this Congregation's inquiry into your work has proceeded according to the *Ratio agendi* which governs such inquiries. In July of 1979 and again in May of 1983, our concerns over certain aspects of your work were expressed in the form of "Observations" to which, in several lengthy communications, you responded. Those replies left no doubt that, as the Observations had maintained, you do dissent from the Magisterium of the Roman Catholic Church on several significant points.

Your most recent letter, of December 9, 1986, to Archbishop Hickey shows perhaps more clearly than before that you continue to maintain your dissenting positions. The Congregation's view, namely that you do dissent, is thus entirely sustained. When we wrote to you in September of 1985, in an effort to invite you formally to withdraw your dissenting positions, we did so to bring this inquiry to a close, always hoping of course that you would in fact revise your views. At that time, the question had been raised whether or not it was thought to be necessary to invite you to a formal colloquium, in accord with n. 13 of the Ratio Agendi. Such an invitation is at the Congregation's discretion in the event that a given author's views remain unclear even after written correspondence. Such was not thought to be required in your case.

That is why, on the occasion of Archbishop Hickey's visit here last month, we distinguished between the formal colloquium and the eventual meeting we might arrange.

We made clear that we would not be opposed to a meeting as long as it was not understood in the sense of a formal colloquium or some sort of ecclesiastical trial, but with a view to clarifying the decision we have reached and which has already been communicated to you. Further, it was to be on the condition that you request it. We prefer to keep this meeting entirely confidential, but if any eventual statement about it were to be made by either party, the statement would have to be agreed upon in advance by both.

You will readily understand that practical considerations will not permit us to schedule such a meeting until March, preferably either the 6th, 7th or 8th. Please let us know which date is most convenient for you.

Regarding your request to be accompanied by some qualified person, I think that would be acceptable if you consider it necessary. Since the discussion would center, I should think, not on the specifics of the moral arguments and the individual dissenting conclusions you have reached, but rather on the ecclesiological foundations upon which our decision rests, the suggestion comes to mind that you might consider being accompanied by the Rev. Carl Peter, a member of the International Theological Commission and a person well known to you. Needless to say, whoever accompanies you shall have to agree to the above mentioned condition regarding the confidentiality of the meeting.

I hope to hear from you at your earliest opportunity.

With my best wishes, I am

Sincerely yours in Christ,
Joseph Cardinal Ratzinger

The
CATHOLIC
  UNIVERSITY of
  AMERICA

Washington, D.C. 20064

February 13, 1986

His Eminence Joseph Cardinal Ratzinger
Sacra Congregatio Pro Doctrina Fidei
Piazza del S. Uffizio, 11
00193 Rome
ITALY

Dear Cardinal Ratzinger:

I received your letter of February 8 on Tuesday evening, February 11, through Archbishop Hickey. I want to respond as quickly as possible so that all the necessary arrangements can be made.

In previous communications I have asked Father Bernard Häring to accompany me to the informal meeting with the Congregation. Father Häring has agreed. Since he was my professor and remains a very close counsellor and friend, I was very pleased by his wanting to accompany me. If you think Father Peter should be present together with Father Häring, I will ask him if he wishes to accompany me.

To protect all involved I agreed to the condition of a joint press release after the meeting. I promise to make no comment to the press beforehand about the meeting and will say nothing else about it in Rome. In fact, I intend to leave Rome the day after the meeting. Permit me to suggest a purely descriptive release along the following lines, with the realization that I am very willing to discuss other alternatives:

> "Father Charles E. Curran asked to be received by the Congregation for the Doctrine of the Faith for an informal meeting concerning his positions on moral theology. The Congregation has graciously received him. The tone of the meeting was cordial and respectful. The Congregation has been in correspondence with Father Curran in accord with the *ratio agendi,* but this was an inforaml meeting outside the procedural regulations of the *ratio agendi.*"

The date of Saturday, March 8, is acceptable to me. Dean William Cenkner of the School of Religious Studies of the Catholic University of America will travel with me to Rome.

I trust all is now in order.

Sincerely yours,
Charles E. Curran

CEC/bg

SACRA CONGREGATIO
PRO DOCTRINA FIDEI
00193 Romae
Piazza del S. Uffizio, 11
Prot. N. 48/66
March 10, 1986

Most Reverend James Hickey
Archbishop of Washington, D.C.
U.S.A.

Your Excellency,

As you know, the meeting we had arranged with Father Charles Curran took place as scheduled on Saturday, March 8, 1986. We agreed on a joint statement which Father Curran was free to publish in the United States, and which we would publish here. I have enclosed a copy of the statement.

There still remains the question of Fr. Curran's definitive written response to the Congregation's letter of September 17, 1985. You will recall that the response he gave to you on December 9, 1985, was only a "preliminary" one. In order that the results of the meeting and his final written reply be brought to the Cardinals of the Congregation as soon as possible, I would be grateful if you would ask Father Curran to forward to you his full reply at once.

With my continued thanks for your invaluable collaboration, and with my best wishes, I am

Sincerely yours in Christ,
Joseph Cardinal Ratzinger


The
CATHOLIC
UNIVERSITY of
AMERICA

Washington, D.C. 20064

April 1, 1986

His Eminence Joseph Cardinal Ratzinger
Sacra Congregatio Pro Doctrina Fidei
Piazza del S. Uffizio, 11
00193 Roma
ITALIA

Dear Cardinal Ratzinger,

Archbishop Hickey forward to me a copy of your letter of March 10. I want to respond expeditiously to your request for a final written reply so that you can bring this reply and the results of our informal meeting to the Cardinals of the Congregation as soon as possible. I will incorporate as part of this final written response the preliminary reply I made in a letter addressed to Archbishop Hickey on December 9, 1985. A copy of that letter is enclosed.

This letter will be primarily a brief summary of the points

brought up at our March 8 meeting. I communicated to you the substance of my final response at that time. However, I understand
your concern to have a written document.

First of all, I want to thank you for the March 8 meeting. I imagine that both of us wished there would have been more true
dialogue, but at least we were able to state our positions to one
another in a respectful way. I did appreciate your explicit recognition of the fact that I have never denied any dogmas or truths of the
faith. Throughout this whole investigation I have tried to point out
the importance of the hierarchy of truths. In my preliminary response of December 9, I tried to pinpoint as accurately as possible
the difference between the Congregation and myself.

After our informal meeting I must reiterate what was said in my
preliminary response of December 9: "I still remain quite disappointed with the dialogue that has ensued between the Congregation and myself on this matter. Both good theology and justice demand that the Congregation explicitly state what are the norms
governing the legitimacy or the possibility of dissent from such
noninfallible teaching and then indicate how I have violated these
norms. In 1979, I proposed five questions and my answers to these
questions in an attempt to find out what might be the norms that
the Congregation is proposing, but there has never been a response
to these questions. Later I expressed my willingness to accept the
criteria for dissent proposed by the United States bishops in 1968,
but again the Congregation was unwilling to accept these norms."

In my judgment public theological dissent on the issues involved
in your investigation of my writings is legitimate. I have carefully
observed the guidelines for public theological dissent from noninfallible teaching laid down by the United States Bishops in their
1968 Pastoral Letter "Human Life in Our Day": "The expression of
theological dissent from the magisterium is in order only if the
reasons are serious and well-founded, if the manner of the dissent
does not question or impugn the teaching authority of the Church
and is such as not to give scandal."

In our correspondence I have pointed out that many other
theologians hold similar positions and that it is an injustice to me
and harmful to the credibility of the Church and its hierarchical
teaching office to single me out when so many others throughout
the world hold similar positions.

In my preliminary response of December 9 to Archbishop Hickey I briefly stated my positions on the four areas of my dissent mentioned in your September 17 letter. I have always discussed and explained the offical hierarchical teaching in these areas with great respect. As mentioned earlier my positions are at times in substantial agreement with these official teachings. Likewise, I have carefully pointed out where my proposals are more tentative and probing. I remain convinced of the truthfulness of these positions at the present time, but I am always open to change these positions in the light of pervasive and convincing reasons.

In conscience at the present time I cannot and do not change the theological positions I have taken. However, I once again bring to your attention the proposal I made in my meetings with Archbishop Hickey and Cardinal Bernardin and which was communicated to you by them and repeated by me in our meeting of March 8. This proposal tries to protect my own integrity as well as the integrity and responsibilities of the hierarchical teaching office in the Church. I would not teach the course on sexual ethics in the Department of Theology of the Catholic University of America, but I would remain a tenured faculty member in this department. The Congregation might also deem it necessary to issue a document pointing out that my position on the issues under discussion are at variance with existing official hierarchical teaching.

I close with the hope expressed by Father Häring in our meeting that a solution can be found which is mutually acceptable and for the good of the Church.

Sincerely yours in Christ,
Charles E. Curran

SACRA CONGREGATIO
PRO DOCTRINA FIDEI
00193 Romae
Piazza del S. Uffizio, 11
Prot. N. 48/66
July 25, 1986

Dear Father Curran:

This Congregation wishes to acknowledge receipt of your letter of April 1, 1986 with which you enclosed your definitive reply to its critical Observations on various positions you have taken in your published work. You note that you "remain convinced of the truth-fulness of these positions at the present time. . . ." You reiterate as well a proposal which you have called a "compromise" according to which you would continue to teach moral theology but not in the field of sexual ethics.

The purpose of this letter is to inform you that the Congregation has confirmed its position that one who dissents from the Magisterium as you do is not suitable nor eligible to teach Catholic Theology. Consequently, it declines your compromise solution because of the organic unity of authentic Catholic Theology, a unity which in its contents and method is intimately bound to fidelity to the Church's Magisterium.

The several dissenting positions which this Congregation contested, namely, on a right to public dissent from the Ordinary Magisterium, the indissolubility of consummated sacramental marriage, abortion, euthanasia, masturbation, artificial contraception, pre-marital intercourse and homosexual acts, were listed carefully enough in the above-mentioned Observations in July of 1983 and have since been published. There is no point in entering into any detail concerning the fact that you do indeed dissent on these issues.

There is, however, one concern which must be brought out. Your basic assertion has been that since your positions are convincing to you and diverge only from the "non-infallible" teaching of the Church, they constitute "responsible" dissent and should therefore be allowed by the Church. In this regard, the following considerations seem to be in order.

First of all, one must remember the teaching of the Second Vatican Council which clearly does not confine the infallible Magisterium purely to matters of faith nor to solemn definitions. *Lumen gentium* 25 states: " . . . when, however, they (the Bishops) even though spread throughout the world, but still maintaining the bond of communion between themselves and with the successor of Peter, and authentically teaching on matters of faith or morals, are in agreement that a particular position ought to be held as definitive, then they are teaching the doctrine of Christ in an infallible manner." Besides this, the Church does not build its life upon its infallible magisterium alone but on the teaching of its authentic, ordinary magisterium as well.

In light of these considerations, it is clear that you have not taken into adequate account, for example, that the Church's position on the indissolubility of sacramental and consummated marriage, which you claim ought to be changed, was in fact defined at the Council of Trent and so belongs to the patrimony of the Faith. You likewise do not give sufficient weight to the teaching of the Second Vatican Council when in full continuity with the Tradition of the Church it condemned abortion, calling it an "unspeakable crime." In any case, the faithful must accept not only the infallible magisterium. They are to give the religious submission of intellect and will to the teaching which the Supreme Pontiff or the college of bishops enuntiate on faith or morals when they exercise the authentic magisterium, even if they do not intend to proclaim it with a definitive act. This you have continued to refuse to do.

There are, moreover, two related matters which have become widely misunderstood in the course of the Congregation's inquiry into your work, especially in the past few months, and which should be noted. First, you publicly claimed that you were never told who your "accusers" were. The Congregation based its inquiry exclusively on your published works and on your personal responses to its Observations. In effect, then, your own works have been your "accusers" and they alone.

You further claimed that you were never given the opportunity of counsel. Since the inquiry was conducted on a documentary basis, you had every opportunity to take any type of counsel you wished. Moreover, it is clear that you did so. When you replied to the Congregation's Observations with your letter of August 24, 1984, you stated that you had taken the positions you have "with a great deal . . . of consultation . . ."; and in the Congregation's letter of September 17, 1985, you were actually urged to continue the use of that very means so that an acceptable resolution of the differences between you and the teaching of the Church could be attained. Finally, at your own request, when you came for our meeting on March 8, 1986, you were accompanied by a theologian of your own choosing and confidence.

In conclusion, this Congregation calls attention to the fact that you have taken your dissenting positions as a Professor of Theology in an Ecclesiastical Faculty at a Pontifical University. In its letter of September 17, 1985 to you, it was noted that ". . . the authorities of the Church cannot allow the present situation to continue in which the inherent contradiction is prolonged that one who is to teach in the name of the Church in fact denies her teaching." In light of your repeated refusal to accept what the Church teaches and in light of its mandate to promote and safeguard the Church's teaching on faith and morals throughout the Catholic world, this Congregation, in agreement with the Congregation for Catholic Education, sees no alternative now but to advise the Most Reverend Chancellor that you will no longer be considered suitable nor eligible to exercise the function of a Professor of Catholic Theology.

This decision was presented to His Holiness in an audience granted to the undersigned Prefect on the 10th of July of this year and he approved both its content and the procedure followed.

This Dicastery also wishes to inform you that this decision will be published as soon as it is communicated to you.

May I finally express the sincere hope that this regrettable, but necessary, outcome to the Congregation's study might move you to reconsider your dissenting positions and to accept in its fullness the teaching of the Catholic Church.

Sincerely yours in Christ,
Joseph Cardinal Ratzinger


The
CATHOLIC
  UNIVERSITY of
  AMERICA

Washington, D.C. 20064

August 27, 1986

His Eminence Joseph Cardinal Ratzinger
Praefectus, Sacra Congregatio pro Doctrina Fidei
Piazza del S. Uffizio, 11
00193 Rome
ITALY

Dear Cardinal Ratzinger,

As a matter of courtesy I want to acknowledge your letter to me of July 25, 1986 which was handed to me at 4:00 p.m. on Monday,

August 18. I note that at the very moment the letter was handed to me, it was already in the hands of the press. I am also enclosing a copy of the remarks I made on Wednesday, August 20th.

Sincerely yours in Christ,
Charles E. Curran

CEC/ddk

## REMARKS OF CHARLES E. CURRAN, August 20, 1986

From the very beginning of the public discussion of my dispute with the Vatican's Congregation for the Doctrine of the Faith I insisted on making this a teaching moment.

On Monday, August 18, at a 4:00 p.m. meeting, Archbishop James A. Hickey, the Chancellor of The Catholic University of America, handed me a letter addressed to me by Cardinal Joseph Ratzinger, the Prefect of the Congregation for the Doctrine of the Faith. Ratzinger informed me that I "will no longer be suitable nor eligible to exercise the function of a Professor of Catholic Theology." The Archbishop informed me that this letter had at that time been released to the press.

In addition Archbishop Hickey gave me his own letter in which as Chancellor of The Catholic University of America he initiated the withdrawal of the canonical mission which permits me to teach theology at this University. The letter also reminded me of my right to request the procedures found in the Canonical Statutes of the Ecclesiastical Faculties. If I do not exercise that right by September 1, he will notify the President of the University that the canonical mission has been withdrawn. In addition, he gave me his press release. He also said that he could give me no answer as to whether or not I would still be allowed to teach at the University in some faculty other than the faculty of theology. That answer according to Archbishop Hickey could only be given by the Board of Trustees.

In keeping with my aim of making this a teaching moment, I

want first to address the issues in Cardinal Ratzinger's July 25 letter to me and then to raise further issues not discussed in that letter. The issues involved in Cardinal Ratzinger's July 25 letter to me are basically three: the moral theological positions I have taken, the legitimacy of my theological dissent, and my criticisms of the process.

First, the letter of Cardinal Ratzinger gives the impression that on the specific moral issues involved in the dispute the official teaching is opposed to such actions and I am in favor of them. That is not the case. I have always developed my moral theology in the light of accepted Catholic principles. My positions on the particular issues involved are always carefully nuanced and often in fundamental agreement with the existing hierarchical teaching. Yes, occasionally I have dissented from the official teaching on some aspects of specific issues, but this is within a more general and prevailing context of assent.

Second, the issue of dissent. The July 25 letter refers to both the infallible and noninfallible magisterium. However, in all the correspondence before 1985 the Congregation for the Doctrine of the Faith recognized that the issue was public dissent from the noninfallible hierarchical magisterium as is spelled out in the very first sentence of the "Observations" sent to me in April 1983. In reality, the July 25 letter refers only to the indissolubility of marriage as defined at the Council of Trent and belonging to the patrimony of faith. However, all Catholic theologians recognize the teaching of the Council of Trent does not exclude as contrary to faith the practice of "*economia*" in the Greek church. I have maintained that the position I propose on the indissolubility of marriage is in keeping with this tradition.

Thus, we are dealing with the noninfallible hierarchical teaching. Here, too, in my writing and recent public statements I have not proposed the possibility and legitimacy of dissent from all noninfallible teaching. In moral matters, all Christians must recognize that the follower of Jesus should be loving, caring, just, and faithful. My disagreements are on the level of complex, specific actions which involve many conflicting circumstances and situations. By their very nature these specific concrete questions are far removed from the core of faith. Recall that official hierarchical teaching does not condemn all sterilization but recognizes that in some situations indirect sterilization is permitted. The 1968 statement of the Canadian bishops about Catholics who cannot accept the teaching of *Humanae vitae* absolutely condemning artificial contraception for spouses is most pertinent. "Since they are not denying any point of divine and Catholic faith, nor rejecting the teaching authority of the church, these Catholics should not be considered, or consider themselves, shut off from the body of the faithful."

In short, I have defended my dissent as being in accord with the norms laid down by the United States bishops in their 1968 pastoral letter "Human Life in Our Day." The Congregation still must answer the questions I have been asking for six years. Does the Congregation agree with the teaching proposed on dissent by the United States bishops or are they claiming that such teaching is wrong?

Third, the process. Most legal systems in the contemporary world recognize that the defendant has a right to the record of the trial including the right to know who are the accusers. No such record has ever been made available to me. The process itself does not allow the individual involved to have counsel in any official meeting with the Congregation or its officials. Cardinal Ratzinger himself maintained that my meeting with the officials of the Congregation was a nonofficial meeting. Ratzinger himself admitted in 1984 that the Congregation had decided to revise its present procedures but workload and time constraints have not allowed this to take place. In this context, I should also point out that I have been given a copy of a letter from a Cardinal member of the Congregation dated July 11, 1986, in which this Cardinal voting member says that he has never received any dossier on my case.

Now I want to raise three issues that are not found in the July 25, 1986 letter of Cardinal Ratzinger.

First, the right of the faithful to dissent in practice from some of the noninfallible teachings with which I disagree. Do the faithful have such a right? What is the ecclesial status of those who so dissent? What does their practice say about the present teaching of the church?

Second, the theological community. The evidence in the last few months has clearly supported my contention that I am a theological moderate and that a strong majority of Catholic theologians support the legitimacy of my position. Over 750 theologians in North America have signed a theological statement of support for me.

This present support from the theological community is in continuity with the support shown for my theological endeavors over the last twenty-five years, most of which have been spent here at the Catholic University of America. The theological community has been in critical dialogue with my positions, but in the eyes of my peers I have been recognized as a significant Catholic moral theologian. My colleagues have elected me President of the Catholic Theological Society of America and of the Society of Christian Ethics. I was the first recipient of the John Courtney Murray Award of the Catholic Theological Society of America for outstanding achievement in theology.

What does this split between theologians and pastors say? This is a pressing problem for the Roman Catholic Church which has always given great weight and importance to the theological community. What action if any will be taken against people holding positions similar to mine? Are all those who maintain the possibility of legitimate theological dissent from some noninfallible teaching not suitable or eligible to exercise the function of a Professor of Catholic Theology?

Third, academic freedom in Catholic institutions. The vast majority of the leaders of Catholic higher education in the United States, including William J. Byron, the President of this University, have claimed that the ability of a church authority to intervene in the hiring, promotion, and terminating of faculty is a violation of academic freedom. Such procedures in Catholic institutions according to these educational leaders jeopardize the very nature of a university or college. Such interventionist procedures are now possible with the Statutes for the Ecclesiastical Faculties of The Catholic University. However, the present universal law of the church already enshrines the same legislation for all Catholic institutions of higher learning. In addition, proposed legislation for Catholic institutions of higher learning spells this out in greater detail.

Before concluding, some other issues must be addressed. My colleagues have urged me to go through the process provided by the Statutes of the Ecclesiastical Faculties if I have the physical and spiritual strength to do so. I would like to honor their request, but there are some problems that must first be clarified. I have written that the existing canonical statutes are themselves a violation of academic freedom. Also in 1982 I wrote an official letter to the University asserting that these Statutes do not apply to me since my tenured contract with the University predates these Statutes and the University cannot unilaterally add anything to my contractual obligations. Only after receiving academic and legal counsel on these points can I make a final decision about the process.

In conclusion, I am conscious of my own limitations and my own failures. I am aware of the consequences of what is involved. But I can only repeat what I wrote Cardinal Ratzinger in my final response of April 1, 1986: "In conscience at the present time I cannot and do not change the theological positions I have taken." In my own judgment and in the judgment of the majority of my peers I have been and am suitable and eligible to exercise the function of a Professor of Catholic Theology.

I remain convinced that the hierarchical teaching office in the Roman Catholic Church must allow dissent on these issues and ultimately should change its teaching. My conviction in this matter is supported by a number of factors. First, the overwhelming support of my theological colleagues has buoyed me personally and strengthened my own hope for the ultimate acceptance of these convictions. Second, the best and the mainstream of the Catholic theological tradition support my basic approaches. According to Catholic theological tradition, the word and work of Jesus must always be made present and meaningful in the contemporary historical and cultural circumstances. The Catholic tradition also insists on the transcendence of faith and the principle that faith and reason can never contradict one another. In addition, Catholic ethics has insisted on an intrinsic morality. Something is commanded because it is good and not the other way around. Authority must conform to the truth.

Finally, some historical examples give me hope. Theologians who have been condemned have at later times been vindicated and their teachings have been accepted. The experience of the Second Vatican Council illustrates this fact.

From a personal perspective, I have been comforted and strengthened by the support of so many. I remain a loyal and com-

mitted Roman Catholic. I pray daily that I might continue to love
and serve the Church without bitterness and anger.

I will continue to work for the legitimacy of some theological and
practical dissent, the need to change some official hierarchical
church teachings, the importance of academic freedom for Catholic
theology, and the need for just structures to deal with the inevitable tensions that from time to time will exist between theologians
and pastors. I believe these are all for the good of the Roman Catholic Church — my Church.

# VII
# FURTHER DOCUMENTS

## Statement of Archbishop James A. Hickey, Archbishop of Washington and Chancellor of the Catholic University, March 11, 1986.

On October 10, 1985, Cardinal Bernardin, as chairman of the board of The Catholic University of America, and myself, as chancellor, met with Father Curran to deliver Cardinal Ratzinger's letter of September 17, 1985. The letter asked Father to reconsider and retract his opinions in several areas of moral theology.

We urged Father Curran to accept the points of the letter as a clear statement of the magisterium in those areas. At issue was Father Curran's continued authorization to teach in the name of the Catholic Church.

In the course of several discussions with the cardinal, Father Curran and myself, we considered various courses of action relative to Father Curran's continuance at The Catholic University of America. These options included among others the compromise proposed by Father Curran and referred to in his press conference of March 11. While we were not in a position to make a commitment to any of these, we were hopeful that some solution could be found which would fully safeguard the teaching of the church while being sensitive to the interests of Father Curran.

Action by the Congregation for the Doctrine of the Faith with regard to Father Curran's license to teach in the name of the Catholic Church is reaching its conclusive phase. Since as chancellor I am directly involved in any proceedings regarding the removal of his license to teach theology at The Catholic University of America, it is inappropriate for me to make further comments at this time.

As the archbishop of Washington, however, I want to stress that it is the right and the duty of the Holy Father and the bishops in communion with him throughout the world to hand on the full and authentic teaching of the church and to ensure that it is presented with fidelity in our parishes and institutions of learning. This fidelity is not a limitation nor a denial of the proper role of theology; rather it is an invitation to discover afresh the very power of the Gospel which permeates the teaching of the magisterium.

At this time of difficulty, I hope and pray that all those involved will work to resolve these questions in ways which serve the church, its teaching authority, the study of theology and the pastoral mission of church.

## Statement of Bishop Matthew Clark, Bishop of Rochester and Fr. Curran's diocesan bishop, March 12, 1986.

I am aware that the Rev. Charles E. Curran, a priest of the Diocese of Rochester and professor of theology at The Catholic University of America, visited the offices of the Congregation for the Doctrine of the Faith on March 8, 1986. I have communicated with Cardinal Joseph Ratzinger on this matter to share with him some of my reflections about Father Curran, about the developments which have led up to this meeting and about some of the pastoral implications which I foresee may result.

I speak now as Father Curran's bishop and friend, as a pastor having the care of the local church of Rochester and as one who, with the college of bishops, shares in solicitude for the entire church.

Father Curran is a priest whose personal life could well be called exemplary. He lives simply and has a remarkable ability to combine a life of serious scholarship with a generous availability to a great variety of persons. My personal observations, supported by the testimony of many, is that Father Curran is a man deeply committed to the spiritual life. I am personally aware of his commitment and know by testimony of others that he is a respected spiritual guide for people who seek counsel in their journeys of faith.

As a theologian, Father Curran enjoys considerable respect not only in our diocese but across this country. He is unfailingly thorough and respectful in his exposition of the teaching of the church. Indeed, I have heard it said that few theologians have a better grasp of or express more clearly the fullness of the Catholic moral tradition. In instances when Father Curran offers theological views which appear to be at a variance with the current official statements of the church, he always does so in a responsible manner. He is respectful of authority in the church in a most Christian manner.

Some members of the Catholic Church have occasionally depicted Father Curran as irreverent, disrespectful, disloyal and unprofessional. I believe that he is none of these. Such judgments of this good priest are sometimes written by those in the church who do not understand the probing and testing nature of the theological enterprise. This will remain a problem in our age of instant communication wherein theologians have no quiet corner in which to attempt to deepen their understanding of our faith. Our concern for this persistent difficulty should not grow out of proportion, allowing fear of confusion to end the necessary growth of theology.

It is, I believe, commonly accepted in the Roman Catholic theological community that Father Curran is a moral theologian of notable competence whose work locates him very much at the center of that community and not at all on the fringe. I believe that perception is true. If Father Curran's status as a Roman Catholic theologian is brought into question, I fear a serious setback to Catholic education and pastoral life in this country. That could happen in two ways. Theologians may stop exploring the challenging questions of the day in a creative, healthy way because they fear actions which may prematurely end their teaching careers. Moreover, able theologians may abandon Catholic institutions altogether in order to avoid embarrassing confrontation with church authority. Circumstances of this sort would seriously undermine the standing of Catholic scholarship in this nation, isolate our theological community and weaken our Catholic institutions of higher education. Alteration of Father Curran's mandate to teach as a Roman Catholic theologian would be an extremely painful experience for all of us and doubly so because the pain would be born of a common and intense love for the church and desire to be fully loyal to the Holy See.

The church in the United States is a church which is struggling mightily to meet the challenge of Vatican Council II. Our bishops, priests, religious and other laity have shown a wonderful generosity and reverence for the church's life and have given themselves unstintingly to her call for renewal. I believe that the vitality, creativity and genuine good-heartedness of our communities is a sure sign that this is true.

We have our faults to be sure, and there have been false starts and mistakes, but we are a faithful people and we will continue to serve God's kingdom in the church with generosity.

My hope is that together we can find better ways to recognize and be faithful to the nature of the particular churches and the communion they form with Rome as their center, and that the Holy See will regard the bishops of our country as ones who can appropriately and ably communicate to the Holy See the shape of and challenges to pastoral life in our particular churches.

My further hope is that an agreement will be reached which will allow Father Curran to continue serving the church as a theologian and will promote resolution of theological differences through the normal channels of writing and debate. I ask all who read these words to pray that God will guide and bring peace to those who are working to resolve this matter in the best interest of the church.

## Statement of Bishop James W. Malone, President of the United States Catholic Conference, March 14, 1986.

The exchange of views between the Holy See and Father Curran has been underway since 1979. His positions have been evaluated in depth by the Congregation for the Doctrine of the Faith. The central issue identified in this process concerns the fact that someone who does not accept the teaching of the Church's Magisterium on crucial points cannot reasonably expect to occupy a position which requires that he teach what the Church teaches. It is clearly the right and duty of the Holy See to safeguard the authenticity of Catholic teaching throughout the world.

I remain hopeful that a resolution of the matter can be reached which respects the integrity of the Church's teaching while also taking into consideration Father Curran's interests. I trust, too, that this controversy will not become an occasion for prolonged confusion and bitterness.

## Statement circulated by FACT (Friends of American Catholic Theology)

We attest that the educational work and Christian witness of Father Charles E. Curran,

— his evident dedication to Catholic Christianity

— his scholarly contribution to Catholic moral theology

— his profound appreciation for the moral traditions of the Catholic faith

— his responsible approach to moral decision making

— his consistent promotion of ecumenical dialogue in ethics

have enriched the lives of American Catholics. His positive influence has encouraged believers to take their faith commitment seriously. It has greatly aided attempts to bring the Christian message to bear on moral decisions. We would deplore any action taken against him.

More than 20,000 people signed this statement.


## Statement signed by some past presidents of the Catholic Theological Society of America and the College Theology Society

The following statement has been drafted and approved by various past presidents of the Catholic Theological Society of America and the College Theology Society. We commend it to you, as our colleagues in one or both of these professional associations, for your public endorsement.

On September 17, 1985, Cardinal Joseph Ratzinger, Prefect of the Sacred Congregation for the Doctrine of the Faith, informed Father Charles E. Curran, Professor of Moral Theology at The Catholic University of America, Washington, D.C., that unless Father Curran retracted certain views on various official teachings of the Catholic Church, Father Curran would not be allowed to continue teaching Catholic theology in the name of the Church. The areas of dissent explicitly mentioned in Cardinal Ratzinger's letter concerned contraception, direct sterilization, abortion, euthanasia, masturbation, pre-marital intercourse, homosexual acts, and the indissolubility of sacramental and consummated marriage. The letter did not specify how Father Curran's writings are at variance with these official teachings, nor does the letter make any claim that any of these teachings fulfill the conditions necessary for an infallible pronouncement. The letter makes clear, nonetheless, that Father Curran's positions "violate the conditions necessary for a professor to be called a Catholic theologian."

The underlying assumption of the letter, therefore, is that dissent from noninfallible teachings effectively places one outside the body of Catholic theologians.

Because many of us are not specialists in moral theology/Christian ethics and, in any case, have not actually seen the Curran dossier, we shall not presume to comment on the specific points of disagreement between Father Curran and the Congregation. However, the letter does raise many serious questions which transcend any specific point of disagreement: (1) Which noninfallible teachings are serious enough to provoke such a result, and how are those teachings determined? (2) How many noninfallible teachings would one have to disagree with before this result would follow, and how is that number determined? (3) If disagreement with *any* noninfallible teaching of the Church is sufficient to provoke this result, on what theological, doctrinal, or historical basis is that principle deduced? (4) If one is declared no longer a Catholic theologian, does that modify in any way the theologian's relation to the Catholic Church itself? If so, how? If not, what does such a declaration mean?

One could leave aside entirely such substantive theological questions as these and still be profoundly disturbed by this letter and the threat of action contained in it. If Father Curran's views on the various issues mentioned in the letter are so incompatible with Catholic teaching that he must be declared no longer a Catholic theologian, justice and fairness would dictate that other Catholic theologians who hold similar views should be treated in exactly the same fashion. Indeed, the credibility of any action on the part of the Congregation would be seriously undermined by a failure to identify and act upon other such cases. The problem is, of course, that there are very many Catholic theologians who do dissent from noninfallible teachings.

This threatened action also raises serious questions about the academic integrity of Catholic institutions of higher learning. For many years, enemies of the Catholic Church in the United States have argued that Catholic colleges and universities are not independent academic institutions, but are nothing more than educational arms of the official Church. If Father Curran were removed from his position as a professor of theology at The Catholic University of America, it would be far more difficult to rebut this charge, and particularly as it might apply to that national institution.

We should like to make one final remark about Charles Curran himself. Father Curran enjoys the complete respect of his colleagues in the American Catholic theological community and beyond. We can think of no Catholic theologian in this country who is more well-liked and personally admired than Charles Curran. He is generous and considerate to a fault, toward colleagues and students alike. There would be much more than professional distress, therefore, if the contemplated action against him were carried out.

Walter J. Burghardt                Luke Salm
Editor, Theological Studies         Manhattan College

Vera Chester                        Gerard S. Sloyan
College of St. Catherine            Temple University

Bernard Cooke                       David W. Tracy
College of the Holy Cross           University of Chicago

Richard P. McBrien                  Rodger Van Allen
University of Notre Dame            Villanova University

Richard A. McCormick
Georgetown University

This statement was subsequently signed by more than 750 theologians.


# Resolution passed by the annual meeting of the Catholic Theological Society of America, June 14, 1986, by a vote of 171-14.

For the good of Roman Catholic theology, Catholic higher education, and the Catholic Church in North America, we strongly urge that no action be taken against Charles Curran that would prohibit him from teaching on the theology faculty at the Catholic University of America.

## Statement of Archbishop James A. Hickey, Chancellor of the Catholic University of America, August 18, 1986.

Today I am authorized to release a letter from the Congregation for the Doctrine of the Faith conveying its final decision concerning the case of Father Charles E. Curran, professor of moral theology at The Catholic University of America. The congregation found that a number of Father Curran's writings are in serious conflict with the authentic teaching of the Catholic Church. For that reason the CDF declared that Father Curran "will no longer be considered suitable nor eligible to exercise the function of a professor of Catholic theology." This judgment has been approved by the Holy Father, Pope John Paul II.

I fully support this judgment of the Holy See. The Holy Father and the bishops have the right and the duty to ensure that what is taught in the name of the church be completely faithful to its full and authentic teaching. The faithful have a right to sound teaching and the church's officially commissioned teachers have a particular responsibility to honor that right. In view of the Holy See's declaration and in accordance with the statutes of Catholic University, I have initiated the withdrawal of Father Curran's ecclesiastical license to teach Catholic theology. Father Curran will enjoy the right to the procedures of due process set forth in the statutes.

The declaration of the Holy See follows a lengthy correspondence which the CDF initiated with Father Curran in 1979 regarding certain errors and ambiguities in his published writings on moral theology. The congregation asked Father Curran to respond to its observations and later asked him to reconsider his positions which dissent from the authentic teaching of the church. Father Curran released this correspondence to the press several months ago.

In 1980, when I was appointed the archbishop of Washington and ex officio the chancellor of Catholic University, exchanges between the CDF and Father Curran were already under way. As chancellor I sought to facilitate that process. As occasion demanded I met with Father Curran and with officials of the university and the Holy See. This past year, when the case reached its final phase, Cardinal (Joseph) Bernardin, chairman of the board of Catholic University, and I met with Father Curran four times to discuss his dissenting opinions in light of his official license to teach Catholic theology.

In the letter to Father Curran, the congregation points out that the authentic teachings of the church, enunciated by the Holy Father and the bishops in communion with him, although not solemnly defined, require a religious submission of intellect and will. The infallible teachings of the church do not stand alone; they are intimately related to all official church teachings and together form an organic unity of faith.

While this decision is surely difficult for Father Curran, it is my hope that his love for the church will prompt him to reconsider his dissenting opinions and to accept the guidance of the magisterium. So also I pray that all of us will grow in an appreciation of that truth and power of the Gospel with which the Lord has endowed his church.

## Statement of Bishop Matthew Clark of Rochester, Fr. Curran's diocesan bishop, August 18, 1986.

In recognition of the ultimate authority of the Holy Father, who has confirmed this decision, and in a spirit of collegiality with him, I accept the decision as the final word on this matter and urge all members of our community to accept it in a similar spirit.

So that there will be no confusion, I state as well that the decision does not affect Father Curran's good standing as a priest of the Diocese of Rochester where he will always be welcome to exercise his priestly ministry.

## Statement of Bishop James W. Malone, President of the National Conference of Catholic Bishops, August 18, 1986.

In a statement last March 14 I said that the central issue identified in the exchange of views between the Holy See and Father Curran concerns the fact that someone who does not accept the teaching of the church on crucial points cannot reasonably expect to occupy a position which requires that he teach what the church teaches. I added that it is clearly the right and duty of the Holy See to safeguard the authenticity of Catholic teaching throughout the world. That remains my position.

Neither I nor anyone else relishes this controversy for its own sake. As I also said last March I hope it will not become an occasion for prolonged confusion and bitterness.

# Home delivery
## from
## Sheed & Ward

Here's your opportunity to have bestsellers delivered right to you. Our free catalog is filled with the newest titles on spirituality, church in the modern world, women in religion, ministry, small group resources, adult education/scripture, medical ethics videos and Sheed & Ward classics.

_____

Please send me a free Sheed & Ward catalog for home delivery.

NAME _____

ADDRESS _____

CITY _____ STATE/ZIP _____

If you have friends who would like to order books at home, we'll send them a catalog to —

NAME _____

ADDRESS _____

CITY _____ STATE/ZIP _____

NAME _____

ADDRESS _____

CITY _____ STATE/ZIP _____